Russia

Germany

England

Switzerland

Italy

Israel

On the Trail
of Martin Frankel

**WALL
STREET
JOURNAL
BOOKS**

The Pretender

*How Martin Frankel Fooled
the Financial World and Led the Feds
on One of the Most Publicized
Manhunts in History*

ELLEN JOAN POLLOCK

A Wall Street Journal Book
Published by Simon and Schuster
New York London Toronto Sydney Singapore

WALL STREET JOURNAL BOOKS

A WALL STREET JOURNAL BOOK
Published by Simon & Schuster, Inc.
Rockefeller Center
1230 Avenue of the Americas
New York, NY 10020

For information regarding special discounts for bulk purchases,
please contact Simon & Schuster Special Sales:
1-800-456-6798 or business@simonandschuster.com

Designed by Deirdre C. Amthor

Endpaper map by Jeffrey Mak

Manufactured in the United States of America

10   9   8   7   6   5   4   3   2   1

Library of Congress Cataloging-in-Publication Data is available.

ISBN 0-7432-0415-8

For Barry and Lily

Contents

Cast of Characters

TOLEDO

Martin Frankel: stock trader/scam artist
    Primary aliases: David Rosse, Eric Stevens
John Schulte: stockbroker and Frankel's first boss
Sonia Howe Schulte: John Schulte's wife; Frankel's first love and
    loyal ally
Dr. Norman Sacks: Frankel's first investor
Ted Bitter: Frankel's first victim

PALM BEACH

Douglas Maxwell: Frankel's first business partner
John Leo Burns: an investor in the Frankel Fund
Anne of Romania: deposed queen of Romania

CREATIVE PARTNERS FUND

Walter Rothschild: salesman for fund
Mark Shuki: salesman for fund

The Thunor Trust

John Hackney: businessman Frankel recruited to run his insurance companies

Gary Atnip: Hackney's chief lieutenant

The Greenwich Mansion

Kaethe Schuchter: Frankel's onetime lover as well as his link to New York's social elite

Karen Timmins: Frankel's office manager

Mona Kim: office assistant

Jackie Ju: office assistant; Frankel's onetime lover

Miriam: Frankel's onetime lover

Frances Burge: office assistant with overwhelming crush on her boss

Cynthia Allison: office assistant with overwhelming crush on her boss

Oksana: Frankel's lover

Greg: Oksana's other lover

David Rosse: Frankel's chief of security

Steve: Rosse's assistant

St. Francis of Assisi Foundation

Tom Corbally: secretive businessman who was Frankel's conduit to the world outside his mansion

Father Peter Jacobs: controversial Catholic priest based in New York and Rome

Monsignor Emilio Colagiovanni: head of the Monitor Ecclesiasticus Foundation in Rome

Thomas Bolan: New York lawyer with ties to the Catholic Church

The Consultants

Larry Martin: New York businessman and fixer

John Yednock: insurance consultant

Larry Brotzge: insurance consultant

Tom Quinn: convicted stock fraud artist

Kay Tatum: lawyer at Akin, Gump
Hugh Alexander: Denver lawyer
Fausto and Alfredo Fausti: Italian businessmen

MISSISSIPPI AND TENNESSEE

Billy Lovelady: Tennessee insurance examiner
Harlan Mathews: former U.S. senator; Frankel's lawyer in Tennessee
Thurston Little: businessman and fixer
George Dale: Mississippi insurance commissioner
Lee Harrell: Mississippi assistant attorney general

CAMEO APPEARANCES

Robert Strauss: former chairman of the Democratic Party and
    ambassador to Russia
Lee Iacocca: former chairman of Chrysler Corporation
Walter Cronkite: former CBS anchorman
Dewi Sukarno: socialite and former first lady of Indonesia
Jimmy Carter: former U.S. President

Prologue: The Fire

It was about seven P.M. on a Tuesday in early May 1999 when George Hannigan's beeper went off as he was pulling into his driveway in Greenwich, Connecticut. The message summoned him to 889 Lake Avenue, in the exclusive "back country" section of the wealthy suburb.

The house at 889 Lake Avenue can't easily be seen from the street. Inspector Hannigan, a fire inspector who was Greenwich's arson expert, had to drive past an apparently unmanned guard hut into a leafy cul-de-sac before he got a good look at the imposing stone mansion. Two fire engines and a police detective had preceded him. The firemen had pried open a sliding door at the back of the house and were already searching for occupants in the heavy smoke that filled its first floor.

They found no one at home. The alarm was still beeping when Hannigan entered, and it seemed as if every five seconds a phone rang somewhere in the house, much of which appeared to have been partitioned into offices. Everywhere were mountains of large plastic garbage bags stuffed with shredded documents. The place looked as if it had been ransacked. In the foyer a dented filing cabinet lay on its side. A table had toppled over and a lamp was on the floor. Scattered about were brand-new suitcases, sales tags still attached, and unused cardboard packing boxes. Three small fires, one in the living room and two in the kitchen, were still burning. The firemen quickly doused them.

The firefighters and police had been summoned by a company monitoring the alarms in the house. When the fire alarm first sounded, an attendant at the command center had phoned the house. A woman

1

answered and explained that although there was some smoke, everything was under control and there was no fire. After some lighthearted
conversation back and forth about having to work late, the attendant
asked for a password, a routine procedure. Suddenly there was some
panicked conversation between the woman and her companion at the
house. Apparently they did not have the password. They hastily got off
the phone. The alarm company then alerted the police and fire depart-
ments, according to standard protocol.

Hannigan had never seen anything quite like the scene at 889 Lake
Avenue, but by walking through the house he could pretty much piece
together what had happened in the moments before the fire trucks
showed up. Clearly, someone had left in a hurry. There was food in the
oven, and the oven was still on. The table in the kitchen was set for two,
with half-eaten food on the plates.

From the number of plastic bags scattered about, Hannigan judged
that whoever was in the house had been shredding for several hours. At
least three shredders had been put to work—not typical office shredders, but elaborate $3,000 German models, the same type used by the
FBI, that could shred documents into unusually tiny pieces. Clearly, the
people working the shredders had gotten tired of feeding the machines
and decided that burning would be more efficient.

They had lit fires in two fireplaces, one in the kitchen and a second in
the living room, where wooden stick matches and matchbooks were
scattered over the tile floor. Empty cardboard boxes and piles of ash in
the fireplaces were evidence that many papers had already been burned.
But the people in the house had had trouble burning documents as well.
File folders placed on a fire don't burn easily, because there is little room
for air to circulate between pages. Hannigan could see that the missing
occupants had sought to alleviate that problem by adding shredded documents as an accelerant.

The situation had gotten out of hand, Hannigan concluded, when
someone got lazy and dragged a large reclining chair into the kitchen,
pulling it too close to the flames, where it was severely scorched. Hannigan found residue from fire extinguishers, and the canisters themselves,
on the kitchen and living room floors, proof that the burners had done
their best to control the fire themselves.

They clearly had not yet finished their work, for near the fireplace was a box of papers waiting to be burned. Among a large number of financial documents was a mutual fund magazine, another magazine with the cover line "Playing the Spy Game: Banks, Bankers and Insurance Learn to Use Computer Intelligence," and a book, *Great Sex,* by Alexandra Penney, the author of *How to Make Love to a Man* and *How to Keep Your Man Monogamous.*

Most curious, Hannigan thought, was a fire set in a file drawer lying in the middle of the kitchen floor. The people burning papers must have panicked after the alarm sounded, he decided. They had simply set alight some of the remaining documents where they were, and fled. Taking a closer look, Hannigan found that many of the documents in the drawer were burned around the edges but not completely destroyed. His first reaction was pride in his firefighters, who had been trained not to use more water than necessary on possible evidence. But when he looked at the business names and addresses on the papers, he grew suspicious. The addresses, he saw, were in residential areas and couldn't possibly be right. The names of some of the firms and investment funds listed were a little screwy, too, as if the companies had been given names resembling those of better-known institutions. To Hannigan, it just didn't add up.

He took a close look at a printer that was connected to the phone system and had spewed out the names of people called from the house. Hannigan recognized some of the names: financial firms; people he knew from high school who had gone to work in the business world. He had only been on the scene for a few minutes, but he suspected that the crime in this strange house was not arson but fraud, a big fraud.

Turning to Detective Steve Carlo of the Greenwich Police Department, he said, "You need help." Carlo responded that someone was on his way to do fingerprinting. That, Hannigan knew, wasn't going to be enough.

"You've got to call your boss, you need to call your chief, the FBI, the ATF, and probably the SEC and the NBA and the NFL," Hannigan replied. "Anything with three initials in it, you call them."

"Why?" asked Carlo.

"Because I'm telling you, this is the biggest case you're ever going to work on in your life," Hannigan said.

. . .

By the next day, the Greenwich police had a search warrant and cops swarmed into the house, gathering evidence of a crime they still couldn't identify. They discovered security cameras everywhere. Some had even been focused to spy on whoever was working in the offices. There were push-button locks on some doors, and thumbprint locks on others. While combing through the garbage, one detective found a receipt for sophisticated night-vision equipment.

In the basement was a setup that seemed to belong in an office building, with more than fifty computer hard drives and a complex phone system—hardly a typical Greenwich home office. Computer servers were linked to a T-1 fiber optic line and several satellite dishes on the back lawn. Some twenty-five computers were wired to receive up-to-the minute market data. Much of the equipment in the basement was connected with a trading room in what had been the living room. There, towers of computers were set up around a large swivel chair and desk. To the right was one of the many phones, which rang incessantly for several days. Every time police personnel answered one, there was silence on the other end of the line.

Two detectives peeked into a bedroom, where they found a stash of condoms and a brochure from a hospital or clinic with instructions about how to treat herpes. In another they discovered pornographic magazines and dildos scattered across the floor, as well as other sex toys whose purpose the detectives didn't know.

Upstairs, the master bedroom had been carefully emptied, but the detectives noted that five-inch rings had been sunk into the bed's wooden frame. They obviously were meant for tying up people.

The detectives busied themselves outside as well. They interviewed a woman who had peered across the fence from next door. She had extremely short red hair, multiple body piercings, and a large tattoo of a spiderweb. She explained that she rented her house from Sundew International, which also owed 889 Lake Avenue. The next day, a moving van pulled up to her house and she vanished.

Two detectives cut open the lock on a shed, expecting to find lawn mowers and gardening equipment. Inside were even more boxes of financial documents. And there were yet more in the three-car garage, which had been converted into offices as well.

The house appeared to be the headquarters of a massive securities trading operation, but the police couldn't figure out why its occupants had fled so suddenly. Still, some of the documents hinted that something puzzling was amiss. The investigators found information about the extradition policies of several countries, including Brazil, and a survey of anonymous banking practices abroad.

One charred document was a "to do" list. Number 1: "Launder money." Number 2: "Get $ to Israel, get it back in." And then there were astrological charts, set up to answer these questions:

1) Will I go to prison?
2) Will Tom turn me in?
3) Should I leave?
4) Should I wire money back from overseas?
5) Will I be safe?

The charts offered no obvious replies, and two days after the fire, the FBI was summoned to try to come up with the answers.

Chapter One

A Real Job

It was a summer day in 1985 when Marty Frankel walked through the doors of Dominick & Dominick, a small discount brokerage office next door to a beauty salon and across from a rare-coin dealer's shop in the Great Eastern Shopping Center, a strip mall in a Toledo, Ohio, suburb. He told the receptionist that he wanted to open an account, and was ushered into the office of Sonia Schulte, a stockbroker who was also married to the head of the office.

Sonia pulled together the necessary paperwork and started asking questions. It was a routine Marty knew well. He had about ten other trading accounts at brokerages around Toledo and spent most of his time thinking about the stock and commodities markets. Marty was almost thirty-one. He'd only very briefly held a job, had never had a real girlfriend, and still lived with his parents in the modest house he'd spent his adolescence in. He told Sonia he was taking courses at the University of Toledo and was on his summer break. He looked the part. Dressed casually, like a college student, he wore comfy loose clothing and wire-rimmed glasses that made him look cerebral. Six feet tall, he weighed only about 135 pounds, just a little more than Sonia did.

The next day he returned to Dominick & Dominick and plunked himself down in Sonia's office so he could watch her stock quote machine. They chatted casually about the market. Marty, Sonia soon discovered, could really talk. In quick but understated tones, he led Sonia on a tour of his theories of the financial markets. His careful study of news events was the linchpin of his theory of trading, he explained. He believed in getting in and out of the market quickly, snapping up even quarter-point gains by exploiting his knowledge and understanding of the news.

Equity markets, credit markets: he knew much more than Sonia did. Marty talked about sophisticated transactions that Sonia and John Schulte had never even heard of, let alone executed for their clients in Toledo. Bull spreads, option spreads, bond option straddles—Marty seemed to understand them all. He didn't appear to be bragging, just very confident. Sonia decided he was very, very smart. She was impressed that he seemed to know many people in Toledo social circles that she and her husband John didn't travel in.

On the surface, they had little in common. About five years younger than Marty, Sonia Howe Schulte was the daughter of a machinist who had worked for the Ford Motor Company for thirty years. A former high school majorette, she was dark haired and attractive, but not stunning. She had put herself through college as a bookkeeper and teller at the Farmers Savings Bank, where she met and began dating John Schulte, a bank vice president. When they married in 1981, their goal was to operate the biggest discount brokerage firm in the city of Toledo. They convinced Sonia's rich great-uncle to invest in their dream, and opened the Toledo branch of Dominick & Dominick that same year. By the time Marty Frankel walked through their doors they felt they were well on their way to meeting their goal; Sonia, at twenty-six, was juggling the administration of the office and the care of a one-year-old daughter at home. "Home" was plush, a four-thousand-square-foot riverside house in nearby Pemberville.

Marty had never met a woman quite like Sonia before. She understood everything he said about the stock market and was willing—actually eager—to learn more from him. He was enthralled. He pulled out a stenographer's notebook and started taking notes as they talked, balancing the notes on his knee. Some of his jottings might turn into ideas for trades, he believed. He could have visited any number of other brokerage firms to keep tabs on the market, but in the weeks that followed he returned to Dominick & Dominick again and again. It wasn't that the firm's services were so vastly superior to the others where he had accounts, but because he just had to see Sonia again.

Next door John Schulte worked in another small office, linked to his wife's by a sliding window they'd installed so they could be in constant communication. Every time he opened the window between the offices, there Marty Frankel would be. Inevitably he was talking away as he checked stock quotes and took notes in what became a succession of steno pads. Schulte was a little annoyed. Weeks after visiting for the first time, Marty still had not put any money into the account he had opened with Sonia, and he had done no trading at all.

One day Sonia marched into her husband's office, Marty close behind. "I have a great idea," she said. "Let's hire Marty."

Schulte was skeptical, but that evening, in the privacy of home, Sonia argued vociferously. "John, let's give this guy a chance. He knows more about the markets than anyone I've ever met," she said. Marty was tied in to all the Jewish money in Toledo, she pointed out, money he would steer into Dominick & Dominick accounts.

That night, as the Schultes huddled, Marty went home and wrote up a résumé on the Apple Macintosh computer he worked on in his bedroom. When Schulte scanned the resume a few days later, one feature stood out: it said Marty had an IQ of 165.

Schulte finally relented and agreed to sponsor Marty for the Series 7 exam, administered by the National Association of Securities Dealers to all would-be stockbrokers. For Marty, taking the six-hour, 250-question test required a nearly superhuman act of will. Tests of any kind sent him into spasms of near hysterical anxiety, something he certainly didn't want John Schulte to see. He failed twice. Schulte, resentful of Marty's increasingly close relationship with his wife, was gleeful. But Sonia was gently supportive and encouraged him to try again. Finally, in November, Marty got the news that he'd passed on the third try, and he had his first job as a stockbroker.

Schulte ordered a small storage closet cleaned out and told Marty that that was to be his office. He didn't want anyone to see him there. It was so small that visitors had to stand halfway outside the door. Schulte supplied his brokers with a single computer screen and limited stock-quote services. On his first morning of work Marty brought in a television set and three extra computer monitors because he wanted additional stock quote services as well as up-to-date Reuters and Dow Jones newswire bulletins.

From the start, Marty had problems with his new boss. There were plenty of reasons why he rubbed Schulte the wrong way. Marty was politically liberal and not shy about sharing his views. He was Jewish. Schulte was a conservative Republican with political ambitions. He saw himself as a strictly "family values" kind of guy. Although he considered Sonia's working as important to their ultimate goal of having the most successful discount brokerage in Toledo, he viewed her primary responsibility to be "in the home," as he put it. Plus, Schulte generally mistrusted Jews.

But more than anything else, Schulte hated the attention Marty paid to his wife and the obvious pleasure she took in that attention. Sonia had been Schulte's only significant girlfriend, and he was a twenty-six-year-old virgin when they married in 1981. Two weeks before the ceremony and honeymoon in Hawaii, he almost called off the wedding when Sonia, twenty-one, confessed that she wasn't a virgin, too. He never quite forgave her.

And Sonia always regretted telling him. She felt sure he would have treated her more kindly if he hadn't suffered what he clearly saw as an insult at the onset of their marriage. At home, she had her hands full with one baby; a year after Marty joined the firm, there was a second. Schulte sometimes drank heavily in the evening and could be a little abusive. Sometimes, she later claimed, he hit her. Even sober, he was sneering and sarcastic. He kept constant pressure on his wife to perform on the job and "in the home."

For the most part, the tension between Marty and Schulte remained under the surface, even as it escalated. Instead, the two men skirmished over petty disagreements. Marty told others in the office that his talent and expertise should give him a pass when it came to office rules like dress codes and schedules. He refused to wear a coat and tie. His boss saw his insistence on wearing shabby clothes as insubordinate. Schulte, himself thin and lanky like Marty, favored polyester double-knit suits or sports coats.

Then there was Marty's idea of a workday. For a while, he worked from two P.M. to midnight. And finally, there was the condition of his office. *Wall Street Journals* were stacked sky high, as was Marty's collection of stenography pads, which he ran through at a rate of about fifteen a week.

The other brokers in the office thought he was a bit of a braggart.

After all, he arrived with no business, and his claims that he could predict shifts in the market, and sometimes even news events, seemed a little silly. "Volcker increased the rates just as I predicted," he announced
one day, as though he were the only one tracking the moves of the Federal Reserve chairman, Paul A. Volcker. At Dominick & Dominick, he
was the odd man out.

Not fitting in was nothing new for Martin Richard Frankel. He had always been a little bit like the odd, brainy kid who sat in the back of everyone's high school class. As one acquaintance from his middle-school
years put it, "He just wasn't quite in the groove. He just didn't fit." Marty
was geeky, and didn't have many close friends, though he wished he did.

In the sixties, in the Old West End of Toledo, the neighborhood kids
swam at the Catholic Club on Friday nights. They ran through the AFL-
CIO union hall, played ball in the alley that ran behind the houses on
Marty's block, and waged "buckeye wars," in which they threw chestnuts
at each other. Marty was there for all of those things, but he would sometimes peel off alone and often came up with ideas or schemes that no
one else in the neighborhood horde went along with.

Years later in Toledo, there were still kids around—now middle-
aged—who remembered the time that Marty ratted on the eleven-year-
old Rzymek twins when he caught them stealing a ten-cent bottle of pop
from a vending machine at the union hall. He also had a habit of tattling
on the large family of brothers who lived in the house next door, and
they returned the favor by constantly beating him up. "When you'd play
football, you'd give him the ball just so you could tackle him," one friend
remembered.

Leon Frankel, Marty's dad, was a lawyer, but not the kind who worked
in a big firm and raked in big fees. He had practiced law in New York,
where he and his wife had two children. But Mrs. Frankel died of
leukemia, and in the late 1940s Leon moved to Toledo and joined his
brothers in their wholesale underwear and hosiery business. A few years
later, he met and married Tillie, called Ty by her friends, who was from
nearby Detroit. She became a mother to his two young children, and the
Frankels soon had two more. Marty was the baby.

Years later, Marty told some of the women who surrounded him at his

Greenwich estate that he had grown up in a slum and that his mother had beaten him. The truth was somewhat different. The Old West End of Toledo, where Marty lived on Winthrop Street, had seen a wave of Jewish settlers in the city from the 1930s to the 1950s. It was an old neighborhood of big rambling houses, the kind that often had front and back stairwells and maid's rooms, though the latter rarely housed maids by then.

By the time the Frankels lived in the neighborhood, it had started changing, with Jews moving out and blacks moving in. The homes were run down and the area was definitely poor, but "it wasn't the slums," says a former neighbor. "There was still a lot of morality in the neighborhood."

The Frankels eventually joined the tail end of the exodus from the neighborhood. When Marty was thirteen, they moved to a modest ranch-style house built on a concrete slab on Stanhope Drive, in a middle-class neighborhood that a few non-Jews—including John Schulte—disdainfully called Little Israel. Most people called it by its real name, the Lincolnshire Addition. It was adjacent to Ottawa Hills, one of Toledo's wealthier suburbs, but was far more modest.

The Frankels' house was decorated for comfort, not style. The furniture was bought in the sixties and never updated. The outside was white, with blue trim, and while the grass was kept trim, there had been no serious attempt at landscaping. Until Marty bought his father a Cadillac in the 1990s, the cars in the short driveway were always far more practical than luxurious.

Leon Frankel eventually left the family business and in the mid-sixties went back to law, as a magistrate overseeing matrimonial cases. He was much respected by the local bar; the story went that he'd rendered some fifteen thousand decisions and never had a single one reversed by a more senior judge. Leon was a big talker, a real storyteller, and that trait was inherited by his younger son, Marty.

Ty was also busy with community affairs. She was a clerk for the City of Toledo and was active in the Jewish community, keeping track of the B'nai B'rith men and women's bowling league scores. She was an accomplished athlete. But while Leon was a sweetheart, with a sunny disposition—he always focused on the bright side of things—Ty's was a darker personality. She could be a little volatile, and she was in some ways unusual—she was one of the rare moms who didn't drive. But Marty's childhood pals did not remember any physical abuse.

In high school, Marty continued to be a bit of a loner, a voracious reader who thought for himself and didn't care what the rest of the pack was doing. He hated tests and was bored by almost all regular classwork, which was too simple for him. By sophomore year he was enrolled in an independent study program that allowed him to do most of his work in his bedroom.

But partway through the year, Marty's English teacher, John Weglian, began to worry. While Marty wasn't actually required to come to class, he should have been stopping by at least every so often. Weglian had no idea what the kid looked like. Also, he was turning in papers that were so well written that Weglian had reservations about whether they could have come from the pen of someone only about fifteen years old.

Weglian met with Marty's parents, who seemed concerned about the situation, and Marty began showing up in class. Weglian was delighted. Marty participated in class discussions, and his teacher thought he was smarter than he himself was.

When the class read *The Caine Mutiny Court-Martial* aloud, Marty wanted to read every part. More than any other student in the class, he understood what the lines meant, and when he thought his classmates didn't quite capture the meaning of the words, he would interrupt them. "You're not reading it right," he'd say. "This is the way it should be said."

In terms of pure intellect, Marty had no peer in the class. And although he got along with some of his fellow students, he was resented by others. There was no question that Marty stood out. While most kids wore tennis shoes and T-shirts to school, Marty was going through a brief—and unusual for him—phase of dressing well, opting for corduroy sports coats along with his blue jeans. It was the right get-up for the stage he was in. The other kids in Toledo were still in a freaky, hippie phase. Marty was more sophisticated politically, Weglian observed, and was focusing on liberal causes.

Weglian lost track of Marty after sophomore year. In fact, his student was again spending more time at home. He stopped going to school for weeks at a time, and although his parents weren't happy about the situation, they couldn't complain too much. Their son went to high school on his own terms, graduating in 1971, after just three years.

Finding their own way was a problem for all of the Frankel children. Several family members were haunted by emotional problems, including depression. All four siblings were considered to be bright, but none appear to have managed to put together a professional life that conventionally succeeded in the long term, and some have at times even had trouble making it financially. None of them is married.

Marty started attending classes at the University of Toledo some years later, and he studied there on and off for years. His test anxiety continued unabated, and when it came time to take final exams or write term papers, more often than not he just froze. He racked up one incomplete after another, and by the end of roughly four years he still had more coursework to finish than he had under his belt.

As he procrastinated on his coursework, he pursued his own studies—in which, of course, there were no final exams. He had many interests and over time considered many possible professions and fields of study. He knew a great deal about biology, physics, and mathematics, but was more interested in the history of human thought, in anthropology, and in the social sciences. The only thing he knew for sure was that he wanted to be known for his brilliance. (Of his brilliance, he was also certain. It was a fact his parents had drummed into him practically since his toddler days.)

For years, he studied ancient religions and early astronomy; those avenues of intellectual exploration led him to a fascination with astrology, which was encouraged by some witches he met at a Toledo boutique. That interest sometimes flagged, but never left him completely. One day a friend's father knocked at the Frankels' door asking for Marty's help. His son had had problems lately, and the man was worried about him. He asked Marty to work up a chart on the young man.

Marty spent more than thirty minutes laboring over the chart and then decided it was best not to tell his friend's father what he'd seen. Extremely disturbed, he told his parents that the charts looked very gloomy. Shortly afterward he learned that at precisely the moment he was confiding in his parents, the young man had suffered a devastating accident.

Marty was freaked out. But the episode solidified his already strong belief. He began to test astrology elsewhere, even applying it to a new interest: the financial markets.

To plot an individual's astrological chart, one needs not only a birth-date, but almost the exact moment the person was born, if possible within about four minutes. Marty began using the same strategy to plot the performance of companies. He would find out when a company was incorporated, even if that was half a century or so before, and then try to research exactly when the incorporation papers were filed. He then made an astrological chart predicting how the company's share price would fare given the way the stars and heavens were aligned. He concluded that his system worked, and so his two obsessions were effectively melded.

Marty eventually discovered that he and Bill Gates shared the same astrological stuff. They were "both lucky and both got things done," he told a friend.

By the spring of 1978, Marty was studying the financial markets seriously. By his own estimate, he spent thousands, if not tens of thousands, of hours reading business publications. He also hung out at brokerage firms, learning how to use machines and sopping up advice from the people who sat around watching stock quotes roll by.

Marty got to know brokers and investors at Paine, Webber, Prudential-Bache, Merrill Lynch, and A. G. Edwards. He opened accounts at these and other brokerage firms, although Prudential-Bache refused to allow him to trade because members of his extended family had accounts there and the brokers didn't want him to lose money. He tracked his favorite stocks in spiral stenography pads and checked back often to see whether his guesses were right. More and more often, they were. He became a voracious consumer of news—not only presidential elections and wars but also arcana, such as crop prices, usually followed by sophisticated traders, not by skinny college students who still lived at home.

Eventually, instead of listening to what others had to say, he started offering free advice. It was almost a game. Marty would make a prediction and, lo and behold, the stock would behave almost as though he had whispered in its ear. "I told people what would happen, and it happened," Marty once explained about that time. "And after a while some of them began to listen to me and I am certain take some of my advice. . . . I didn't do it for monetary gain, I did it with the aim of becoming a broker and eventually having these people as clients."

Ed Krauss, a friend of Marty's older brother, Bob, liked to stop by the house on Stanhope and watch over Marty's shoulder as he labored over his Apple Macintosh. Krauss was mesmerized, listening to Marty analyze the news, connect seemingly disconnected events, and come up with predictions about the way stocks would behave. Marty would announce that a certain stock was going to go up, and two hours later it inevitably would. Krauss noticed that Marty himself never seemed to buy. Once in a while he would ask Marty why he wasn't following his own advice about a stock. "I just want to watch it a little longer," Marty would answer. Still, he was always confident in his own powers. "What you should do every day is ask me what's going up tomorrow," he told Krauss.

Over the several years before he became a broker at Dominick & Dominick, Marty did invest. But the money was a pittance, a couple of thousand dollars at most in stock and commodity options. And he only broke even over the years.

Dr. Norman Sacks was an ophthalmologist who lived in Ottawa Hills, in a large house with a pool; he had a successful practice in a building at the Westgate Village Shopping Center, not far from Marty's home in the Lincolnshire Addition. Occasionally, between patients or on his lunch break, Sacks would leave his office and walk down the hall to visit A. G. Edwards, where he had a brokerage account, and watch the stock quote machines.

There, in 1985, he met a scrawny young man who seemed to be a font of information about the market. Sacks didn't even know whether the young man had an account at A. G. Edwards. He gave the man his name and pretty much forgot about him.

Shortly after he got his brokerage license, Marty gave Sacks a call, and the doctor agreed to open an account with him at Dominick & Dominick. Sacks had some experience in the market, and was not about to immediately turn over his entire portfolio for Marty to manage. He gave Marty a few thousand dollars but absolutely no discretion: Sacks chose all the stocks he wished to buy.

Marty knew that Sacks had more to invest, and was hopeful that he could convince the ophthalmologist to pour more money into the account. He started dropping by the Sackses' in the evening, often arriving while the family was still eating dinner. He waited patiently near the pool or on the porch until Sacks was free to talk. The family liked to joke that Marty was hanging around like a pesky puppy.

At first, Sacks thought Marty was brilliant. The young broker had read up on all the market wizards and said that one day he wanted to be a money manager. He told Sacks all about a highly successful businessman in Nebraska, Warren Buffett. Sacks had never heard of him.

Shirley Sacks, the doctor's wife, thought Marty was sensitive and gentle, if a little odd. They chatted about Irish literature and he took the time to read her own poetry. It was wonderful, he gushed. One night, he confided to her that he'd lived for a time in a hut on the Maumee River, which runs through Toledo. When she was preparing to take courses at the University of Toledo, they discussed professors and he made suggestions.

Sacks finally did give Marty more money, and at one point the account had a few hundred thousand dollars in it. He actively traded stocks and options. But he was reluctant to give Marty any more discretion over his money. For one thing, he began to feel that Marty wasn't the genius he made himself out to be. Sacks remained impressed at the sheer number of facts Marty had at his disposal. But he didn't think Marty reasoned all that well. Market junkie that he was, Marty continually complained that he couldn't quite get himself to "pull the trigger," as he always put it, and actually make a trade on his own. Sacks also thought Marty was not totally honest. It was nothing major—only that, as he later put it, "I caught inconsistencies. In other words, lying."

Sacks wasn't overly impressed with Dominick & Dominick either. He thought Schulte cared more about churning accounts than about his clients' welfare. He also wasn't comfortable with the way Sonia kept track of accounts. She seemed a little inefficient, he thought.

Marty tried to reassure him. "She's wonderful," he crooned about Sonia. "Schulte's no good, but Sonia's a wonderful person."

Eventually, Sacks began to find Marty just plain annoying. When Marty claimed that he wanted to write a book about blind people, Sacks saw the "plan" for what it was, a way to curry favor with an eye doctor. Needless to say, it didn't work.

One day Sacks came home from his medical office only to find Marty's ancient and beat-up Chevy blocking his driveway. Sacks gently nudged the car out of the way with his own car and came into the house and told Marty what he'd done. Marty erupted, shouting "I'm going to sue you for wrecking my car!"

"Marty," the doctor replied, "do me a favor and go, will you please? I can't stand it." Sacks had had enough. A few days later he called Marty and fired him as his broker.

Several days after that, Sacks walked into the surgical suite's coffee room while between eye operations at the Riverside hospital. There was Marty. He was wearing a cheap suit, which is to say he was unusually well dressed. Sacks was still in his surgical scrubs.

"Why would you want to abandon me?" Marty asked, crying. He told Sacks that the doctor was his number-one account. "I'm just getting going," Marty said, sobbing. "I need your account." Sacks thought to himself that it was a little odd that Marty didn't try to argue how good a broker he was. And then he told the young man that their professional relationship was over, and he should remove himself from the surgical suite.

Sacks was the only really big client Marty brought to Dominick & Dominick, but he did have other clients. Originally from a farm family, Ted Bitter was a tool and die maker from Millbury, Ohio. He spent his days making machine parts to exacting specifications at a small plant in Perrysburg, half an hour or so outside Toledo. About five years older than Marty, he was slowly accumulating a retirement nest egg for himself and his wife, Sharon. He kept it at Dominick & Dominick because he had known John Schulte for years from St. John's Lutheran Church in Stony Ridge, where they both worshipped. Occasionally, he stopped by the brokerage to watch the quote machines and check on his portfolio.

One Sunday, Bitter ran into Schulte after church. "I hired a genius," announced Schulte, who despite his misgivings could not deny that Marty was unusually smart. He suggested that Bitter come by and introduce himself to Marty someday soon.

On his next visit to the brokerage firm, Bitter made sure to seek out

Marty in the broom closet. His first impression was that Marty seemed to be "very timid," even "a nebbish." He was *too* courteous, Bitter thought, and unnecessarily apologetic.

"Oh, this place is so dirty, but please come in," Marty said, as he invited Bitter as far into the cubbyhole as was possible.

Bitter began to swing by Marty's office often. He became convinced that Marty was brilliant, and he thought him extremely well spoken. Like Ed Krauss and others who took the time to actually listen to Marty's rantings, he was impressed with the young man's market expertise. Marty would predict how a stock would perform, and sure enough the stock would do what he said. Bitter decided to give Marty $8,000 to invest. At first Marty just dabbled in the market with the money. Although the results were nothing special, Bitter was tantalized by Marty's quiet and nonstop patter. Marty made him excited about trading and Bitter couldn't wait to see more. Soon he gave Marty more money—roughly $50,000. It was his life's savings.

Marty was petrified. Being Sacks's broker had been easy; the doctor made his own decisions about when and in what he wanted to trade. Bitter was happy to turn over those decisions to his genius broker. He soon learned, however, that while Marty could recognize solid trades, he always wanted to wait and watch a little longer. "I realized this was a pattern that he was having a real tough time breaking," Bitter later said.

"We would have made ten thousand today if we'd made that trade," Marty said, the day after one of his predictions came true. And Bitter thought, "One of these times he's going to do it."

But even Bitter began to get discouraged. There was no place to sit in Marty's closet—in fact, there was barely enough room to peer over Marty's shoulder at the computer screens piled one on top another. One day Bitter got down on his knees and just begged Marty to just do something.

It was under that kind of intense pressure that Marty finally decided to make a buy using Ted Bitter's retirement money. One day he bought eighteen bond calls in the futures market for about $20,000, about a third of his client's money. Immediately, he was in anguish, a complete mess. He worried out loud whether it had been the right call. Leaving his tiny office, he paced back and forth. The next day, when the other Dominick & Dominick employees arrived at work he was still there worrying, and they wondered whether he had gone home at all. Finally he couldn't take it anymore and sold the calls.

Schulte was livid. "You're out of your mind," he said. "You just lasted one day!"

In fact, Marty had called it right. The net gain on Bitter's account for the one-day position was about $18,000. Marty was triumphant. He called Bitter, who congratulated him on being a "genius." The Bitters took Marty out to Cousino's Steak House, in a Toledo suburb, and showered him with gifts. "I thought it was a harbinger of things to come," Bitter later said.

Just a few weeks later, at about 11:40 a.m. on January 28, 1986, mundane news being spewed over the news ticker was interrupted with the bulletin that the space shuttle *Challenger* had exploded over the coast of Florida, only seventy-four seconds into its flight. Seven crew members died, including the New Hampshire elementary-school teacher Christa McAuliffe.

Marty Frankel was thrilled. That morning before coming to work he had worked over his astrological charts and predicted a crash. As the news broke he ran out of his office.

"I knew it this morning when I woke up!" he shouted. "I should have shorted bonds." He exhorted his fellow brokers to "short bonds, sell the market!" (Investors who short bonds borrow the security and then sell it, betting that the price will fall and they will be able to buy the bond back at a cheaper price, and thus realize a profit.)

In fact the bond market rallied, influenced apparently by the Bank of Japan's discount rate and not the tragic crash. His fellow brokers were sore and fed up with his predictions and bravado.

John Schulte was losing his patience fast. "John was aggressive and bossy," Bitter later explained. "Marty is the exact opposite. He's passive and stays to himself. Marty hates being pressured." Schulte would sneer at Marty and attempt to shame him into trading. Marty would wait until John had retreated to his own office, then let forth a string of expletives under his breath.

The bickering between the two men kept escalating. Schulte continued to chafe over the clothes Marty wore to work and the condition of his workspace. He finally told the cleaning lady just to sweep up around the piles in Marty's office, and bits of Marty's old lunches remained on his desk for days.

"I don't have to listen to anything you say," Marty hollered at Schulte one winter day, sounding more like a child than an employee.

Schulte, too, could sink to petty gestures. When Sonia insisted that Schulte accompany her to dinner at the Frankels' house, he choked on the food prepared by Tillie Frankel and insisted on leaving early, later telling Sonia that the house was too dirty for him.

Of course, there were serious issues, too. Marty was not generating much business. Sacks was gone, and once the excitement over his fortunate trade for Bitter died down it was increasingly apparent that Marty was doing very little except talking.

Schulte was also angry because, without his permission, Marty had ordered expensive equipment and news services, signing his own name to contracts as though it were he who ran the office. These were bills that Schulte was then responsible for, and Marty was not generating enough income for the firm to cover the expenses.

About a month after the *Challenger* disaster, Schulte finally exploded. The showdown came after yet another battle over the state of Marty's office.

"Get the hell out!" Schulte screamed, telling Marty he had to be out of the office by five P.M. that day. He threatened to throw Marty's equipment into the parking lot, and yelled about his "lack of production" and "insubordination."

Marty told Schulte to "take a flying leap," and Sonia ran out of her office to try to get her angry husband to back off.

"I don't give a damn!" Schulte screamed at her. "This guy's out of here, and he's out of here today." Sonia retreated into her office, but as the din shifted to the firm's tiny lobby, Dominick & Dominick's brokers and customers could hear the flinging of curses back and forth as the two men argued.

"You're a no-good bastard," Marty finally screamed. "I'll get you." He swore that he would prove to the world that Schulte was "no good."

About an hour later, Leon Frankel arrived to take his son home. Marty watched as his elderly father carried his computer monitors out to the parking lot, and then the two got into the car and drove away.

Several days later, Schulte heard from Marty's lawyer, who threatened to sue him for wrongful termination. Marty eventually received about $5,000 from Schulte, roughly what was owed him in commissions on Sacks's trades.

It seemed, at the time, that the two men's relationship was over, and that they would never see each other again unless they bumped into each other accidentally as they went about their business in Toledo. In fact, though they rarely met again, each became a driving force in the other's life.

Chapter Two

Marty's First Fraud

The firing was only a temporary setback. Soon Marty had regained his confidence and was thinking ahead again. Being a broker, after all, was only a single step on the road to his greater ambition of managing large sums of money—and proving to the world that he had a special knack for it.

"It is my thesis that, since Wall Street is a place where the lunatics often run the asylum, one must keep a weather-eye on the gurus of the moment, for the simple reason that when one is in Rome one must be careful to note what the current lunacy is, for such lunacy is often adopted as truth, and thus becomes, if only for the short term, a self-fulfilling prophecy," Marty wrote to prospective clients on his handy Macintosh computer.

His best shot at getting back into the game, he decided, was Ted Bitter. One Saturday morning in December 1986, he called and asked Ted to meet him at the Westgate Village Shopping Center, not far from the Frankels' house.

Bitter drove the half-hour or so to Toledo from Millbury, parked his car at the mall, and waited. He had already heard that Schulte had fired Marty, and had no idea why Marty wanted to speak to him.

Soon the car door opened and Marty slipped into the passenger seat. He was calm and even upbeat. He explained that he'd affiliated with LaSalle Street Securities, a discount brokerage based in Chicago, and that he would now be working out of his bedroom in his parents' house. He wanted Bitter to switch his account from Schulte's office to LaSalle.

Bitter knew he would be Marty's first client, and maybe his only one. But the $18,000 overnight windfall was still fresh in his mind and he wanted to believe Marty could do it again. So, a few days later, he opened an account with LaSalle.

For Marty, setting up shop on his own had turned out to be easy. He saw an advertisement LaSalle placed in *Registered Rep,* a trade publication, and just called them up. He wasn't required to come to Chicago for an interview, and he didn't have to do much more than fill in a one-page questionnaire and submit to a few cursory phone interviews. Marty felt he needed professional equipment, Telerate and Reuters services, and these turned out to be his only big expense. He piled all his new equipment, and his computer, on his mother's old card tables.

Hour after hour he sat in front of the screens, tracking stock prices and making predictions. Each time he hit it right, he felt a thrill. So did some of the people he spoke to each morning by phone. Bitter, and a few others, would call in the morning and Marty would tell them what stocks were sure to go up by the end of the day. One Toledo-area executive who became a client kept tabs on Marty's predictions and told him he was 90 percent accurate. Still, Marty rarely actually made a trade, and money quickly became a problem.

Although he was living at home, he ended up eating into his nest egg—roughly $15,000, including his meager Dominick & Dominick commissions—to pay for his machines and news services. Continually overdue on the monthly fees, he did his best to put his creditors off. Finally he set up a corporation, Winthrop Capital, named after his old street in Toledo's West End, to contract for the services and shield him from personal liability. He used a mail drop as the company's address, and the name James Spencer, borrowed from a friend apparently without his permission, for its president. That was Marty's first alias.

Marty rarely left his bedroom, which soon resembled a slightly larger version of his cubbyhole at Schulte's shop, complete with three-foot stacks of *Wall Street Journals* on the floor. Tensions in the Frankel household escalated. Leon had been hoping that his son would go back to college and had even been telling friends that Marty would soon finish his degree. Tillie began getting on his case about the mess and his failure to do chores around the house. Often they had screaming battles over her refusal to just let him be.

Bitter believed he was Marty's only visitor during the months after the firing. Typically, he dropped by on Saturday afternoons, around one. Marty would take Bitter up to his room, where they would look at the computer screens stacked up against one wall. On more than a few occasions, Bitter witnessed fights between Marty and his parents, especially his mother. Bitter thought Tillie was rough, and not very ladylike, but in general he thought the Frankels seemed pretty much like an ordinary couple. Marty kept telling him that he was "stressed out." He needed peace, he said, and his parents were distracting him from his true work. But Bitter didn't put much stock in Marty's ranting about his parents.

Then they would take off for Barry Bagels at the Westgate Village Shopping Center—or sometimes, for a change of pace, the Olive Garden at the Southwick Shopping Center—so they could get a sandwich and talk. Over and over again, Marty told Bitter that he was a genius, or "near genius." He was smarter, he insisted, than many of his college professors and was always the brightest in his class. Bitter thought he was just "fluffing up his own ego."

They talked about politics and religion. Marty was the first Jew whom Bitter had ever known well, and he was very interested in what he had to say. Marty insisted that he was an atheist. But although he was not a practicing Jew, he had great appreciation for his roots and traditions. Bitter asked about the Holocaust, and with great authority, Marty went into long explanations of what had happened.

Marty would move on, and talk about stocks, commodities, and option trading, subjects generally over Bitter's head. In any case, it was hard to hear him because when they talked business, Marty always dropped his voice to a whisper. He worried constantly that someone was listening and would steal his ideas.

But no matter what they were discussing, Marty always returned to a topic that Bitter found increasingly frustrating: Marty's trading problem. How could he use his talents to circumvent his "trading block"? he asked again and again, not really expecting an answer from Bitter. Long after his sandwich was finished and he had pushed away his plate, he tried to analyze the problem. He likened it to his anxiety about tests and his inability to finish college. Perhaps, he said, psychological help, some sort of therapy, would help.

Even as he struggled, Marty started bringing in more clients. In

March 1987, John and Shirley Herlihy saw an advertisement in the Toledo yellow pages that attracted their attention. "Super Discount Brokers," it said. "Very Low Commissions." The ad promised that the brokerage's accounts were insured.

John Herlihy had recently retired as a salesman for Sears, Roebuck, and he wanted to invest his retirement savings safely and conservatively. He gave Marty a phone call at the number listed, which was his parents' house. Marty wowed Herlihy with his sophisticated patter about the financial markets. Clearly the young man was very intelligent, very sensitive to his customers' needs. It wasn't long before Herlihy surrendered his employee stock ownership plan holdings to Marty, some 4,538 shares of Sears stock. Marty scrawled a one-page receipt in all capital letters on a blank piece of paper without letterhead. He sold the stock for $231,178. Soon afterward, Herlihy turned over more money, approximately $63,000. He was Marty's biggest client.

Possibly because he so rarely went out, Marty became an inveterate phone caller, a habit that persisted for years to come. One day in late 1986, through a phone acquaintance, he met Douglas Maxwell. The owner of a small brokerage firm, Maxwell traveled between Nashville—his hometown—Chicago, and Palm Beach, Florida. He called initially because he wanted Marty to put some of his clients' money into some penny-stock companies he had underwritten. Marty refused, but the two continued their conversations.

Marty told Maxwell that he oversaw several million dollars, although even after Herlihy signed on he had a little under $500,000 in client money. He did lots of trading, he told Maxwell, and made big commissions. And he bragged about his system, his knack for correlating market moves with news events and getting in and out of the market at lightening speed.

A few years younger than Marty, Maxwell had a bit of the hustler about him. He liked to think big and was anxious to expand his firm, PDS Securities. He told Marty he had done several underwritings and that he cleared his trades through a big New York Stock Exchange firm, Mesirow Financial. He knew some of the richest people in the world, he added, former employees of Exxon, Texaco, and Getty Oil, people who lived in Switzerland, the queen of Romania.

Hooking up with Maxwell, Marty thought, could be his big chance. He liked the idea of becoming the protégé of the owner of a brokerage firm. Maxwell thought really big, and in that sense they were kindred spirits. But the negotiations went on and on. Maxwell thought that the best investment vehicle for Marty to run would be a limited partnership or mutual fund. That, he explained, would allow Marty to keep a percentage of the profits. But setting up such an investment vehicle would cost between $50,000 and $150,000. Marty didn't have that kind of money—but he didn't want to tell Maxwell so.

In May 1987, Maxwell told Marty to expect a phone call from John Leo Burns, a former Exxon executive and a distant relative of his by marriage. Burns, Maxwell explained, was worth $7 million. Burns called Marty in Toledo and they chatted for more than an hour. Marty talked mainly about his philosophy of jumping in and then out of the market quickly. It was his view, he explained, that "news ruled the markets." And, using this approach, he was making 20 to 30 percent returns on an annualized basis.

"He really struck me as very bright, a sort of genius type who was quite capable of doing day trading. That's what he was really into when I met him," Burns said later.

Marty followed up by mailing Burns a twenty-page disclosure statement, the one in which he described Wall street as "a place where the lunatics often run the asylum." He went on about the theories of John Maynard Keynes, John Kenneth Galbraith, and Warren Buffett, and about Robert Prechter's championing of the Elliott Wave Principle, an arcane system of technical stock market analyses, which, he pointed out, has an "epistemological underpinning akin to astrology or Tarot." His own system, he wrote, placed "supreme importance on swift interpretation of and action on news events and media reports. To this end he [that is, Marty himself] employs a sophisticated, costly array of news retrieval systems. . . . Marty Frankel has developed his own proprietary indicators; he uses these indicators as critical action-triggering signals in his system of 'informational analysis.' "

Burns was convinced that Marty could make him some significant money. In June 1987, he liquidated his existing investments and deposited $561,580 in an IRA account at First Trust, a Denver bank. From there it was transferred to Marty Frankel. Despite Maxwell's assertion that Burns was worth $7 million, the money Marty was now managing for him represented about a third of his holdings.

The Burns money, and that of John and Shirley Herlihy and Ted and Sharon Bitter, went into the Frankel Fund, a new limited partnership set up by Maxwell and Frankel. (The fees and legal work associated with setting up the fund were paid for by the investors, without their express permission.) Each investor's funds were to be kept in a separate account, and Marty was to be fully in charge of how the money was traded. He had hit the big time.

But he was frozen. He couldn't, as he always put it, "pull the trigger" and buy stocks. One Friday in June, when the Frankel Fund was not yet a month old, Burns called him to ask what he had been doing with his money. Marty hadn't done a thing, and Burns made it perfectly clear that he wanted to see some action.

"You've got to make a trade to his account," Maxwell said when he called Marty later that day. "You've got to trade. You've got to make a trade. You must do it."

Marty balked. "I don't want to do anything right now. It's my account. I have control. I will decide when."

If Marty wasn't going to trade, he, Maxwell, would trade for him, Maxwell insisted. A week or so earlier, Marty had predicted that Eastman Kodak would go up. And it had, by about eight points, although, of course, he hadn't invested. So Maxwell proposed that he would buy Kodak. Marty objected. It had gone up already, he pointed out. Off the top of his head, he suggested that Maxwell buy shares of the pharmaceutical firm Merck & Company instead, because there had been an article about Merck in the morning papers.

Maxwell got off the phone and bought 3,000 shares of Kodak and 1,000 shares of Merck.

Marty was frantic. He worried all weekend and could barely sleep. On Monday, he was so nervous he couldn't even read the newspapers, a practically unheard-of departure from habit. And then he sold both stocks. He had lasted in the market for one business day.

Despite the haphazard way in which the stocks were bought and then sold, Marty and Maxwell had actually done okay. It wasn't exactly a windfall, but they made $1,000 for Burns's account. With Marty on the line, Maxwell called Burns to report the victory. His response was "Great. Get me more."

Maxwell had learned that he needed to be able to ride herd on Marty. He began to try to convince Marty to move to Palm Beach, where Maxwell then lived, so that he could keep a closer eye on his trading and support him when he was stuck in his periodic bouts of insecurity and doubt.

Never having spent more than a short time without his mother and father, and never having lived away from home, Marty was reluctant. But Maxwell was pretty persuasive. He could introduce Marty to prominent people in Palm Beach, and the wealth there was ready to be mined for accounts. And, he promised Marty, there were plenty of women around, and he was sure to have sex, including oral sex.

That for Marty, was definitely an added draw. His sexual experience was extremely limited; much of what he knew came from reading *Playboy*, copies of which he kept in his parents' living room. In this respect, he was like an adolescent boy, ricocheting between terrified prudery and lurid obsession.

For a while, he'd had a crush on a woman who worked at a newsstand near his parents' house, but he'd barely been able to bring himself to talk to her. When Bitter took an extra look at an attractive woman they saw in a coffee shop, Marty was aghast. "You're married!" he said. "What would your wife say?"

Finally, in 1987 Marty decided to make the break and move to Florida. He and his parents were comforted by the decision of Marty's older sister, Amy, to accompany him. Amy would act as his housekeeper and helper. Maxwell also brought his own sister, Elizabeth, to Palm Beach to help with the venture.

Maxwell found Marty a house. Actually, it was in West Palm Beach, Palm Beach's somewhat lower-caste cousin, but it belonged to King Michael and Queen Anne of Romania. King Michael, then in his sixties, had been deposed by the Communists in 1947 and was living in exile with his wife and daughters in Versoix, Switzerland, on the shore of Lake

Geneva. Over time he'd tried his hand at farming and in the investment business. He and Queen Anne, who was of French royal extraction, spent part of each winter in West Palm.

The house, which was built in about 1940 and has since been torn down, sat on the Intercoastal Waterway. Its layout was a bit odd; it had six bedrooms and four baths, and had been added on to rather haphazardly over the years by more than one owner. It could be closed off into four discrete apartments, each with its own entrance; the king and queen, a little pressed for cash, rented parts out.

The exiled couple lived in an upstairs bedroom, which had lovely views of the water and a magnificent tentlike silk ceiling that gave it the feel of a movie set. But the king and queen cooked on a hot plate in the room and stored their food in a small refrigerator like those found in hotel or dorm rooms. When in residence, their daughter, Princess Sophie, lived in the former living room.

Marty took over several rooms, and set up shop in what had been a downstairs bedroom, adjacent to the Florida room. An electrical conduit was put in around the walls of the room, with plugs every six or so inches for his equipment. About fifty phone lines were also installed.

Marty and Maxwell discussed their need for stock quote and other services—Reuters, Telerate, Dow Jones news services, and Automatic Data Processing machines. Marty said they had to be in Maxwell's name because he owed Reuters and Telerate money under his own.

"Pick an alias. What alias do you want to use?" Marty later reported Maxwell saying.

"What alias do you want me to use?" Marty asked.

"No, you pick an alias," Maxwell insisted.

Marty had already used the name of his friend James Spencer, so he changed the first name to Paul. That, apparently, was fine with Maxwell, who, Marty later said, confided that he had previously used the alias "James Duncan." Maxwell then also used the name "Paul Spencer" to install phones in Queen Anne's house.

From the start, Marty was a wreck. He discovered that Maxwell had bought and then sold Texas Instruments stock, losing about $7,000, without telling him. Again and again, Maxwell would buy securities and Marty almost immediately would sell what Maxwell had just bought. It was not exactly a coherent trading strategy.

Marty often sat in the house, or in an office they briefly occupied, chastising himself for not buying a certain stock. "Here's what, here's what I should have done with X, y, z," he told Elizabeth Maxwell. "And see, I had it picked and I meant to, I should have bought, or I knew I should have bought a thousand shares. . . ."

Elizabeth thought Marty was just "verbally flailing around." He complained endlessly about Maxwell. "Doug, all Doug does is just tells me to trade. 'Just force yourself, Marty, force yourself to trade,' " he said.

He couldn't get the newspapers in West Palm Beach as easily as he did in Toledo, he griped. More than once, he told Elizabeth Maxwell that he was moving home to Toledo that night, only to announce the next day that it was "not so bad, I'm getting settled." At one point he even tried to convince Ted Bitter to move to Florida, because he always found Bitter a stabilizing influence, but Bitter refused.

Perhaps the high point for Marty was that he did indeed get to meet a few members of what he called the "Palm Beach crowd." Maxwell knew a woman whose sister knew a young relative of Queen Anne. Marty studied up on Romanian history, reading several books on the subject, so that he could talk intelligently with the queen about her country.

Anne was a handsome woman, and Marty was particularly taken with her. He described living in her house as "the best time of my life" and said her company was like "a breath of fresh air." He told the queen that she was "one of the most thoughtful and caring people I have ever met."

Marty also was enchanted with one of the queen's daughters. "I kissed the hand of a princess!" he bragged breathlessly to a friend back in Toledo. He seemed to think the princess might consider him seriously as a suitor.

Although no romance developed, he must have made some sort of impression on the royal family. After some discussion the queen agreed to invest $50,000—in cash—in the Frankel Fund. In nearly inch-high capital letters, Marty scrawled a two-sentence receipt, forgetting King Michael's name and squeezing it in as an afterthought.

With the queen's contribution, the Frankel Fund had had turned over to it $1,024,522, by far the most money Marty had ever managed. But after less than a year of operation, the fund was losing money. Marty calculated that it had suffered $130,000 in trading losses, which he blamed entirely on Maxwell, even though he was certainly as responsible.

There were other losses, as well. Marty was paying his personal expenses directly out of the various Frankel Fund shareholder accounts. He paid his $3,000 monthly rent and the fees for his ADP machine out of the accounts. He also wrote a check to his sister for $4,294, and another to "Mrs. Leon Frankel," his mother, for $5,000. He even tapped the shareholder accounts when he needed $500 spending money.

In January 1988, John Herlihy started getting worried about the nearly $300,000 he had invested with Marty. He wasn't receiving statements regularly, and when he called Marty in West Palm Beach, he found the number had been disconnected. Alarmed, the Herlihys called Marty's father, who simply told them that Marty was no longer living at home. Leon then wrote his son that one of his clients was trying to reach him, and Marty finally returned the phone call.

By that point Herlihy was pretty upset, and he asked for his money back. Marty immediately flew to Toledo to try to persuade him to change his mind. He arrived at the Herlihy's home with strange gifts, ashtray-type items that looked as though they had been lifted from a nondescript hotel room. Marty insisted to Herlihy and his wife that the Frankel Fund had been very successful and that their money was safe.

He promised even more. He told Herlihy that he would guarantee them against any losses as of January 27. "Furthermore," he wrote them after he returned to Florida, "this letter guarantees that your principal shall earn an annualized rate of return of 10 percent." Marty sent the couple a statement, drafted as usual on his Macintosh, stating that as of January 27, their account was worth $327,451.83, up more than $21,000 from the beginning of the year. The Herlihys were satisfied with the statement. A month or so later, they received another, which told them that they had earned an additional $2,960.53 on their account; a month after that, in March, they were informed that the account was worth $333,428.59.

What the couple didn't know, until several years later, was that on January 29, Frankel had transferred $307,200 out of their account and into the account of John Burns to cover trading losses and Marty's other expenses.

The money never made it back into Herlihy's account. In February,

Burns wrote Marty a brief note: "Dear Marty, This is my written notice to redeem $500,000 worth of my partnership interests in April. Very truly yours, J. L. Burns."

Why Burns wanted to withdraw his money is not quite clear. "I don't know why I did it except I didn't trust it anymore," Burns said more than ten years later. "I started asking him, 'What are you doing now in terms of future use of these funds and if I want to withdraw some of these funds let me know how you do that.' And he said, 'You don't need to do that . . . we'll double your money.' No way he could have done that in the time he said he could do this. I said okay, I'm out of this."

Like Herlihy, Burns had some trouble reaching Marty and had not been receiving statements on a regular basis, although in early January he got one that said he now had $628,000 in his account.

But something else was going on as well. Maxwell was looking for new business for PDS, his firm; he enlisted Burns, who had an ownership stake in PDS, to travel with him to Australia to scout opportunities. They apparently thought they might need Burns's money elsewhere.

Did Maxwell, Burns's relative by marriage, encourage him to take his money out of the Frankel Fund? "We probably talked about it because he was concerned as I was," Burns recalled. "It was a combination. We were looking at better using the funds with PDS, but it was also the fact that Marty was not giving us reports. We didn't know what he was doing and so forth." PDS never did do any business in Australia.

But even though Burns had informed him of his decision to remove the money, Marty exploded when it finally happened two months later, in April. The transfer occurred while Marty was in Santa Monica, California—he said at Maxwell's behest—making television ads for the Frankel Fund. When he returned to West Palm and listened to his answering machine, he heard a message from an official at the financial institution at which the Frankel Fund money was actually kept. He returned the call and was told that the $500,000 had been wired out of the Burns account.

"I didn't wire any money out," he said, panicking. "You crazy? What are you talking about?" When he was given the details of the transfer, he began screaming into the phone. "Get that money back, is there any way we can get that money back? . . . Stop that wire! That wire wasn't authorized by me! . . . Get that money back!"

Marty was told that the money had already been wired into Burns' IRA account at a bank in Denver. He called there and resumed his diatribe. "I think a crime may have been committed!" he screamed.

Marty desperately tried to reach Maxwell, even calling him at his mother's home in Tennessee. It turned out Maxwell was in Florida. When they met, he tried to remind Marty that he had known the money was going to be removed from the account, and he explained that it was going to be used in some way to attract rich investors from Australia. Eventually, Maxwell said, it would be returned to the fund.

They argued for hours, but finally Marty started screaming. "Just get the money back! Get the five hundred thousand back! Get the money back!"

Suddenly, Maxwell mentioned that there were other problems brewing as well. Someone they worked with had discovered that the Frankel Fund was allocating trades—that is, making trades and then assigning them, after the fact, to particular clients. Though not necessarily illegal, it potentially opened them up to breach of duty claims by investors, and might have to be explained.

Faced with the possibility of legal problems, Marty called the bank in Denver to smooth things over. He said there had just been a mixup and everything was fine.

But even after Maxwell left, Marty was hysterical. Thinking he was dying, he called 911. The paramedics diagnosed a panic attack and decided it was not necessary to take him to the hospital.

Over the next several days, Marty had to reckon with a situation that he realized was very grim. The $500,000 was firmly in Burns's hands. The money had actually come from the accounts of several different clients, whose missing funds ultimately would have to be explained. Phony statements had been sent to Herlihy and Burns, and the Frankel Fund might also be in trouble for other legal infractions.

Marty's immediate concern was that he had recently sent Burns a phony statement to the effect that he had almost $700,000 in his account. What would happen if Maxwell went into the other Frankel Fund client accounts to make up the difference?

Frankel's solution was to wire the money into his own, personal account at a Florida bank. In other words, Frankel Fund money belonging to several of his clients was now in Marty's name.

By now, Amy Frankel was extremely concerned about her brother's emotional state. She knew next to nothing about how his business worked, but she did know that Marty was a mess. It would be better, she believed, for him to be under their parents' care in Toledo. Within just a few weeks she had convinced him to leave West Palm Beach and head north. He returned heavyhearted.

Shortly after Marty returned to Toledo, Ted Bitter came to see him at the house on Stanhope. Bitter was struck by the change in his friend. Marty could barely speak, and when he did he was almost incoherent. His conversation no longer flowed smoothly. Instead, he jumped here and there and didn't form complete, thought-out sentences. Later, Bitter would describe it as a "state of nervous hysterical depression and anxiety."

It was a brisk spring morning, but they drove in Bitter's car to the nearby Crosby Gardens and sat outside on a bench. The Frankel Fund had collapsed, Marty explained. He said that Doug Maxwell had stolen money and that some had been lost in bad trades. But, he said, Bitter's money was safe in an interest-bearing account.

It was only a month or so later, over the telephone, that Marty finally told Bitter the truth: that his money was mostly gone. Bitter wanted to wring Marty's neck. He and his wife had planned a trip to Dayton for the weekend, and as they drove he broke the news to her: their savings were gone.

"A disaster has befallen my life," Marty wrote to Queen Anne, who had invested her $50,000 in the fund only about six weeks before its collapse. In a nine-page typed letter informing the queen that her money was gone, Marty said that his life was "utter chaos," and that he felt "as if I was a woman who was raped." He set the blame for the mess squarely on the shoulders of Doug Maxwell. In the letter, he likened himself to H. J. Heinz, the founder of the ketchup company, who went bankrupt "early in his career, at a very young age. In his early thirties, he drew up a list of what he called 'moral obligations.' He resolved that even though he was bankrupt, he was going to pay back every single moral obligation, and this he did." Like Heinz, Marty promised, he would pay back "every penny" to his clients.

"I am a man of honor; I am a man of honesty," Frankel wrote the queen. "My whole life has been based on the idea that when clients entrust money to me, it is a sacred trust." He described himself as being "shaken to my roots," and said that he "will regret to my dying day" his decision to discontinue trading on his lawyers' advice. "I know now that with my talents it would have been very easy for me to recoup all the clients' losses simply through trading with the remaining client funds."

"I vow to repay all my investors double their initial investment," he continued. "My only goal in life is to work for the satisfaction of my clients. I entered this profession because I believe that managing money and making money for clients is a noble profession. I still believe this to be true; my experience shall not kill me, only delay me."

Meanwhile, Marty had turned over $249,000 to his cousin, a Toledo lawyer, for safekeeping (the money was put in a trust account and later turned over to the SEC), and had hired a law firm in Chicago, Goldstein & Koch. On a regular basis, Tillie Frankel would drive her son, now almost thirty-four years old, to Chicago to see his lawyers. The trip was five hours long, and when they arrived, Mrs. Frankel insisted on joining her son in the meetings.

The lawyers began to try to figure out what actually had happened in the roughly one-year life of the Frankel Fund. It was all a huge, huge mistake, Marty's story went. He only had his clients' best interests at heart, he explained; Maxwell had stolen $500,000 and ruined everything. But he strained his lawyers' credulity when he told them about his peculiar genius for always picking the right stock at the right moment. Out of a hundred picks, he told them, he would get it right a hundred times.

When the lawyers doubted Marty, they had blustery Mrs. Frankel to deal with, asking how they could "dare" question her son's truthfulness. Getting a straight answer about anything from Marty was difficult. They were seeing very much what Bitter had seen just a few weeks before. At times, Marty was almost incapable of answering a question, or even of finishing a sentence. He reminded one participant of Billy Bibbit, the stuttering character in *One Flew Over the Cuckoo's Nest* who is finally driven to suicide by Nurse Ratched.

Mrs. Frankel frequently brought Marty's lunch along to the law firm in a brown paper bag. When things got too tense, or her son was upset, she would announce, "He needs his lunch now." She interrupted so often that the lawyers insisted that she go sit outside the conference room. But every fifteen or twenty minutes she would knock on the door and ask whether Marty needed some water. She was "so overbearing, so egotistically powerful that there was no room for Marty," a participant later said.

Marty and his lawyers eventually agreed that the best way to forestall worse trouble was to voluntarily approach the SEC. In late May, and again in July, Marty sat down in a conference room in a Chicago federal building and spilled his guts. In the process, he thoroughly frustrated and sometimes confused the SEC lawyers doing the questioning. His intention appeared to be to prove himself innocent and pin the blame solidly on Maxwell, but in his three days of testimony, he admitted violating several federal securities laws. By telling investors that he had successfully managed several million in individual accounts, he had concealed the fact that he had never had more than $500,000 under his management. He had falsely told investors that he had averaged yearly returns of over 20 percent. He had told investors that only he would manage Frankel Fund accounts, when in fact he had "help" from Maxwell. And he had sent investors false statements showing that they were making impressive profits when, in fact, the Frankel Fund was a dog.

The SEC thanked Marty for his time and kept investigating. It wasn't until August 1991, almost three years later, that the commission sought a permanent injunction barring Frankel and Maxwell from the securities business, and the two men would not actually lose their licenses for another year after that. No criminal charges were ever brought.

In the wake of his visits with the SEC, Marty spent hours in his bedroom, scribbling notes to himself. On a sheet of paper on which Maxwell apparently had made a list of Marty's expenses, Frankel scribbled:

TYPICAL EXAMPLE OF DOUG'S INSTRUCTING MARTY TO STAY IN PB [PALM BEACH] BECAUSE OF ALL THE ADVANTAGES OF BEING WHERE "MONIED PEOPLE COULD VISIT." MARTY WANTED TO BE HOME IN TOLEDO THE ENTIRE TIME. . . . MARTY HATED BEING IN PB—SPENDING MONIES HE HADN'T EARNED BECAUSE OF HIS TRADING BLOCK.— TOO FAR FROM PARENTS, OLD CLIENTS—NO FRIENDS AND NO GOOD SERVICES WHICH HE INCIDENTALLY HAD FREE OF CHARGE IN TOLEDO—HE JUST WORKED DAY &

NIGHT & NEITHER WENT TO DINNER NOR RENTED
VIDEOS. EXCEPT FOR CANNED FOOD HE HAD NO PRIVATE
EXPENSES: SO HE WAS NEVER INVOLVED IN SQUANDERING
CLIENTS FUNDS. . . .

Another note read: "I wish I had never gone to SEC . . . extraordinarily depressed. . . . Since April—life into shambles . . . listening to lawyers bad advice . . . emotionally unstable . . . suicidal."

Although, having lost his savings, he too was feeling down, Ted Bitter continued to visit. One day Marty told Bitter that he was considering hanging himself with a cord that was holding up a picture on his bedroom wall. Bitter saw that the cord probably wouldn't even hold ten pounds. "Marty," he said, "that wouldn't do it."

Marty's thoughts turned to flight. He talked several times with Bitter about Robert Vesco, the financier who fled the United States, and other money managers who had stolen their customers' assets. He told Bitter that he had files on Vesco and the others, including clippings that detailed how they went about engineering their escape.

He even had some money. It belonged to another client, for whom he had created what he called the Jupiter Fund just after the Frankel Fund collapsed. Marty told his parents that he was going to take $125,000 of this money and disappear into the mountains of Colorado. That plan did not remain workable for long, however. In early August, the client, who was the son of a former Texaco chairman and managed his family's money, heard from Maxwell about Marty's troubles. He quickly demanded his money. He eventually received a portion, $189,000, and a promissory note for $71,000, the rest of what he'd invested.

Frantic with worry, in the late summer of 1988 Marty's parents decided to have him admitted to the psychiatric floor of St. Charles Hospital, a Catholic hospital in Toledo. Marty didn't want to go. Bitter recalled that during a visit he paid Marty, a doctor came in and told the patient sternly, "We don't want to treat anyone who doesn't want to be cooperative. If you don't want to be here, go. We don't want you here unless you cooperate."

Another time Bitter got a desperate phone call from Marty in the hospital. "Only you can help me," he said. He was terrified that the doctors were going to insist he take drugs that would ruin his brain and his talent for picking stocks. His plan was to break out. He asked Bitter to go to the University of Toledo theater department and find someone with acting experience. The idea was to get that person to dress up like an Orthodox rabbi and come to the hospital. Then the actor would switch clothes with Marty, and Marty would walk out in rabbi's garb—a free man.

"Life is not a James Bond movie," Bitter told Marty. "There's no way I'll be a part of that."

When Sonia Schulte heard that Marty was in the hospital, she was torn. She wanted to see him—but she knew it would anger John, who had just lost a hotly contested Republican primary race for state senate.

Sonia sought the advice of a friend who knew them both. "Marty's my friend," Sonia said. "I want to go see him, but I'm afraid, because John wouldn't want me to go."

The friend counseled her to talk to her husband and do whatever he wanted. Sonia followed the advice and told John that she wanted to go to see Marty. He agreed to go with her, but he was livid, so mad, he later said, "I could have spit bullets."

Schulte went up to the psychiatric ward with his wife. Marty was in the visiting room, sitting on a small chair pulled up to a table meant for preschoolers. Sonia went in and pulled up another tiny chair and sat across from him. To Schulte, the scene was positively "goofy."

The next time they visited, the Schultes fought bitterly in the parking lot outside the hospital. John was getting more upset about her continued interest in their former employee and her belief that he was a good guy. "Maybe I should be admitting *you* to the hospital," he told her. Sonia was furious and went upstairs to see Marty on her own while John fumed in the car.

Marty's stay in the hospital was brief. He returned home still depressed, and Bitter continued to visit, sympathetic because his friend was such a mess. One day, he arrived at the Frankels' to find Marty, ensconced on one end of the living room sofa, acting depressed and carrying on miserably, as usual. Bitter just let him talk. The phone rang and Marty rose to answer it.

Suddenly, he was a changed man. With the person on the other end of the line, he behaved as though he were on top of the world. He was cheerful. He told the caller "things are going great." He said he was making money. Bitter was flabbergasted, and Marty refused to meet his eyes.

The episode was a revelation. "Marty," Bitter finally said. "I'm not the least bit concerned about you. There's a whole world of suckers out there, plenty of suckers for you to put the screws to just like me." Marty just looked at him.

Soon after, Bitter called a lawyer. Although he had never met the Herlihys, they teamed up and hired one of Toledo's biggest law firms, Shumaker, Loop & Kendrick. The case was not the kind the firm usually took on, because it was not a money maker. It involved relatively modest amounts of money, and was so complex it would require many hours of lawyers' time. But several of its lawyers were so appalled at what Marty had done that they doggedly pursued the case for years.

It was after deciding to file a lawsuit that Bitter saw yet another side of Marty. When Bitter told him that he was going to take him to court, Marty turned mean. He would "fight fire with fire," Marty said, and he was going to "defeat" Bitter. "Nobody does that to Marty Frankel," he told his former client. If Bitter won, Marty went on, he would refuse to pay damages and would deplete Bitter's remaining resources by maneuvering in court. He vowed that the suit would motivate him to be successful in his business from then on. That was the way, he promised Bitter, he would get his revenge.

But even after he officially filed suit a year later, Bitter had mixed emotions about the man who had lost him his life savings. On November 19, 1989, shortly after signing a sworn statement that he knew would contradict Marty's account of the demise of the Frankel Fund, Bitter wrote a letter addressed, "To whom it may concern."

"I've known Marty Frankel many years and do not wish to cause him harm," he wrote. "I ask you to be sympathetic to him. In spite of what has happened I remain convinced that Marty has many good and caring qualities. Respectfully, Ted Bitter."

Chapter Three

A Creative Partnership

Marty's return from Florida coincided with an especially troubled period in the Schulte marriage. Tension was escalating between Sonia and John. One day their brokerage firm's secretary, Anita Boyer, invited Sonia out for lunch at Frisch's Big Boy, a fast-food place near the Great Eastern Shopping Center where they worked. Boyer considered Sonia to be not only her employer but her friend. She told Sonia that John had been making sexual advances toward her, even putting his hands on her legs. Boyer was repulsed. She called John's behavior "creepy crawly."

Boyer had thought long and hard about telling Sonia about the advances and she was apprehensive about the lunch. But she was much relieved at Sonia's steely response. Sonia told her that she was glad Boyer was "woman enough to tell her," and said she knew Boyer would not "succumb" to her husband's "little games."

They returned to the office to find a furious John Schulte, who apparently had guessed what had transpired between the two women. He called his wife into his office and shut the door. Boyer heard the sounds of Sonia being knocked around and slammed against the walls of the tiny office.

The couple's problems continued to worsen. Shortly after the lunch, while the two women were visiting the Lucas County sports and family activity center with their children, Sonia tearfully confided to Boyer that her husband had raped her one night when he returned home drunk. More than once, Pemberville police were called to the Schulte home to help sort things out. Over time, Sonia left John seven times, often calling her husband's father to come pick her up. Usually she retreated to her parents' home in Elmore, some fifteen minutes away, only to return to John after a day or so, sometimes asking his forgiveness.

It took Sonia quite a while to see how untenable her situation really was, and when she did it was with the help of Marty Frankel. Increasingly, Sonia's thoughts turned to divorce. She knew precious little about the subject, and the first person she considered consulting was Marty, because his father was a referee in the local divorce court. She was not in regular contact with him, but when she phoned him at his parents' house he seemed more than happy to help. He consulted Leon and got back to Sonia with the names of three reliable divorce lawyers.

Marty, who had been sitting at home nursing the remnants of his depression and contemplating his next move, was thrilled to hear from Sonia. He wanted to keep her on the phone and asked how she was doing. "Is John still beating you up?" he asked. The question startled her, even though Marty had once heard her crying in the office and seen her bruises after she'd had a particularly grueling run-in with her husband. They talked awhile about the state of Sonia's marriage. "You're a battered wife, Sonia. You've been abused," he told her gently. To Sonia, it was a revelation. She had never thought of herself that way before.

They continued their conversations on nights when Schulte bowled or attended Republican party activities. Slowly, over time, Marty helped Sonia realize that her situation was dangerous and that she needed to take action against their mutual nemesis.

One night in late 1988 it was John who picked up the phone when Marty called the Pemberville house. "What the hell are you doing calling here?" he demanded.

Marty sounded oddly cheerful. "I have a great opportunity," he told his former boss. "You can buy and own the bank you've always wanted to own." He went on to explain that he had a contact who could help with the acquisition of a bank. When it became clear that the rather annoyed—and perplexed—Schulte had no interest in conversation, Marty asked to speak to Sonia. It was only then that Schulte realized that Marty had meant to talk to Sonia in the first place, and had not expected to find John at home.

Schulte hung up on him and went upstairs to find his wife. It was late;

Sonia was already in bed. "Dear," Schulte said tersely, "what in the hell is going on?"

"We're friends," she answered. "He checks up on me and I check on him. We're friends."

Schulte was fuming. "Jesus Christ. You gotta be out of your mind," he said.

As far as Schulte knew, Marty never called again. Everything seemed to be "hunky-dory," and dinner was on the table on time every night for the next six months.

April 14, 1989, was a Friday, and Schulte returned home from work at about 8:30 P.M., as he usually did. As he rounded the corner he saw Sonia's gray Chevrolet station wagon in the driveway and had the thought that it was "always nice to know that the home was solid." Sonia was in the kitchen and she brought their three-year-old into the family room, telling Schulte that it was his turn to watch the kids. The older girl, then five, reported that they'd had pizza for dinner, and there was a cold box of leftover pizza lying nearby.

Schulte asked Sonia to warm some up for him and settled down to watch *Wall Street Week* on PBS. But the girls wanted to watch a video, and the older girl popped *Cinderella* into the VCR. A soap opera appeared on screen: someone had taped over *Cinderella,* and the girls were crestfallen. "Your mommy must have ruined the video," Schulte told them.

For Sonia, it was the last straw. She stormed into the room and slapped her husband across the face. It was cold outside and she began bundling the little girls into their coats. Both girls were screaming. "What do you think you're doing?" Schulte demanded to know.

"I'm leaving," Sonia retorted.

"Where are you going?" he asked.

"None of your business," she said. "We're never coming back." She grabbed a child under each arm, like sacks of potatoes, and walked out the door.

"Call me later tonight and let me know when you're coming home," Schulte called after them. But Sonia was gone, and she never did come back.

. . .

For the Schultes' business, the timing could not have been worse. From the outside, the couple seemed to be thriving. They were still living in a large house by the river, and John drove a white Cadillac. But despite their apparent prosperity, they'd had some serious setbacks. Their brokerage had suffered mightily in the 1987 crash, and a dispute between the firm and one of Sonia's clients resulted in legal fees and a settlement they could ill afford. They had been ditched by the New York headquarters of Dominick & Dominick and had affiliated with Thomas F. White & Company, a San Francisco discount brokerage. Shortly before he and Sonia broke up, Schulte had negotiated an agreement to merge their business into the Illinois Company, a brokerage based in Chicago, which agreed to buy them out. It was a heady moment for the couple, as they flew by private plane to Chicago to meet the prospective buyers. The understanding was that Sonia would become a branch manager of a new office on Secor Road, not far from the Frankels on Stanhope.

Sonia did indeed open up shop as planned on May 1, just two weeks after she had left John. Shortly afterward, Schulte walked into her new office to try to negotiate a reconciliation. Sonia was sitting behind her branch manager's desk, in a private office, looking proud of her fledgling operation. They talked awhile and John told her how wonderful and powerful she looked. Then he noticed an application for a new brokerage account sitting on the corner of his estranged wife's desk. The name on the application was Martin R. Frankel.

"What the hell are you doing with this guy?" John asked.

"He's important to me" was all Sonia would say.

John took off his wedding band. He placed it in the center of her desk. "Dear, I obviously don't need this anymore," he said. "Let me know when you want me to be your husband again."

Sonia told the Illinois Company that she was no longer interested in doing business with her husband, and soon its executives were calling Schulte, trying to figure out what had happened to the happy husband-and-wife team they had been about to make a deal with. John gave them an earful. He explained that Sonia had been involved in the misuse of client funds at their old firm, and that she was now involved with a man named Frankel who was up to no good.

The Illinois Company canceled the deal and severed its ties with

Sonia. She accused her estranged husband of having caused her trouble, but in fact it is unclear whether the firm took him seriously or simply decided to cut its losses rather than get involved in what was gearing up to be a messy divorce battle.

Shortly after the Illinois Company debacle, the friendship between Marty and Sonia took a romantic and sexual turn. For Marty, it was a complete revelation. He had never had a real girlfriend before. One Saturday afternoon, shortly before Bitter filed his court papers and toward the end of his increasingly tense friendship with Marty, Bitter was sitting in the Frankel living room when Marty suddenly stopped chatting and just stared at him. "I don't know why I'm telling you this," Marty said, "but I'm in love with Sonia."

"Does she feel the same way?" Bitter asked.

"Yeah," Marty answered, drawing out the word, and sounding almost as if he didn't believe it himself.

For Bitter, the conversation was "a total bombshell." He simply couldn't imagine that any woman could be sexually attracted to Marty. "I couldn't conceive of the idea," he said later. "There's nothing that anyone, of any gender, would find attractive about Marty Frankel. He's not the alpha male." He thought of Marty as "almost a Stephen Hawking kind of guy," referring to the theoretical physicist with crippling Lou Gehrig's disease. He considered Marty's bad posture, his shuffling and his inability to pick up anything that weighed more than twenty pounds, and thought, "You gotta be joking."

What Sonia and Marty had in common was that they were both victims of John Schulte, she confided to her friends. Unlike John, she told her friend Anita, Marty was a nice guy. He wasn't controlling, he didn't beat her up, and he really cared about the kids. He was concerned about them and that really touched Sonia's heart. As a precaution, she had introduced Marty to her daughters as "Michael," so that they wouldn't talk about him by name on their visits with their father.

Those visits, like all aspects of the Schulte divorce, grew increasingly tense. Frequently, Sonia drove the forty-minute round trip to Toledo to pick Marty up and bring him to Elmore, where she'd moved into a trailer next to her parents' house. They spent hours talking, plotting her next moves against John Schulte. During one such discussion, Marty showed Sonia how to wrap her hands around her own neck, squeezing hard enough to create a bruise. His idea was that she could use the tactic against Schulte with the police if things got too hot.

On the night of January 1, 1990, Schulte dropped the little girls at the trailer and—champagne bottle in hand—tried to enter Sonia's tiny trailer with the idea of trying yet another reconciliation. What happened next was a classic he-said, she-said tale.

John claimed that Sonia tried to push him out the door and that he left voluntarily and went back to his car. Sonia's version of events was quite different.

She said he tried to kiss her; she pushed him away and asked him to leave. He then attempted to force his way in, grabbing her by the neck and pushing her into a coat rack.

The police were called and they found a red mark on Sonia's neck. John was taken into custody and spent the night in the Ottawa County jail. He wondered later whether Sonia had hit the clothes rack during their tussle at the door or inflicted the bruise on herself.

With Sonia's professional life in turmoil, and Marty still reeling from his Frankel Fund fiasco, both were trying to figure out how to make a go of it financially. For the rest of their time in Toledo, their businesses would be intertwined.

Just a few months before the incident at the trailer, Marty had launched a new fund, Creative Partners. "Never a Down Month," shouted a flyer he composed on his computer. He drew up other charts showing that $1,000 invested with Marty Frankel in January 1985 would now, in the fall of 1989, be worth $252,427. Lengthy disclosure statements and brochures came rolling off Marty's printer, which was still stationed in the bedroom of his parents' house on Stanhope.

"It may come as a surprise to many of our investors that, on average, we are in the market only ten to thirty percent of the time. For example, out of twenty trading days each month, we may be in the market on only two to six days, on average," he wrote in a brochure soliciting clients.

"We believe a portfolio manager should fly over the investment universe like an eagle, searching for trades that appear like diamonds amongst the coals," Marty wrote. "Then he should swoop down and scoop up his profit very quickly. He then can return to his search, knowing his capital rests safe and secure in the bosom of a money market fund." Marty's brochure also quoted Warren Buffett and Will Rogers.

His bio claimed that he had scored 194 on the Stanford-Binet IQ test as a young child, and noted that "a score of over 140 is considered a score of 'genius or near-genius.' " Touting his 92 percent to 96 percent accuracy, he went on to say that at Dominick & Dominick he had generated "approximately $70,000 a month in gross commissions, but he left this job in order to concentrate more on money management than retail brokerage.

"Marty Frankel's prowess at investing is powerful. For five years Marty Frankel has placed in the top rank of money managers in the United States. . . . Frankel believes the job of money manager is a sacred profession," his bio concluded, "like that of a doctor, and he approaches his clients with this same degree of care." In another document he said that a minimum investment of $10,000 was required.

While clients didn't exactly line up, there was a slow trickle of investors coughing up checks. Some of them came through Marty's first employee, Walter Rothschild. A broker for some thirty years, first at Investors Diversified Services, Inc., which became part of American Express, and then at Smith Barney, Harris Upham & Company, Rothschild was seventy years old and on the verge of retirement. Sheldon Frankel, Marty's cousin, was his dentist. Rothschild's son, Steven, had recently gone through a bruising divorce, and Marty's father had been helpful to him. One day Walter ran into Leon and told him, "I want to thank you. I think you helped Steve a great deal. If I can ever do anything for you, let me know."

Sometime afterward, Leon called Walter to ask him to meet his younger son. Walter dropped by the Frankels' and took Marty, who was then without a car, out to coffee. Marty told him that he'd worked in Florida, and spelled out his credentials. He'd hired a lawyer to work on his disclosure statements to clients and would be investing mostly in commodities. He wanted Walter to be Creative Partners' first salesman. Walter was receiving a retirement income from American Express; his attitude was, simply, "What do I have to lose?"

He began to worry a little when Marty appeared to be doing no trading in early 1990. "Marty, get off your duff," said Walter. "You better do something." But a month later, Marty produced statements showing solid gains. "Look at the statements," Marty said proudly. "Look at what I'm doing!"

Walter took the statements at face value and began to persuade clients to invest in Creative Partners. All told, he put roughly fifteen clients into the fund, and they invested about $300,000 in all. Some put in $20,000 or $50,000; one couple put in $120,000 of their savings. Walter Rothschild also put in $100,000 of his own money. Suddenly Marty was in business again.

Things also were looking better for Sonia. Around the time Marty started Creative Partners, in the fall of 1989, Sonia had set up a new Toledo office of Thomas F. White & Company, in the same quarters she'd rented for her Illinois Company operation. She was competing with John Schulte's Thomas F. White office just twenty minutes away.

Initially, Sonia had hoped that she could hook Marty up with Thomas White as well. Together, they had flown to San Francisco to meet White and others at the firm's headquarters. White understood Marty to be Sonia's boyfriend and was willing to listen to his pitch and read his prospectus. Marty's numbers, White thought, "were pretty good. Really spectacular." The problem, he later said, was that "they were entirely unreasonable." When he asked Marty for some verification of these stunning returns, Marty was able to produce nothing. To White's mind, Marty's schemes were "absolutely pie in the sky" and "ridiculous." He decided to take a pass on hiring the genius stock picker.

The setback was only temporary. Soon, several of Sonia's brokers were putting their clients into Creative Partners; to some degree, the matter of who worked for whom became, in the word of one person familiar with the operation, "fluid."

One thing that had not changed was Marty's penchant for secrecy. As Ted Bitter had noticed during their endless Saturday meetings, Marty constantly worried that someone would steal his trading secrets. These days he had a lot more to fear than that. First, there was his trading block, which he needed to hide from his new investors and salesmen. Looming even more ominously was the slowly moving court case filed by the Bitters and Herlihys, whose lawyers were trying to unravel exactly what had happened to the Frankel Fund. And then there was the specter of the SEC's investigation of the Florida debacle. The commission, too, was moving very slowly, but there was the distinct possibility that eventually it would try to shut Marty down.

With those problems in mind, Marty slowly started making it easier to cover his tracks. He opened bank accounts in different names in at least three states: Ohio, Michigan, and Texas. These accounts were in the names of "Creative Partners Fund," "CPI," and, in the case of an account at the Frost National Bank in San Antonio, "The U.S. Government Securities Savings Fund." On some accounts, Sonia was a cosigner.

Endlessly drafting documents on his computer, Marty carefully tried to distance his own name from Creative Partners. In an investment summary he sent to his customers, he wrote that the general partner of Creative Partners Fund II was Rothschild International Investments, Inc., that its chairman and president was Eleanor Rothschild and its treasurer and controller was Steven Rothschild, C.P.A. Eleanor was Walter's wife, and Steven was their son. Neither had anything to do with Creative Partners, nor did they know that Marty had borrowed their names.

One of Marty's efforts to cloak his little operation in secrecy backfired badly. One day Marty had been having a rare lunch out, at a restaurant named Charlie's, when he bumped into Walter Rothschild, who was lunching with another broker, Harold Gauthier. Rothschild introduced them, and when Marty and Gauthier ran into each other several times afterward they exchanged pleasantries.

Some time later, Gauthier inexplicably started getting mail for Marty Frankel and Creative Partners at his condo in Perrysburg, coincidentally the same Toledo suburb where Ted Bitter worked. Mystified, Gauthier phoned Marty at home. Marty said it was all a mistake, and explained that he needed a mailing address. Gauthier told him to stop using his address and Marty promised to take care of the problem. Some months later, though, more mail arrived at Gauthier's place, including a letter from the IRS. Gauthier put his lawyer on the case and the mysterious mail stopped.

In his final effort to minimize scrutiny of his little empire, Marty flew to Europe, telling Walter Rothschild that he wanted to meet with contacts in Luxembourg and Switzerland. There, he set up a bank account in Switzerland, which is famous for the secrecy and confidentiality it accords bank customers.

Returning from Europe, Marty stepped with gusto into a new skir-

mish between Sonia and John. For several uneasy months, Sonia's
Thomas F. White office had coexisted with John's branch of the same
firm. On March 1, John had notified the brokerage's headquarters that
he intended to resign in a month so he could affiliate with another firm,
Great Lakes Equities Company. But before the month was up, he was
fired: Thomas F. White headquarters accused him of mishandling
clients' funds.

On March 16, Sonia distributed a flyer that reads as though it was
heavily influenced—if not actually written—by Marty. "We want to let
you know that John Schulte is no longer associated in any way with
Thomas F. White & Co. In fact, he has been fired by our company for
your own protection, because he committed irregularities detrimental
to his clients. . . . Thomas F. White & Co. only wants brokers who apply
the highest standards of ethics in their relationships with clients. . . . Associates of John Schulte may ask you to sign certain documents. We advise you: Do not sign any of these documents."

The flyer went on to tout Sonia's operation: "We have hired new staff
whose function is solely to monitor the fast-breaking news in order to
protect your capital and make it grow."

Furious, Schulte immediately had his lawyer call Thomas F. White &
Company in San Francisco. On March 19, just three days after Sonia's
salvo, the firm tried to distance itself from the Toledo brouhaha by sending out its own letter, informing its Toledo-area customers that the
Schultes had recently separated. Sonia's flyer, the firm wrote, "was not
authorized by our firm. . . . We are embarrassed by and apologize for
any misunderstanding the above unauthorized letter may have caused."
The dispute became the talk of Toledo, fodder for the front page of the
Toledo Blade's business section.

It was shortly after this episode that Walter Rothschild became
alarmed about what Marty was up to. He'd returned from a stay in
Florida to discover several disturbing developments in Toledo. First and
foremost was Marty's use of his wife and son's names. But there were
other problems as well. Marty had promised that he would have a Chicago lawyer review the disclosure statements sent to investors; Rothschild did a little poking around and learned that no lawyer had been
involved. When he started checking on other things that Marty had told

him, he learned that Marty was not properly registered as required by the SEC.

Finally, he was unable to get Marty to come up with audited certified financial statements to send clients, even though such statements had been promised in the original offering documents. The only statements clients got were generated on Marty's computer. In fact, Walter had no actual evidence that Marty was trading at all. "Everything was hush-hush," he later recalled. "Nobody could get near him." The only one Marty seemed to confide in was Sonia, and Walter didn't like her or the other brokers in the couple's circle. He especially had problems with Robert Guyer, whom he wanted Marty to fire, in part because he didn't think Guyer dressed professionally.

Over the course of a few months, Walter's attitude became "Hell, this is for the birds." He'd been a licensed broker for thirty years. He knew only one way of doing business, and this was not it. In August 1990, Marty presented Walter with a $10,000 commission check. Walter thought Marty was trying to placate him; he told Marty he didn't want the money.

A few weeks later, on the evening of Labor Day, Walter told Marty they had to talk. He picked Marty up and drove him back to his condo in nearby Sylvania. Sitting in the den, Walter and his wife, Eleanor, told Marty that they wanted out of Creative Partners. This was no way to do things, they told him. They said they wanted him to dissolve Creative Partners and return the money to the investors.

Marty balked. Liquidating the fund was absolutely unnecessary, he argued; everything was fine. But the Rothschilds had made up their minds. As the evening went on and on, Marty finally got angry. "I have connections," he said. "I can get the Mafia on you."

"You're full of hot air," Walter replied.

It was about two A.M.; they had talked and argued for more than five hours and gotten nowhere. Walter drove Marty home. It was a very quiet car ride.

Walter hired a lawyer, and a day or two before Christmas his clients got letters by certified mail explaining that he had severed his ties to Creative Partners and advising them to get their money out. Also, Walter immediately asked for his own investment back. It took roughly six months, but he finally got a check for $150,000, a 50 percent gain over his initial investment. While some of Rothschild's clients followed his example, others were pleased with the fund's performance and stayed put.

Rothschild's defection put only a minor damper on Marty's new confidence. His fund was up and going and he'd found more contentment than he'd ever had before with Sonia and her children, who he increasingly viewed as his own. For the first time since his brief foray to Florida, Marty was thinking of leaving his parents' house. Briefly, he considered buying a mansion on about two acres of land in Ottawa Hills. The rear of the house suggested a Tudor-influenced English country cottage. A sort of turret served as a front vestibule, and the signs of the zodiac were carved into its ceiling.

But in the end, he decided on something far more modest. On June 20, 1990, he set up the Donar Corporation, listing himself as president. A day later, Donar purchased a house at 3415 Stanhope Drive, in Toledo. Marty paid the purchase price, $70,000, in cash. At almost thirty-five years old, Marty had bought his first house, just diagonally across the street from his parents'. The place was a modest one-story painted gray with white trim, on a small lot studded with mature trees. Marty moved the satellite dish from the roof of his parents' house to his own, and put up a swing set in the backyard for Sonia's daughters.

Setting up housekeeping was a totally new experience for Marty. He furnished the living room with six La-Z-Boy chairs, on which the plastic remained for months to come. A small portion of the living room was curtained off. There Marty worked, with a bank of computers and a television spewing news at all times. Often, he kept this area dark, like a control room; he sat in a easy chair facing the monitors that stood against the wall. It reminded one rare visitor of the Pentagon. Marty had news wires and Quotron and all kinds of arcane services hooking him into obscure exchanges that one would have expected to find only in a large brokerage house.

Sonia also moved, abandoning the mobile home in Elmore and moving into a two-story apartment building in Ottawa Hills. She and Marty were only about five minutes apart by car, and she and her children spent much of their time at Marty's house. They drove back and forth in a Mercedes-Benz, Marty's first new car. It had been bought for a little more than $68,000 by the SEBA Corporation, which Marty had set up especially for the purchase.

Sonia took on the task of seeing to it that Marty was not disturbed or interrupted, and the brokers putting their customers into Creative Partners typically dealt with him through her. Marty still complained to his infrequent visitors that he had a trading block, but Sonia told confidants that she believed he was just slow and methodical.

For Sonia, the move and the relationship with Marty were a breath of normalcy in an otherwise hectic life; she was trying to make a go of her business while pursuing her bitter divorce. Marty respected her, she told friends, and he loved her kids. He was much more generous than John with money, too. She exclaimed to one friend that she didn't have to drink Tang anymore, she could drink real orange juice. When she'd lived with Schulte, she had had to make her own clothes to save money. But things were changing there, too. "Do you know what an Armani suit is?" she asked a friend, who was left with the distinct impression that Sonia had just acquired one.

True normalcy was impossible, however, in part because Schulte kept the pressure on. Aggressive as Sonia and Marty were in their battle against him, John was unrelenting in his pursuit of them. It seemed as though he had not yet given up hope that she would return to their home, and yet everything he did was alienating, if not downright scary. Over the first two years or so after she walked out on him, he left her three hundred phone messages. He dug up a stash of postcards he'd had printed for his unsuccessful state senate campaign in 1988 and sent one a day to each of his daughters for a full year. The postcards showed the intact Schulte family, the daughters wearing polka-dot outfits and each sitting on a conservatively dressed parent's knee. Neither daughter was old enough to read or really understand their father's messages, but the postcards kept coming. "Mommy's crazy. . . . She doesn't know what she's doing. She's mixed up with evil forces," one friend of Sonia's later remembered the postcards as saying. One addressed to Sonia's father said, "Hope that Frankel doesn't blow up."

Schulte often parked down the street from Marty's house to observe the comings and goings. He hired a private investigator to track the couple's movements. During 1991, the investigator would sneak onto the property at night and collect Marty's garbage, which he then turned over to Schulte for review. There were Creative Partners documents, discarded envelopes, and score cards kept by Frankel for games he played with Sonia's kids. One night an astrological chart turned up.

Some of the information Schulte tried to use in his ongoing divorce and custody battle with Sonia, in which he kept trying to make her relationship with Marty an issue. For his part, Marty jumped into the fray with a combination of affection for Sonia and deep resentment of Schulte. He accompanied Sonia to her lawyers' offices to discuss the status of the case. Over time, he paid one of the lawyers at least $54,000 and another at least $254,000, mostly in wire transfers from his Swiss bank account. Marty had more knowledge of divorce law than most laymen, having lived with his father for more than three decades. Sometimes he himself cracked open law books to help Sonia with her legal strategy. When decisions came up as to how to pursue the case, Frankel would get on the phone with Sonia's lawyers and remind them to "do things by the book . . . You have to do it legally."

The most strife-ridden aspect of the battle was Sonia's allegation that Schulte had sexually abused the children. John had bathed naked with the girls, and Sonia repeated in court hearing after court hearing that he had engaged them in inappropriate games, having the children "grab a wash cloth which he had laid across his penis," as one court document described the allegation.

John denied the abuse. He denied that he had raped Sonia and he denied that he had hit her. ("We might have had our jostling matches," he admitted years later.)

The case dragged on for years. Experts testified. Reams of documents were filed. Visitation was suspended, reinstated under supervised conditions and debated endlessly. At one point a court referee concluded that "the credibility of both parents is in question" and cited, among other things, Sonia's apparently misleading testimony that she had no business association with Marty.

Finally, Marty and Sonia went to the Wood County prosecutor's office to ask him to criminally charge Schulte. The prosecutor involved, Gary Bishop, didn't feel he had enough evidence, so Sonia and Marty left in frustration. That night Marty tapped out a detailed summary of "our meeting" with Bishop on his computer. Later that night, Schulte's private eye scooped up Marty's garbage, including a printout of the memo, alerting Schulte to his wife's new strategy.

Sonia and Marty became convinced that they would not be able to get a fair hearing in Wood County. The area was predominantly Republican, and John was an influential member of the party, although he had usually been frustrated in his quests for public office. (He was president of a local board of education from 1981 to 1985.) Sonia started pushing for the appointment of a special prosecutor and ultimately was successful. A criminal investigation was finally launched.

Marty was anxious to expand Creative Partners' reach beyond a small group of Toledo-area residents, many of whom were retired. With Rothschild gone, he hooked up with two young Chicago brokers, both in their twenties, whom he met through other broker acquaintances.

Mark Shuki was a part-time broker who supplemented his income by bartending and at the time was earning roughly $1,500 a month. He was happy to accept Marty's invitation to come to Toledo so they could talk about Creative Partners and arrived with his friend Eric Jensen, also a broker.

The two spent a couple of weeks in Toledo because they wanted to check their prospective boss out. At first, Shuki was not too impressed. Marty didn't spend much time talking with him, and the setup in Toledo was a little strange. "If this guy is such a big superstar," Shuki wondered, "why does he live in just a regular little house?" Finally, he "wrote it off": "If you're a money manager, then maybe you're just weird."

Also, Shuki was very impressed with Marty's claim that he made 100 percent profits because, as he later said, "I know that's hard to do." One of the brokers working for Sonia also bragged to him about Marty's incredible profits.

There was other evidence of Marty's powers. The market was suffering a severe slump at the time, but a recent mailing to Creative Partners' clients, citing the fund's results as of October 1990, showed that it was up 99.21 percent over a twelve-month period. "So far this year, Creative Partners Fund has outperformed every publicly traded mutual fund in the nation!" Marty had tapped out on his Mac. "We are up 81.94 percent this year!

"In the past few months many investors have suffered severe losses because they placed their money in funds whose value fell with the overall stock market. Public mutual funds are down, on average, 14 percent so far this year—compare that with our track record." He went on to attack one of the year's best-performing funds, Fidelity Select Biotechnology, up 25.8 percent, because it was unable to "go 100 percent into cash when the managers think it's a good time to step out of the market. . . . By contrast, your fund is flexible, because it has the whole universe of financial investments open to it." Still, whereas virtually all funds tell their customers where their money has been put, Marty provided no information on what sectors or companies he had invested in.

Shuki was sold. When he and Jensen returned to Chicago, they rented a small office with a couple of desks, some computer equipment, and a few chairs from which clients could watch stock quote services that cost about $1,000 a month. Marty footed all the bills.

Over the next year and a half or so, Shuki put about fifteen clients into Creative Partners, with investments totaling several hundred thousand dollars. His understanding with Marty was that he would earn a percent of the profits on his account. Although Shuki believed his boss was trading stocks, he had little detail beyond the vague statements issued from Marty's computer in Toledo each month showing healthy profits. Clients would call, hoping for tips from their reclusive investment guru. "What [stocks] does he like? What does he like?" they asked Shuki. He had no answer, but went so far as to call Sonia's office in Toledo to ask if they had any "confirms," confirmations that are generated by the clearinghouses that process trades. None were forthcoming and Shuki was told that Marty kept all the trading paperwork at home.

In fact, Shuki didn't usually talk with Marty, although the boss once took Shuki to lunch when he visited Chicago to meet with his lawyer. All the paperwork for new accounts, commissions, and other matters went through Sonia, whom Shuki thought of as "the Gestapo of the operation." Sonia seemed very busy and sometimes a little harsh. She would call periodically to tell Shuki and Jensen about the partnership's returns.

In early 1991, Shuki's clients got a package of information from their fund manager showing that Creative Partners had gained 159.23 percent over a fifteen-month period. Marty claimed that $10,000 invested on November 1, 1989, would be worth $25,923 on February 28, 1991.

For Shuki, life was good. Marty was paying him well, and he didn't have to bartend to make ends meet. In the office he had access to ADP to monitor stocks and every news service he wanted. Prospecting for new clients was easy; mostly a matter of word of mouth. He started spending a lot of time playing golf. Marty, Shuki later said, "was making money and that's all that mattered to us."

Chapter Four

A Special Trust

Marty Frankel began 1990 the way a lot of other people did, in bed with the flu. Laid up at his parents' house on Stanhope, he was absolutely miserable despite his mother's attentive care. Fever, sore throat, aches—he had them all, and so did some 50 million other Americans that particularly bad flu season.

As he wallowed in his misery, Marty worried over the other problems plaguing him. Not only did he have the stock market to obsess over, and Sonia's ongoing divorce, he also had his own defense in the case filed by the Bitters and Herlihys to worry about. The litigation was in full swing, and Marty was trying to save money by handling much of it himself. He did research, drafted documents, and procrastinated. The flu came at a bad time. He had briefs and motions due in federal court and a big, aggressive law firm on the other side.

"While in the process of preparing his brief in this case, defendant Frankel, on Tuesday, February 13, 1990, was stricken with an acute case of the 'A-Shanghai flu,' a viral infection that totally incapacitated him, leaving him with a fever of 102 degrees," Marty wrote a federal judge, asking for an extension. "Four days bed-rest was prescribed, along with medication. Defendant was advised that if his condition did not improve and his fever continued after forty-eight hours, he was to return to see his physician. . . . Defendant has suffered from repeated bouts of fever from his illness, and thus defendant is unable to complete his brief at the present time."

Soon after he recovered, Tillie Frankel drove him the fifteen minutes or so to his deposition at Shumaker, Loop, the law firm for the Bitters and Herlihys, which was headquartered in an imposing building near Toledo's courthouses. Marty spent much of an afternoon fielding questions from four lawyers. Question after question he answered with the refrain, "Upon advice of counsel, I respectfully refuse to answer all your questions; I'm exercising my rights under the United States Constitution." Every so often he would launch into an attack on Jeffrey Creamer, the lawyer conducting much of the interrogation. Several years before Marty had consulted Shumaker, Loop very briefly because he was considering buying a candle company, a deal that went up in smoke almost immediately. Marty apparently believed that the firm had no right to oppose him now.

"Isn't it true, sir, that your law firm has engaged in the past in severe conflicts of interest?" he demanded. "Isn't it true, sir, that you, in the past, represented me in this matter and I have paid you several thousands of dollars to your law firm, and when you could not extort further monies from me, sir, you have turned on me and represented these parties in an action against me and this is a classic conflict of interest that you are representing me in a case in which you previously represented me and took monies from me? Do you consider that as a conflict of interest, sir?" He went on to accuse the firm of similar misconduct in an unconnected case involving union pension funds.

Creamer warned Marty that he might seek court sanctions against him and litigation expenses for his refusal to answer questions.

"I'm present. I'm answering your questions and responding with parts of my answers," Marty snapped. "If I answer with a question that is a way that, if you ask my father Leon Frankel, he will tell you that it is a very common way to answer—it is a—it is an acceptable way to answer; I can answer your question with a question."

The other lawyers in the room, local counsel for Doug Maxwell and the brokerage firm Marty had been affiliated with at the time of the Frankel Fund, picked up their newspapers and began to read. Finally, Marty asked for a break to go to the bathroom. One of the lawyers put down his newspaper and looked at Creamer, his opposing counsel. "If you just want to haul off and punch him," he said, "neither one of us is going to say anything."

. . .

Marty knew that eventually the SEC would probably shut him down. With his Swiss bank account and numerous domestic accounts already in place to launder or hide money, he now took additional steps so that if necessary he could operate in the securities world undetected. In 1990 he paid $8,000 to acquire Frisch Investments, Inc., which had been registered as a broker-dealer with the SEC in 1986, but was pretty much inactive. A year or so later he changed its name to Liberty National Securities and installed William Kok, a broker who worked for Sonia, as president to run its day-to-day operation. Although Liberty National was doing little or no actual business, he ordered letterhead, listing Kok, Sonia, and several other brokers. Marty's name was not listed anywhere.

John Schulte had dumped a load of garbage, papers painstakingly plucked from Marty's trash, at Shumaker, Loop. They could see that Marty had gotten back into the investment business, and they were none too pleased. When a lawyer from the Chicago office of the SEC called and asked them about Creative Partners, Shumaker, Loop was more than willing to make a case that Marty needed to be stopped immediately.

In a letter to the SEC, Shumaker, Loop's Terrance Davis provided what he said was evidence that Marty had hidden some of the Creative Partners money in Swiss bank accounts, that he had given or was thinking of giving control over those accounts to Sonia, and that he was now using an alias: Marty Rothschild.

Davis also pointed out the similarities between the Frankel Fund and Creative Partners, noting that documents for both funds were produced on Marty's computer and "contain the same philosophical discussions of Frankel's trading system."

"I have also enclosed a copy of another document Frankel was distributing late last year explaining how Creative Partners Fund, L.P. was returning profits of approximately 100% as of November, 1990," Davis wrote. "As you can imagine, our clients, who have suffered so greatly at Frankel's hands in the past, are somewhat bewildered by the fact he is still operating so flagrantly within the Toledo area. Hopefully, you will be able to put a stop to that shortly."

But the SEC made no attempt to shut down Creative Partners. In the complaint it finally filed against Marty in 1991, all the allegations and charges stemmed from the SEC investigation of the Frankel Fund. The complaint demanded that Frankel and Maxwell "disgorge" their "ill-gotten gains," and not engage in any similar activity. But no special action was taken to protect Creative Partners investors, even though there was evidence that Marty was using aliases and hiding assets.

It is not completely clear why SEC lawyers didn't take more decisive action against Frankel when they realized he had started a new fund—or years later, when the agency again was alerted to his activities in the securities industry. He was one of about fifteen oddball scamsters with whom the SEC's Chicago office had to contend from time to time in the late 1980s and 1990s. He was memorable to enforcement lawyers, one recalled years later, mostly because he was the rare con artist who lived with his mom.

For the SEC's Chicago office, the amount of money involved in the Frankel case was a pittance. Like most federal agencies the SEC has limited resources and not enough lawyers to handle a very complicated caseload. Often in Chicago they faced political pressure to chase the big-money cases and either drop the smaller ones or leave them for state authorities to pursue. Given that pressure, and the relatively small sums of money involved, says a former enforcement lawyer, the thinking was probably "You bring [charges based on] what you have without endlessly investigating," and then file contempt proceedings down the road if the defendant violates a court order.

Another SEC veteran notes that the agency often is loath to bring a case that is not a sure bet. Because Creative Partners investors were, for the most part, happy customers, enforcement lawyers may have decided that filing such a case was not worth the risk.

But an opportunity was lost to shut Marty Frankel down before his cottage-industry fraud became an empire.

In any case, Marty was already several steps ahead of the feds. By the time they filed their action stemming from the Frankel Fund—more than a year passed before Marty was officially banned from the securities industry—he was already in the final stages of hatching a new game plan, one that would hoist him into a whole other financial league and allow him to leave the world of small-time investing in Toledo forever.

The trick for Marty was to find a new source of funds that he could tap into without using his own name at all. Although his name didn't appear on all the Creative Partners offering documents, it appeared on some of the early papers. And some of his investors had been Sonia's clients going back to the Dominick & Dominick days. Marty also needed to find a way to pay back the Creative Partners money, thousands of which had been spent on his still modest (but definitely improving) lifestyle. Finally, Marty wanted a bigger pool of money because he still had faith in his own trading prowess. He still wanted to trade. And he never gave up hope that his trading block would ease and he would prove to himself—and the world—that he was as good a trader as he believed himself to be.

One morning as he read the daily newspapers, trying to keep tabs on news events he could use to predict market moves, Marty came upon a small advertisement in *The Wall Street Journal* that piqued his interest. It offered for sale banks in the southeastern United States. Marty called the number in the advertisement and was connected to the small office of John Goodhue, a lawyer in Nashville, Tennessee. He told Goodhue that he was interested in acquiring a midsize community bank. He had an interest in the stock market, he explained, and had a special knack for stock picking.

Brokering the sale of financial institutions was just one of the things Goodhue was doing at the time. He was trying to resurrect his career in the wake of his suspension from the practice of law in 1990. While representing the buyers of a Kentucky manufacturing business, Goodhue had forged the signatures of two of the sellers on a purchase agreement in an effort to get financing for his clients. Although no actual damage resulted from his actions, he was suspended from practice for a year. When he reapplied to practice in 1991, at roughly the time he was dealing with Marty, his request was denied. He never reapplied again.

Goodhue sent along the preliminary paperwork, which Marty filled out and returned along with a $50,000 check as a retainer. The understanding was that if Goodhue found a bank, Marty would pay him more to conduct a legal and financial review of the institution.

The project, however, stalled. Goodhue did find a bank and began work on a possible acquisition, but Marty balked at paying his second bill. There were other problems as well. Goodhue sent Marty a ream of forms to fill out for the acquisition, but although the two had several conversations about the detailed information requested, no documents were forthcoming from Toledo.

Then Marty called Goodhue with an odd request. For various reasons, he explained, he was thinking about not putting his own name on the documents. Instead, he was thinking of putting the bank in a trust. Did Goodhue know anyone honest in Tennessee whom he could appoint as trustee?

Goodhue was losing patience with this strange man whom he'd never met, but who took up lots of time on the phone. He explained that it was against the law to hide the ownership of a financial institution. Despite many conversations in which Marty insisted to Goodhue that he would be forthcoming with names of board members and other information, Marty just let the deal languish. When it became clear that he had no intention of paying the bill either, Goodhue sent him a letter terminating their relationship.

Goodhue was fed up. But then John Hackney, a friend who was working for him while between jobs, offered to take a crack at getting the money out of their deadbeat client. Goodhue told him to give it a shot. Marty was weird, Goodhue told Hackney, but he appeared to have real money. "If you can keep him focused, he can be incredible," Goodhue said.

When it came to the uncollected bill, Hackney had no better luck than Goodhue. But Hackney and Marty began a long series of phone conversations—talks that took place over the better part of a decade before they actually met in person. One day Marty mentioned that perhaps a bank wasn't such a good idea; maybe he should look at insurance companies. John Hackney knew next to nothing about insurance. His professional background, to the extent he actually had one, was in banking. He had helped run a company that did "back-office work" for banks, and was fresh from a humiliating and unsuccessful attempt to start a bank.

Flipping through the yellow pages, Hackney found a little insurance company that caught his attention mostly because it was headquartered in the small town where he lived, Franklin, Tennessee. He made a few phone calls and learned that Franklin American Life Insurance Company was a slumbering, if not ailing, company that specialized in selling what is euphemistically called "pre-need burial insurance." The firm contracted with funeral homes to sell its policies to elderly folk who didn't want their families to get stuck with big funeral bills a few years down the line.

The company, it turned out, was open to an acquisition, and Marty was intrigued. An insurance company has cash assets, which it needs to invest conservatively so that it has ready money to pay out policies. This was just the kind of pool of cash Marty was looking for. Marty told Hackney to go ahead and make the deal, the caveat being that he wanted to remain anonymous. Unsure of how to structure such a transaction, Hackney went to a local attorney, John Jordan, and explained that he had an investor who for legitimate reasons wanted to remain anonymous.

Jordan told him that that was possible as long as the investment vehicle was designed as an irrevocable trust, with Hackney in charge. As trustee, Hackney would vote the investors' stock and decide where the company's money went. They would have to find "grantors" to officially supply the money for the purchase of the insurer. Hackney reported all this to Marty, and reminded him that he'd have to come up with a name for the trust.

A few days later Marty called back with the name Thunor, the Anglo-Saxon name of Thor, the powerful Scandinavian god of thunder and lightening. He told Hackney that he just liked the name.

Finding "grantors" was a lot trickier. There were few people Marty really trusted, and he didn't want his name anywhere near Thunor because he wanted to be able to trade without attracting the attention of the government or his other enemies. Sonia would definitely work as one grantor, but he was unsure about whom else he should name. Then he thought of his two young salesman in Chicago, Mark Shuki and Eric Jensen. The only question was how to convince them to sign the trust document. In the summer of 1991, as he finalized his plans to buy Franklin American, Marty told the two young salesmen that he had a plan to go after bigger investors and possibly institutional investors as well. He was going to form a new kind of partnership. Shuki, then twenty-eight, thought to himself that he was going to be Marty's "boy there just like I was his boy at Creative Partners." A document from Marty soon arrived at the small Chicago office.

Soon afterward Shuki walked into the office and was told by his fellow salesman Jensen that Sonia had called to say they should expect a call from a man named Hackney, from Tennessee. Hackney spoke to Shuki and Jensen over the speaker phone. They were going to set up a new operation so that they could invest the way insurance companies did, he told them. "We need you people to be in the organization," he said. "All you need to do is sign [the paper] and fax it back to Sonia."

Shuki and Jensen discussed the new plan. " 'We'll see how it goes and in the meantime, let's help them out,' " Shuki said, describing his reasoning. "He was taking care of us, he was helping us out, all he wants us to do is sign this one piece of paper and help him out." Shuki didn't even bother to read the paper he signed. "It was like paperwork. It was like if your dad said, Sign this, you say, 'Okay, dad,' " he later said.

But then suddenly, Marty changed course. He announced to his two young employees that he was retiring and shutting down Creative Partners. "Wait a minute," Shuki said nervously. "You can't do that without sending back my customers' money." Marty and Sonia promised that all the investors would get their money back. Shuki came away from his conversations with Marty and Sonia with the impression that Marty had decided that the "Creative Partnerships" were getting too big, and that if more people subscribed he would have to register with the SEC, which Marty told Shuki he didn't want to do. Besides, Marty was sick of dealing with small customers. He was getting out of the money management business completely.

Shuki, who suddenly needed to find a new job, simply forgot about the paperwork he had signed. "It just kind of drifted into the sunset," he later said.

Actually, it was firmly in Marty Frankel's hands. Marty decided it was best not to use both of his salesman as grantors, perhaps because he wanted to impress insurance regulators and thought he needed someone else with better credentials. He chose to keep Shuki; for Jensen, he substituted Ed Krauss, his brother's friend, who once upon a time had peeped over his shoulder at the Macintosh computer in wonderment over Marty's stock-picking prowess.

Marty's conversations with Krauss were infrequent. He sometimes saw him when Krauss visited from Columbus, where he worked as the director of a training and employment program administered by the chamber of commerce, and they occasionally chatted by phone. On one of their rare talks, Marty told Krauss that he was interested in buying insurance companies and investing their assets to generate a profit. He asked Krauss if he would be willing to supply a character reference, and Krauss readily agreed.

Still, he didn't have Krauss's signature. Sonia's and Shuki's were ready to go, even stamped by notary publics. But Marty knew that Krauss was a lot more likely to read a document and ask questions than Shuki had been. He solved the problem himself, apparently by signing Krauss's name and affixing Leon's notary public stamp on the document. It was done.

The Thunor Trust Agreement was dated September 19, 1991. A month later, the Thunor Trust purchased Franklin American Life Insurance Company and installed its trustee, John Hackney, as chairman and president. The purchase price was $3.7 million; Thunor told Tennessee regulators that Shuki had put up $900,000; that Sonia had put up $2.5 million; and that Krauss had contributed $500,000.

A little scrutiny would have revealed how improbable those numbers really were. Sonia's divorce also became final in 1991, and divorce court documents stated that she earned $25,000 a year. Shuki had been making between $1,000 and $1,200 a week and spending more. Krauss later said that he didn't have that kind of money to invest in an insurance company or anything else. He insisted his name had been forged.

In fact, none of the three had contributed a cent. Marty had simply wired the $3.7 million from his account at the Frost National Bank in San Antonio to purchase Franklin American. Although the money trail is not easy to follow, Marty seems then to have used Franklin American's money to pay back the Creative Partners investors.

The scheme apparently worked this way: Franklin American had roughly $18 million in assets. Almost immediately after the acquisition closed, Marty asked Hackney to transfer all of that money to Liberty National Securities, and on November 19, Hackney did. A portion of the money ended up briefly in an account at the Republic National Bank of New York. Marty transferred a little more than $11 million from Republic to a bank in Michigan. From the Michigan bank he transferred $1.2 million to a Creative Partners Fund account at a bank in Toledo, and $8.9 million to the Frost National Bank account.

He then ordered Frost National to issue checks to the Creative Partners investors.

The process was convoluted, as it was intended to be. Marty was now an experienced money launderer and he had created a confusing trail of wire transfers to throw off regulators and other investigators attempting to sniff out fraud. But in this case, nobody was even looking. Although the government had been alerted to Marty's involvement in Creative Partners, there is no indication that the series of money transfers was ever questioned.

And none of Creative Partners' investors raised a fuss, either. In fact, they were pretty happy. Some of Shuki's investors made 70 or 80 percent, though most saw more modest gains. The Reverend George Freeland, a friend of Sonia's who invested in Creative Partners through her Thomas F. White office, made 20 to 30 percent on roughly $40,000 of his and his wife's retirement money. Freeland didn't know what Marty had invested in, but he welcomed the opportunity to get the kind of returns that big hedge-fund investors got. "He did well for those I knew," Reverend Freeland later said.

The closing down of Creative Partners took care of one big problem in Marty's life, but the other—John Schulte—was still very much on the loose. Marty was increasingly nervous about his safety and that of Sonia and her two daughters. He began interviewing security consultants, one of whom suggested that he install sheets of bulletproof steel siding on his house. Finally, through a referral, he met David Rosse, a former auxiliary police officer who had been raised in New York State and had lived in northern California. His advice was dramatic, but it made increasing sense to the beleaguered lovers. It was simply this: Get out of town.

In the summer of 1992, that's exactly what they did. They vanished. Sonia quietly and suddenly moved to Los Altos, in northern California, and Marty spent some of his time there. He talked daily with John Hackney about plans for Franklin American to acquire more insurance companies and thereby increase the amount of money he could invest.

But within a year, the couple had some serious setbacks on the Schulte front. For one thing, Schulte found them. He turned up in California unannounced, and after many consultations with psychological counselors and lawyers, he was allowed to see his daughters in a carefully supervised setting. The girls were escorted to meet their father by a phalanx of guards recruited by David Rosse and paid for by Marty.

But Sonia and Marty were dealt a greater setback by a Wood County Common Pleas Court judge who acquitted John Schulte of molesting the two young girls. "The amount of pain that these children must have gone through in the past several years is beyond comprehension to me; caught as they were between two parents and all this conflict," Judge Richard B. McQuade, Jr., said on April 5, 1993. But while he shook his head at the notion of a father bathing with his daughters, the judge said, "I believe that this indictment was built on a house of cards, and I believe those cards are crumbled. . . . I cannot say that I am firmly convinced of the truth of these charges."

John Schulte rejoiced. On the twenty-foot marquee-style sign in front of his brokerage office in Oregon, Ohio, he displayed the message "The Truth Is Now Known." Much of Toledo knew what he meant, for the long legal wars had been covered extensively by the *Toledo Blade*. Schulte went back to concentrating on his business, Great Lakes Equities, even setting up the Great Lakes Stock Average, an index that Schulte told the *Toledo Business Journal* reflected "the northwest Ohio and southeastern Michigan business environment." He did a weekly radio commentary on the market.

But only a month after his acquittal, Schulte was summoned to the SEC's Chicago office, where a staff attorney basically accused Schulte of using his clients' money for personal expenses. The accusation was true. Schulte admitted to the SEC that before the divorce, he and Sonia had used the "float" on client funds—taking, in effect, short-term free loans of clients' money during the period after the clients wrote the brokerage a check and before the money was actually invested.

Schulte had other things he wanted to discuss with the SEC. He spent much of his visit talking about Marty and Sonia, insisting that they were the ones who should be under investigation. Finally the lawyer wearied: "We're not here about Mr. Frankel. We're here about you," he said, exasperated. "Mr. Frankel has already made his statement." He went on to say that both Marty and Sonia had talked to the SEC about Schulte.

For Schulte, this was a stunning confirmation that Frankel and Sonia were out to destroy him. And, indeed, Sonia later bragged to her friend Anita Boyer that Marty had caught her ex-husband in wrongdoing and reported him to the SEC. Marty led at least one other confidant to believe that he and Sonia had ratted out Schulte to the SEC and IRS.

The government's investigation into Schulte seemed to fade away, however, until one day six months later. At 8:30 on the morning of November 11, Schulte was backing his white 1988 Mercedes out of his driveway when he noticed unmarked blue police cars in front of his small brick house. "Who are they going after?" he wondered.

It turned out to be him. With a federal search warrant in hand, they pulled apart his car as though he were a drug dealer, and they searched his house. More cars were waiting at his office, where FBI and IRS agents confiscated files and office equipment. Schulte couldn't believe it. He almost couldn't move.

Having spent some $150,000 defending himself in the child abuse case, Schulte was broke. His father had had to mortgage the family farm to help pay his legal bills. He had nothing left to defend himself with. The feds seemed to know who his twenty-five largest clients were, and he was certain that the list had come from Sonia and Frankel.

Schulte sent his attorney, Jay Milano, a package of information, much of it gleaned from the garbage cans on Stanhope, that he thought incriminated Frankel. Milano, in turn, forwarded it to the U.S. attorney prosecuting Schulte. And that lawyer sent it on to a special agent of the FBI. But much of the information in the packet related to Creative Partners. It was stale and nothing ever came of it.

Conveniently for Sonia, the allegations against Schulte concerned a period that began in 1989, the year the couple separated, and ended in 1993. The feds had found evidence that Schulte had taken some $115,000 from six clients and used it for himself instead of making investments as he'd promised. He had created false confirmation slips and monthly statements. On May 24, 1994, Schulte pleaded guilty to one count of mail fraud and two of income tax fraud. He served seven months and seven days in the federal prison in Bradford, Pennsylvania. About a month after his release, while he was living in a halfway house in Toledo, he filed a motion asking the government to turn over its papers related to his case. He wanted to know for sure whether Marty and Sonia had informed on him.

"Defendant's former wife, acting in conjunction with one Martin R. Frankel, set out on a conspiracy to ruin defendant personally and in business," he wrote. He accused Sonia of wrongdoing in their joint business from 1986 through 1989, and he claimed her misdeeds resembled Frankel's in the Bitter matter. "The government must be aware of the involvement of defendants [*sic*] wife and Mr. Frankel's activity, though attempts by the defendant to inform the government of such went unheard."

The U.S. attorney's office refused to turn over the documents and a federal judge ruled against Schulte. By the time he was released from federal custody in 1995, Frankel and Sonia had abandoned their homes in California and Toledo. Sooner or later, Schulte believed, he would pick up their scent again, and he would track them down.

Chapter Five

Phone Pals

Every year the Tennessee Funeral Directors Association held its annual meeting at the Opryland Hotel in Nashville. Delta Air Lines promoted its body-transporting services. Embalming-fluid companies handed out free samples of lotion to soothe the chemically roughened hands of embalmers. And Franklin American set up a booth touting its burial insurance.

One of John Hackney's biggest innovations after he and Marty took over Franklin American was to host an ice cream social at the annual meeting. It quickly became a tradition. Ice cream was cheaper than liquor. Hackney reasoned that funeral homes were usually family-run businesses, and "If we could get the kids in there, when they take over ten years from now they'll remember that ice cream." He dished out sugar-free ice cream, too, for diabetics. The first year about fifty people showed up, but after that the numbers grew steadily to four hundred and five hundred people.

Hackney loved running Franklin American. He relished the prospect of restoring the ailing company to financial health, and he liked to watch deer grazing from the windows of his office, as some fifteen employees busily processed claims and chatted on the phone with small-town funeral directors outside his door.

For John Hackney, who was forty-two when he slipped behind the president's desk, taking charge of Franklin American was more than just the pinnacle of his career. It was a total relief. Quite simply, in just a few short months, Marty Frankel had changed his life. Hackney had been broke when they first talked on the phone; he didn't have a real job, and he was living off friends. Almost immediately after he'd hooked up with Marty, the financial pressure eased.

Even before Hackney found Franklin American for Marty to buy, Marty put him on a $5,000-a-month retainer. "That's nothing to me," Marty told Hackney over the phone from Toledo, where he was still living at the time. "I make more than that in an hour. I make that in no time at all." Hackney believed that he was just a small cog in Marty's massive financial empire.

Hackney was a smallish man, a little bit round and a little bit bald. At home he had a very attractive wife, a small son, and a second baby on the way. Now, he felt, he could finally do right by them. Ann Hackney came from a "good family" in Guntersville, Alabama, where her father had retired from a successful insurance business. Ann was Hackney's greatest blessing, and he wanted to be able to give her the kind of life she'd had when she was growing up in a big lakeside house in Guntersville.

Hackney hailed from Lawrenceburg in southern Tennessee, about halfway between Memphis and Chattanooga. It had fewer than 9,000 people when he left for college. His dad was a dentist and his brother became a plastic surgeon. Many of the friends Hackney made at Middle Tennessee State University went on to successful careers as lawyers and entrepreneurs. Bart Gordon, a good pal from his freshman year, even became a U.S. congressman.

But Hackney had a harder time finding his way. Friendship was probably his greatest gift. As social chairman of his fraternity, Kappa Sigma, John had been the one to hire the bands and order the food for some legendary toga parties. When the movie *Animal House* came out, a few years after he graduated in 1972, old frat brothers in several states called him to say, "Remember doing that?" His buddies—and he had plenty of them—liked to joke that he'd served as best man at least twenty-five times before becoming a groom himself. That was probably true. He was a football fan, a hunter, and a teller of jokes, some of them a little bawdy and most of them unbearably hokey. He'd call friends and just start rattling jokes off, without introducing himself. It didn't matter; they all knew the slightly halting, slightly nasal voice on the other end of the line.

His joke-telling, of course, couldn't be parlayed into a career. Hackney began graduate school in business administration but didn't quite finish after his mother's death threw him into a tailspin. He moved to Nashville, rented an apartment, and went to work as a records clerk for the Tennessee state senate. But he knew that would lead him exactly nowhere. And more than anything, John Hackney wanted to be a successful man. He just wasn't sure at what.

He was somewhat interested in banking, and after a short, and unsatisfying, stint selling respiratory therapy equipment to hospitals, he got a job supervising purchasing for the First American Bank in Nashville. The bank was growing rapidly and Hackney did much to update its archaic purchasing systems and save it some significant cash. The bank's comptroller, Richard Herrington, became a mentor of sorts.

The two left the bank and with several other partners founded Hickory Financial Systems, which specialized in handling back-office work for small banks. Hackney lived next door to its offices and poured his heart into keeping expenses under control and trying to sell bank executives on the company's services. "People liked him," Herrington later recalled. "John could meet somebody and within thirty minutes the person would tell him his whole life story."

But eventually Hickory Financial ran into problems. The company split in two; part of it was acquired by a savings and loan, which itself fell victim to the growing S&L crisis. Ultimately Hackney was out of a job.

Herrington was putting together a group of investors to start the Franklin National Bank, and Hackney did his best to help, organizing some early meetings. He was hoping for an ownership stake, but when he couldn't come up with the $50,000 or so he needed to invest in the venture, Hackney found himself closed out of the deal. The bank needed lending officers and tellers. He had no experience as a lender and was too experienced to be a teller. Even as an employee there was no place for him at the bank, and he was deeply resentful. (One of the first things Hackney did after the Franklin American buy was sever Franklin American's ties with its bank—Herrington's Franklin National—and take its business elsewhere.)

After several painful love affairs in his twenties and thirties, Hackney married Ann when he was thirty-eight. ("Nobody could be that sweet," remarked a friend of John's after meeting her. She soon decided Ann was.) They moved from a condo in Brentwood, a Nashville suburb, to a brick house in a subdivision of exclusive and tony Franklin. Hackney had some sizable bills to pay and financially he was in a jam.

John Goodhue came to the rescue. Hackney had met the disbarred lawyer through Gary Atnip, a certified public accountant with an office near Hickory Financial. Goodhue and Atnip once had worked together at a firm that had tried to develop technology to enhance the taste of diet food. Goodhue helped Hackney with a few house payments and other living expenses and told him he could work for him.

But then came Marty Frankel. Shortly after Goodhue let Hackney take a crack at getting Marty to pay his overdue bill, the two men went their separate ways. Hackney told Goodhue that he was putting together a group of investors to buy Franklin American Life Insurance along with a local lawyer, John Jordan. He chose not to mention that Marty was involved. Marty, of course, was desperate to cloak his acquisition in complete secrecy. But at play were other sensitive issues. Goodhue could easily have argued that he was entitled to a finder's fee or some other piece of the action. And there was the unpaid consulting bill to consider. As it was, Goodhue didn't find out that Hackney had run off with his client until many years later.

It was an act of desperation by a man hungry for success. Hackney realized that if he wanted to be a success, he was going to have to shed his good-ol'-boy ways and be a little more aggressive in business. As one of his friends put it, he "tried to swing for the home run."

And it looked as if he'd hit a good one. He went from near unemployment to CEO. Once the deal was closed, Hackney was on salary, at about $80,000 a year. There was the promise of bonuses if he succeeded in acquiring additional insurance companies for Marty. And nobody except Jordan, the lawyer who set up the Thunor Trust, and Gary Atnip, whom Hackney installed as his right-hand man, knew that there was someone else behind the scenes, pulling the strings.

As soon as the acquisition was complete, Marty called Hackney and asked him to send all of Franklin American's $18 million in assets to a series of accounts at Bear Stearns, Dreyfus, and several other firms. As Hackney and Atnip understood it, Marty and Sonia were liquidating

Franklin American's portfolio so that they could invest it more wisely for the company.

Over the phone, Hackney and Atnip briefed Marty on the laws that governed the investment of insurance company assets. Marty didn't like what he heard. The laws in Tennessee stipulated that only 10 percent of an insurer's admitted assets, those recognized by regulators, could be invested in anything other than government securities, which certainly was going to put a crimp in his trading: "I'm really good at bonds, but I'm better at equities," he whined. Hackney and Atnip sent him copies of the law, and insisted that he read them very carefully. Finally they convinced him to steer a conservative course and invest only in bonds.

Hackney was no great market expert, and Marty spent hours explaining and re-explaining his bond-trading philosophy. If there are 32 ticks in a point, he explained, and if he earned an average of a ½ point a month, all he needed was less than a tick a day. Then all you need is an extra tick a month and that gives you another 6 percent. On a bond yielding 7 percent you pick up an extra ½ point a month, and that's 16 ticks and a yield of 13 percent.

He could get 2 points a month, "no problem," Marty said. If he thought bonds were going to pop up 2 percent, he'd go in, trade, get his gain, and put the money back in cash for the rest of the month. Hackney didn't quite get it, but he figured that didn't matter so long as Marty knew what he was doing.

A Franklin American filing with state insurance regulators explained the company's investment policy this way: "The market is to be observed on a daily basis. When market conditions make it favorable to sell the security, a sell order is placed in the morning for the highest price possible. That same day, if the market is favorable, the security or one that is in accordance with this investment policy will be bought back at the lowest price possible."

Just a month after Thunor bought Franklin American, Hackney got a November statement from Liberty National Securities, Marty's brokerage firm. He opened the envelope and saw that Marty had made a gain of nearly $200,000 in just one month. Hackney was ecstatic. He and Atnip rejoiced. The company hadn't made a monthly profit like that in seven or eight years.

Hackney still hadn't met Marty face to face. Much earlier, before they'd bought Franklin, Atnip had traveled to Toledo for a day to help Marty with some accounting problems. Sonia had picked him up at the airport in nearby Detroit and driven him to the house on Stanhope. Atnip had reported back to Hackney that Marty was very sloppily dressed, wore thick glasses, and seemed "real studious." The place, he had told Hackney, was not very clean. Hackney and Atnip spent considerable time trying to figure out just how much Marty was worth, assuming that he was investing huge sums of money for himself and others.

Most of what Hackney knew about Marty he learned from the man himself. Hackney thought his boss had a lot of quirks, but he didn't let himself ask any tough questions, the most obvious being, Why all the secrecy? In his heart, he knew that the money put up to buy Franklin had not come from Sonia Schulte or Ed Krauss or Mark Shuki. He knew it came from Marty Frankel and he knew that Marty would control the company. Later, he chastised himself for not asking more questions. "But it was like looking a gift horse in the mouth," he said. "I think I was so happy to have someplace to go to work at."

Marty explained his need for secrecy by regaling Hackney with stories about his feud with John Schulte. He wanted to destroy Schulte. He claimed that Schulte had molested Sonia's daughters and that he was going to protect them no matter what. Marty talked about spoiling the little girls, and Hackney, a devoted father himself, thought he really cared about them.

"Refer to me as Eric Stevens," Marty instructed Hackney. "Don't call me Marty in the office." Marty found the word "alias" distasteful. He liked "nickname" better. Marty asked Hackney to tell people who were curious about how he'd gotten hitched up with Franklin American that he'd met Sonia, who had been interested in buying a bank.

So Hackney called his boss Marty on the phone, or when he was closeted with Atnip or John Jordan, their lawyer, because both were privy to Marty's real identity. But around the office he referred to Marty as "Eric," and he was vigilant about never slipping up. He went so far as to create a persona for "Eric." He was a very wealthy eccentric, Hackney told his staff. The Thunor investors were four or five rich Jews in New York, including "Eric" and Sonia. Around the office, staffers referred to the company's owners as "the Jewish investors," or "the Thunor Group."

Hackney even made up a story about a summer trip he and Ann took to Europe with the investors, confiding that "Eric" had had a huge bank of computers and monitors installed in his hotel room in Venice because he needed to monitor the markets and news even on vacation! He'd been very demanding of the hotel employees.

That "Eric" was demanding, the Franklin American staff already knew. They'd heard from the switchboard operator that Hackney spent hours on the phone each day with "Eric." Usually, "Eric" did most of the talking, and sometimes Hackney put him on the speaker phone, hit the mute button, and carried on the firm's business, talking to Atnip and signing checks as his boss droned on and on. Forty-five minutes later Marty would suddenly ask, "Are you there?" Hackney would take the phone off mute and continue the conversation.

In 1992, about a year after Thunor bought Franklin, Marty began to mention—almost in passing—that he'd been "messed over" by the government. Some guy named Doug in Nashville had stolen his clients' money and had "hung him out to dry," he said. But Marty had paid back every cent, he insisted. Marty's explanation was unclear to Hackney, but it finally dawned on him that Marty had lost his broker's license. What Hackney didn't realize was that the money with which Marty had paid back his clients came from Franklin American's coffers.

Marty finally had made a deal with the SEC. When it became clear that the commission's case against him was airtight, he agreed to pay a fine and relinquish his broker's license. (Maxwell turned in his license as well.) Marty also settled with the Herlihys and Bitters, but only after an arbitration panel of the National Association of Securities Dealers dealt him a devastating defeat. In August 1992, after a hearing in Cleveland that Marty had not bothered to attend, the panel awarded the Herlihys $622,000 in damages and the Bitters $176,632 in damages. Attorneys' fees were awarded as well.

The lawyers at Shumaker, Loop practically ran to federal court to get an injunction freezing Marty's assets. Marty was beside himself, and the next day they heard from his local lawyer, agreeing to settle in order to get the injunction lifted. Jeff Creamer and the other lawyers at Shumaker, Loop were nervous. They worried that whatever money Marty came up with to pay the settlement would be stolen money—although from where, they had no idea.

Marty insisted he was penniless, but he told the Shumaker, Loop lawyers that he could get a loan from relatives. The lawyers wanted him to swear to it—in writing. "I do not own, whether in my name or otherwise, either directly or indirectly, any property, cash or other assets other than personal effects having a value of less than $10,000," Marty attested. "I have obtained a bona fide loan of $175,000." The affidavit was notarized by Leon Frankel. The money covered part, but not all, of the two families' losses.

In the end, Shumaker, Loop's fears proved to be correct. Franklin American footed the bill for Marty's Frankel Fund fiasco. The money to pay the Herlihys and Bitters was simply wired back to the United States from Marty's Swiss bank account, where he had parked it. And what Marty had neglected to mention in his affidavit, of course, was that he had a multimillion-dollar insurance company chugging away down in Franklin, Tennessee, with what on paper was a bond portfolio swelling as a result of his supposed financial prowess.

Down in Franklin, Hackney wasn't too worried about Marty's muddled account of his run-in with the SEC. He told himself it didn't matter that Marty no longer had a broker's license, because Marty really owned Franklin anyway, so all he was doing was trading his own assets. "If it's your own money, you're extra careful," Hackney told himself. He didn't ask many questions about the details of Marty's operation, but he more or less thought that Marty wasn't technically making trades anyway. He was telling someone at Liberty National Securities to execute the transactions.

Besides, Marty told Hackney that he had a lawyer in Chicago who was trying to get his license back, and he mailed the paperwork to Franklin American to prove it. In fact, nothing ever came of the lawyer's efforts.

With the Frankel Fund shenanigans firmly behind him, and Creative Partners dissolved, Marty had virtually cleansed his business life of his name; he began to build his new empire, with Hackney as front man. Starting in February 1994, and continuing for another five years, Marty and Hackney went on a buying spree, purchasing six insurers based in Mississippi, Oklahoma, Missouri, and Arkansas. They formed two holding companies, Franklin American Corporation and International Financial Corporation, to own the firms, which sold "pre-need" burial polices and some regular life insurance policies. Both holding companies were in turn owned by Thunor and run out of the offices in Franklin, Tennessee.

With each new acquisition, it seemed to Hackney that Marty was relying more and more on astrology to guide his business decisions. First, Marty wanted to know the exact time of Hackney's birth. Hackney happened to have his birth certificate in the office and quickly dug it out. Marty happily reported that their signs "matched up."

"Perfect, great, terrific," said Hackney, who had little patience for the stars. Nevertheless, a short time later he asked Marty whether he'd "worked up a chart on him." Of course, Marty had.

"I didn't want to tell you this," Marty said a bit sorrowfully, "but you'll get a divorce and you'll have an awful marriage." Hackney decided that the chart was probably referring to his previous, unhappy relationships and Marty agreed that that was possible.

Marty wanted to know the birthdates of the other executives in the burgeoning little company, and he wanted similar data on the lawyers Hackney retained to help buy the other companies. Hackney felt a little silly collecting the information and managed to avoid the assignment. But it became increasingly difficult for Hackney to ignore Marty's zodiac obsession. When Hackney was trying to acquire First National Life Insurance Company of America, which he then moved from Alabama to Mississippi, Marty wanted to pick an astrologically correct date on which to close the deal.

"You can't do that!" Hackney wailed into the phone, thinking of all the regulatory and business personnel who had to be marshaled in preparation for closing. But Marty insisted that the deal "would crash and burn" if the date was wrong. He insisted that certain documents be filed with state regulators on special dates, and sometimes he even stipulated the time of day.

"You've got to be careful," he ominously warned Hackney, trying to explain something crucial about the positioning of Mars.

In his hokey way, Hackney tried to joke Marty out of it. He talked about billboard "signs" and stop "signs."

"You're being too silly," Marty finally said. "It's my quirk. I'm the one who has to invest my money. Just do it." Before he got off the phone he added, "It really does work."

The silliness continued. Marty seemed to have time to explore a wide range of issues with his chief executive. When Marty decided it was time to leave Toledo behind, Hackney suggested he move down south. Marty instead chose Greenwich, Connecticut, an hour outside New York, complaining that he wouldn't be able to get his *Wall Street Journal* or Bloomberg magazine fast enough if he moved south of the Mason-Dixon line. The two men spent hours debating Marty's growing belief that Southerners were just plain dumb. To him, they were all bigots, narrow-minded and anti-Semitic. "You're one of the new Southerners," Marty told Hackney. "You're not a bigot." The two launched into what became a series of discussions about the Civil War, with Marty arguing that it was fought over slavery and Hackney insisting that the core issue was states' rights, noting that only 10 percent of Southerners had ever owned slaves.

Always, Marty had the upper hand in these discussions. He insisted that Hackney listen to his theories that eating dried peas and ejaculating often—by masturbation if necessary—prevented prostate cancer, one of his particular bugaboos.

"That is not something I want to know," Hackney told his boss. "It really grosses me out when you talk about this."

Hackney never stopped to wonder how Marty had time for these discussions, given that he was supposedly day-trading government securities. Even when Marty began to complain that he couldn't get himself to trade, and confided that he was seeking the advice of a psychiatrist because he just couldn't get things done, Hackney didn't take him seriously. When Marty referred to his "trading block," as he still called it, he was usually talking about stocks, not bonds. So Hackney wasn't too worried.

He had ample reason *not* to worry. Every month statements rolled in from Liberty National Securities confirming Hackney's belief in Marty's special talent for timing the market in U.S. Treasury bonds. In March 1996, for example, the statements showed that Marty had made forty transactions. On March 3, he bought bonds at $112\frac{2}{32}$. The next day he sold them at $112\frac{8}{32}$, making a tidy little sum. The reports Hackney received from Liberty National showed that Marty was making his family of small insurers a very healthy profit of almost 15 percent a year.

Even without the investment income, Hackney's companies were thriving. He was a soft touch for a raise, a hands-off manager, and his employees loved him for it. Franklin American had been on the ropes when Marty and Hackney bought it, as were many of the other companies the Thunor Trust acquired. The company's policies were sold through funeral homes. Before Thunor came along, these clients had abandoned Franklin American in droves because it often didn't pay funeral costs on time, leaving funeral directors in a lurch. Hackney made sure that bills were paid promptly and that claims were dealt with fairly. He made it clear to customers that a change was at hand. Slowly the funeral directors—mostly small business owners in rural areas—came trickling back.

"John [Hackney] did not micromanage," Jerry Poindexter, his chief salesman, later said. "John let you go. He let you do what you knew how to do, which I thought was one of John's strong points. He did not know a whole lot about the business. If you did things right, John didn't bother you."

In 1992 Franklin had about $1 million in new premiums come through the door, but by 1998 that had increased to about $14 million, and that was for Franklin American alone—without the new companies that had been added to the Thunor empire. Jerry Poindexter, who along with his wife, Janet, traveled around Tennessee wooing funeral directors, projected that new premiums were going to hit $20 million by 1999.

That meant a whole lot of policies were being sold. The average policy cost a little less than $5,000, which paid for a nice, but not glitzy, funeral. Most buyers were seventy to seventy-two years old, lived in small or rural communities, and paid a single premium. For the most part, they were relatively unsophisticated and didn't realize that an insurer would earn the interest on the money they'd saved up for their funerals when the money could have remained in their own bank accounts.

Under Hackney's regime, Franklin American did anything and everything to court the funeral directors and their families. Janet Poindexter once ran out to buy a doll's bonnet to fit over the head of a tiny baby born without a brain, so that a funeral director client could present the baby's body in an open casket for the grieving family.

Hackney talked to Marty endlessly about his efforts to boost sales and create a familylike atmosphere in the growing empire's home office. Although Marty was far more interested in Hackney's acquisition plan, he listened and even offered to help entertain a group of funeral directors when they came to New York.

The five funeral directors, their wives, and one mother-in-law were part of a larger church group that had decided to tour New York at Christmastime. Most of the group got off the plane and filed onto tour buses, but the funeral directors and Janet Poindexter were met by two of Marty's limousines, which had traveled the hour or so from Greenwich to pick them up. Inside each limo were bouquets of flowers and each funeral director's favorite liquor, including twelve-year-old Old Charter whiskey for the mother-in-law. "The associates just want you to enjoy yourselves," explained one of the limo drivers, Sheldon, who was Marty's personal chauffeur.

Late one night, after attending a Broadway show, the funeral directors decided they wanted to go to Tavern on the Green, the well-known restaurant on the edge of Central Park. But when they pulled up to the Christmas-light-festooned restaurant, they found that the kitchen had just closed for the evening. There was a chorus of disappointment in the back of the limousine and Sheldon made a phone call back to headquarters in Greenwich. There was a fifteen-minute wait while something— the funeral directors weren't sure what—was negotiated. Then suddenly the funeral directors were invited inside and served dinner by a somewhat disgruntled waitstaff. Outside once more, they remarked that they hadn't been served coffee. Sheldon got on the phone again and, lo and behold, coffee was served out in the limos. By then it was about three A.M.

The group decided that it wanted to see the famed Apollo Theatre in Harlem. Sheldon was skeptical, implying that it wasn't safe. But the next day he arranged it. As the limousines turned onto 125th Street, it appeared to Janet Poindexter that the street had been closed to traffic. Men in black coats lined the street, waiting for them. When the limousine pulled up to the theater, its moon roof was opened and the funeral directors snapped pictures. They were allowed about five minutes, and then the cortège pulled off again.

In response to the funeral directors' wonder and gratitude, Sheldon responded obliquely, "It's just the associates, ma'am." For three days, "the associates" paid for everything, from a fake Gucci watch to lunch in the Oak Room at the Plaza Hotel. The limousines pulled up to the Frank E. Campbell funeral home, which buries Manhattan's elite, so the funeral directors could take a look and engaged its dignified staff in a technical—but heated—argument about Jacqueline Kennedy Onassis's embalming.

"Damn, these people really do have pull," Janet Poindexter thought to herself about "the associates." "These are some really rich Jewish people and they're nice Jewish people. We always heard Jewish people were stingy."

Back in Franklin, Janet Poindexter and the funeral directors wanted to thank whoever had made their trip so successful, but Hackney refused to give them a name. He told them that the Thunor Trust had just wanted to entertain them and no thanks were necessary. "They're not like that," he told Janet Poindexter. Finally, they drafted a note addressed, "To Whom It May Concern," and Hackney promised to "get it to them."

By the mid-nineties, Franklin American's attentiveness to clients was paying off. Hackney's staff had swelled from about fourteen employees to nearly eighty. The empire's assets were approaching $200 million. They'd acquired Family Guaranty Life Insurance Company (Mississippi), Farmers and Ranchers Life Insurance Company (Oklahoma), and International Financial Services Life Insurance Company (Missouri) in 1994. The next year they acquired Franklin Protective Life Insurance Company (Mississippi). In 1997, they bought First National Life Insurance Company (Mississippi), and in 1999 they bought Old Southwest Life Insurance Company (Arkansas).

And Hackney was reaping the benefits of his loyalty to Marty. As a bonus for acquiring several of the new insurance companies, Marty bought him a house in 1994. John and Ann Hackney chose a beauty. Built in 1874, it was called the Blackburn House after its original owner, who had personally picked every piece of wood used in it. The house stood just a short walk from downtown Franklin, a historic town centered around a picturesque square. The price was $515,000 and Hackney knew that he could not really afford the taxes on it. John Jordan, Franklin American's lawyer, was all set to form a trust in order to lighten the financial burden, when Marty came up with another idea.

Marty suggested that a company called Middleburg Investments Ltd., which Marty had registered in the British Virgin Islands, should officially own the house. "It's something that I have," Marty explained. "There's nothing in there." He wired money from his Swiss banking account to an escrow account controlled by Jordan's law firm, and the house on Third Avenue South in Franklin became Middleburg's only asset and Hackney's home.

When the Hackneys moved out of their nondescript house and into their new, large place just a few minutes away, they ascended to a new social stratum in Franklin. The pretty town had a certain snob appeal. Home to horse farms, a country club, and country music stars, Franklin had a lot of hometown pride and was enthusiastically committed to historic preservation. The Blackburn House was next door to the house where the headmaster of the town's elite private school lived, and John Hackney quickly befriended him. He was friends with Franklin's police chief and the town's best-connected lawyers and businessmen. Suddenly, Hackney had become the man he had always wanted to be. He was economic development showcase cochairman for the Williamson County–Franklin Chamber of Commerce, a board member of the prestigious Heritage Foundation (devoted to local historic preservation) and president of the Downtown Franklin Association. Friends talked about his behind-the-scenes contributions to the town's shelter for battered women. He received do-gooder awards. And he and Ann were frequently mentioned in the society columns of *The Tennessean:* "Harpeth Academy rocked around the clock last weekend at its annual auction party," according to one such column, which went on to note that Ann and John were among the rockers at the " '50s evening." Another column, in 1996, referred to Franklin American's CEO as "insurance wizard John Hackney." He was playing, as one friend put it, "in the big leagues."

Ann fixed up the house so that it was picture perfect, with green-and-white-striped kitchen walls and a dusky pink living room that was filled with antiques, as was a study across the hall. The Hackneys mostly lived in the back part of the house, where there was another large living room, but the front was opened for their annual Christmas party, one of the town's hottest social events.

Several years later the Hackneys used $375,630 in bonus money from Marty to buy a house on the big lake in Ann's hometown. Decorating in warm yellows, Ann adopted a sort of Southern Martha Stewart approach to the house. The Guntersville property stretched down to a dock with a panoramic view. Marty even okayed a loan from Franklin American to Hackney's brother, who wanted $400,000 for his plastic surgery business.

Hackney wasn't the only one who benefited from the money Marty controlled. Gary Atnip, who presided over Franklin's books and called Marty by his real name, received cash bonuses, including an investment in World Christian Online, a Christian website that was his pet project. He bought a house on the grounds of Dolly Parton's mansion in Brentwood, Tennessee.

And finally, John Jordan, the lawyer who knew Marty's real identity and had helped form the Thunor Trust, pulled in impressive fees for his law firm. At one point his firm was making about $20,000 a month. Given that most of Franklin American's legal work required regulatory expertise, not Jordan's bailiwick, and was farmed out to other lawyers, it seemed like an awful lot of money to employees like the Poindexters, who couldn't quite figure out Jordan's role with the company.

The money seemed plentiful. "John [Hackney] was so wonderful to us about anything we would ask for," Janet Poindexter later said. "I was never told no in five years." When one employee asked where all the money was coming from, Hackney replied. "We don't know. We just say what we need, and we get it."

There seemed to be few signs that the flow of cash would ever stop. Sometime in 1996, Jerry Poindexter visited with Thomas (Tad) Trantum, the president of Mastrapasqua & Associates, a money management firm in Nashville. Trantum, a portfolio manager with an M.B.A., wanted to pitch Franklin American for its investment business. Poindexter explained the company's strategy—the buying and selling of U.S. Treasury bonds—and told Trantum that the company was earning about 14 percent on its investments.

That sounded a little funny to Trantum, who knew that the bond market generally was yielding only about 7 percent. He called Poindexter a few days later and said that his firm had tried every which way to figure out how Franklin's current portfolio manager could have gotten such stunning results. They had no clue how he'd done it. "Let me look at the portfolio; let me see what's been done," Trantum asked.

The conversation worried Jerry Poindexter. He went to see Hackney and told him what Tantrum had said. "Maybe they just don't understand the kind of investments we have," Hackney said, not taking it too seriously. Poindexter decided that that was probably the case, and went back to visiting funeral directors.

Chapter Six

Domestic Bliss

John Hackney dialed the 800 phone number Marty had given him and was connected with the financier's new headquarters in Greenwich, Connecticut. He had only routine business to discuss, but Marty had other things on his mind. He was ranting: he had just arrived at his new house, and everything was in turmoil.

While Marty was still in Toledo, Hackney had warned him that his office should be set up properly before the spring 1993 move so that he could just walk into his new place and start working. It hadn't happened that way. As Marty complained to Hackney over the phone, he broke off to gripe at Sonia about how the phones weren't set up right and to scream at David Rosse because the computers were not up and running and he couldn't access his files.

With all the tumult, Marty complained, he just couldn't trade.

"Just calm down and get everything settled down and you'll be ready to roll," Hackney told Marty, attempting to talk his boss down from his attack of extreme agitation. The way Hackney saw it, the worst-case scenario was that Marty would lose a week's worth of trading. If that happened, he thought, he would simply make it up the following week, month, or quarter. There was nothing to worry about.

But Hackney could not fully appreciate the anxiety Marty felt at moving far from his family to start a new life that, he hoped, would escape John Schulte's detection. David Rosse had helped Marty find the house. The security chief had grown up nearby in New York and knew the area well, so he searched for houses and then summoned Marty to look at a few serious prospects. For Rosse, it was a maddening experience. Marty was afraid to fly and insisted on traveling from Toledo to Greenwich by train, an overnight trip that took more than fourteen hours. Not only that, but he was extraordinarily picky. He refused to consider some houses because he believed the direction they faced was unlucky. Finally he settled on a twelve-room stone mansion at 889 Lake Avenue and agreed to rent it from the family of the architect who had built it, for about $20,000 a month. He chose it not so much because he liked the looks of the place, but because he felt it was secure.

The house had five bedrooms, eight baths, and, in its public rooms, soaring cathedral ceilings. Floor-to-ceiling windows let in vast quantities of light. The house sat on four acres in what was known as the back country of Greenwich, one of the most exclusive neighborhoods, in one of the most exclusive suburbs of New York City. Greenwich was home to financiers and venture capitalists. At last Marty had a home among his peers.

Security and secrecy were his top priorities. Marty did not use his name on any of the documents related to the house. Instead he had one of his corporate entities, Sundew International, lease it. When he eventually bought the house, for $3 million of Franklin American's cash, he made sure the closing took place at the astrologically correct moment.

Happily, Marty's fixation with safety meshed nicely with David Rosse's James Bond–like tendencies. Rosse came from a close-knit family with an interest in the law. While one sister became a lawyer and another a paralegal, Rosse became obsessed with the more technical side of law enforcement. After a stint in the military and as an auxiliary cop in California, he started his own small private-detective agency, which allowed him to indulge in his passion for high-tech security devices. Marty was a godsend. "The Boss," as Rosse called him, was willing to pay for any fancy gadget Rosse's heart desired. Soon he was happily installing all kinds of expensive equipment around the compound. He topped fences with big floodlights. He installed alarms on the doors, as well as sophisticated cipher locks that required anyone opening them to punch numbers into a key pad. Security cameras were placed inside and outside the building. Rosse ruled over a command center set up in the garage to monitor the cameras. Meanwhile alarms were hooked up to a monitoring company that called and demanded passwords whenever trouble was electronically detected.

Marty felt more secure than he had in a while, and he owed it largely to Dave. Shortly after the move, Marty treated Dave to a Harley-Davidson Dyna Wide Glide motorcycle that cost a little more than $13,000.

Marty had other special security needs as well. His various corporate entities needed anonymous-sounding addresses to shield him from scrutiny by the SEC, insurance regulators, and, of course, John Schulte. Liberty National Securities, his brokerage firm, used a mail drop on Wall Street in Manhattan. Two other companies, AWV Corporation and RMI Investments, Inc., had addresses at a Mailboxes Etc. in Katonah, New York, just a short ride from Connecticut. Marty had an account with the New York Stock Exchange for MDS devices, providing up-to-the-second stock prices, through a firm he named Gates Investments, apparently after Bill Gates, whose career he avidly studied. Invoices from the exchange were sent to "Mike King, 1st Floor, 889 Lake Avenue," making it look as though the Greenwich house was actually a business establishment. Gates International also had a Telerate account for lightning-fast foreign-exchange-rate quotes.

Marty closed off most of the living room and turned it into his trading room. His mother's card tables, the same ones he'd used since he'd operated out of his bedroom in Leon and Tillie's house, also had made the move to Greenwich, and he piled his growing stack of computer monitors on them. David Rosse, who reveled a bit in his boss's weirdness, warned him that the tables were going to collapse, perhaps dumping thousands of dollars' worth of computer equipment on top of him. But Marty thought the tables brought him good luck and was willing to take his chances. The tables and towers of monitors formed almost a semicircle around the large chair he sat in. Hating to feel confined, he usually wore jeans several sizes too big for his scrawny frame and kept his fly unbuttoned and unzipped while he sat in front of the computer bank. When he stood up, he would simply put himself back together again.

The rest of the house was furnished sparsely, and the only comfortable chairs were the recliners he'd moved from the house on Stanhope. They looked a little out of place in their palatial new surroundings.

Sonia and her two children had arrived at the mansion with Marty. The couple was officially engaged and they did their best to settle in as a real family. A cousin of Sonia's came to help take care of the girls, who began to play with other children in the neighborhood.

After Marty and Sonia had been living in Greenwich for a few months, a neighbor whose children played with Sonia's asked the family over for a barbecue. Marty introduced himself as Mike King. Wearing a pair of khakis, his hair disheveled, he blathered on in his stream-of-consciousness way about security. He talked about his fear of bandits who converged on rich families at dinnertime, tied them up, and stole their money. Sonia's ex-husband, Marty explained, was a very bad guy and was looking for them. That was why they needed extra security and bulletproof glass. He mentioned that he always stayed on the ground floor of hotels because he worried about fires.

The neighbor, who also worked in the financial world, thought the safety obsession was a bit excessive. "Lots of wealthy people live in Greenwich," he thought, "but they're not *this* paranoid." Marty had represented himself as a rich private investor who did his own trading. But when this neighbor dropped by the house, he thought it somehow didn't look like a real trader's setup. The kind of data Marty had up on his screens just didn't make much sense for a trader. The neighbor's antennae went up. The whole thing was a little odd, he thought; but, he decided, "everybody does things differently."

Marty had Hackney and the operation in Franklin, Tennessee, under control. But almost as soon as he moved in, he had to deal with a sticky logistical problem that threatened to topple his operation. William Kok, his front man for Liberty National Securities, decided to return home to Singapore. Back in Toledo, Marty had done his best to keep Kok happy. When the young man had married, Marty had hosted and paid for a twenty-five-person party at a Chinese restaurant on Central Avenue. Sonia's friend George Freeland, a minister and Creative Partners investor, had officiated at the ceremony.

But now Marty had to start over, cultivating loyalty in another broker who wouldn't mind babysitting Liberty National and hiding its real owner from securities regulators. It had to be someone not apt to ask a lot of questions, so that Marty could continue to "trade" Franklin American's assets without obstacles. He turned to Robert Guyer, who had worked as a broker for Sonia after she'd split from Schulte. Guyer, fifty-five, was a deeply religious man, who had taken wedding pictures and sold insurance before turning to stockbroking late in his career. Marty called him in mid-1993, explaining that Kok was returning to Asia and that he needed someone to replace him as head of Marty's little firm. "I just need a place to land when I get my license back," Marty explained, telling Guyer he could run the company any way he wanted until then. Was Guyer interested?

He was.

Guyer knew Marty, although not well. Sometimes Marty had come into Sonia's Thomas White office to hold meetings. He'd been impressed with the success of Creative Partners, in which he had invested. Marty's offer came at a good time. Guyer wasn't generating enough in commissions to pay office overhead in Toledo. So for him, it was a definite plus to be able to retreat to his three-bedroom house in nearby Dundee, Michigan, and set up shop as Liberty National Securities on the enclosed front porch. He even took the so-called Series 27 license test so he could manage a brokerage office.

Guyer made himself a pretty good deal. In 1994, Marty started paying him $2,000 a month to run Liberty National. Guyer spent most of his time servicing his own small group of retail clients. As Marty's employee, he had relatively few duties to perform. He filed a so-called Form BD, by which brokers/dealers seek regulatory approval to do business, but hid the fact that Marty owned the firm. He installed an 800 telephone number and forwarded the line to Greenwich. When some of Guyer's clients ended up reaching Greenwich by mistake, Guyer got another phone number for them. Occasionally, mail for Marty would arrive in Dundee, and Guyer would simply forward it to Greenwich.

Marty remained convinced that he could conquer his trading block. He continued to match wits with the markets—on a theoretical basis—and he continued to find that his predictions were often on the mark. Ultimately, he believed, he would be able to trade and catch up with his phony results. He would pay back the money he was siphoning out of Franklin American's accounts.

Another "trading" problem was also nagging Marty. For years, he had created simple brokerage statements on his computer. But in his new role as asset manager for a real insurance company he needed to come up with statements that looked more professional—especially since insurance regulators were now looking over John Hackney's shoulder.

Marty delegated David Rosse to find someone to print forms for the statements. Rosse found a printer in Westchester. Still, the statements were hard to create, and Marty could do it only with help from Sonia. The trick was to search bond market prices for opportunities in which he *could* have taken advantage of minor upward fluctuations, had he been emotionally up to the task. Then enough "trades" had to be pinpointed to make it look as though in most months Marty had earned a respectable profit. The data were typewritten onto the forms, which were then photocopied. The results didn't look quite right.

And making up statements wasn't always easy. Sometimes Hackney called asking why the monthly statements were late. Several times, Marty sent David Rosse to Franklin with statements and a box of confirmation slips. Rosse flew into Nashville, drove the half-hour or so to Franklin, carried the box into John Hackney's office, said hello, and immediately returned to Greenwich.

Eventually, through a contact at Bear Stearns where he had an account, Marty met Mark Burgess, a Wall Street professional and computer whiz. Burgess visited Marty in Greenwich and the two talked about Marty's theories of the market. Burgess was dazzled and came away thinking that Marty had a business mind like that of Bill Gates.

He signed on as a freelancer, creating a software program that helped create professional-looking statements using real closing prices. Marty's hope was that the statements would now be audit-proof. Still, someone—and it had to be someone Marty trusted—had to input information about the phony trades. Most of the time, that someone was Sonia.

On the domestic front, Marty also had plenty of distractions. He believed wholeheartedly that peace and quiet would go a long way toward curing his trader's block. But as he started his new life in Greenwich, he was overtaken by a new obsession: sex. Years before, Doug Maxwell had promised that there would be sex aplenty if Marty made the move to Florida. But that angst-ridden sojourn in West Palm had yielded nothing in the girlfriend department. Since then Marty had rarely lived more than a few yards from his parents' probing eyes. Socially, he was completely at sea. He didn't really know how to make friends. George Freeland, the minister, even likened him to a "deprived child" who "really didn't mix well with too many people."

Besides, his relationship with Sonia was getting a bit rocky. Their war with John Schulte had brought the couple together, but it also had taken a toll on them; although Marty cared deeply about Sonia and her children, whom he regarded almost as his own, the relationship wasn't completely satisfying him. With all Sonia's domestic problems, theirs was hardly a free and easy romance. He'd always lived a life subservient to his mother and especially to his personal demons. Now he wanted to explore. Marty wanted a little fun.

Racked with fears and phobias as he was, partying or even just plain going out was out of the question. As he fantasized about what he really wanted in a woman, Marty stationed himself where he was most comfy, in front of his computer screens, pants unzipped. There he did research on the Internet, studying the array of sexuality available outside the sphere of his parents' world in Toledo. He scanned personal ads in New York's *Village Voice* and on the web. After hours of surfing he came upon an organization called The Eulenspiegel Society. Originally established by a group of sexual masochists in 1971, TES, as it is known, eventually became a full-fledged S&M organization devoted to "sexual liberation as a basic requirement of a truly free society," as its official creed explained. (The organization was named after Till Eulenspiegel, a "foolish yet clever lad" in a German folk tale cited in Theodore Reik's *Masochism in Modern Man,* a classic of psychoanalytic literature.)

Though he was ashamed of such thoughts, Marty felt powerfully attracted to sadomasochism. The possibility that he could dominate a woman was titillating and liberating.

Marty subscribed to TES's quarterly magazine, *Prometheus,* and through a personal ad in it found a woman who appealed to him. Miriam, a married TES participant who lived in Manhattan, was a good match for Marty in many respects. A onetime stockbroker, she was smart and well read. She was also emotionally volatile and a dedicated submissive sexually. She and Marty had long phone conversations in the summer of 1993, just months after he'd arrived in Greenwich. Marty was intrigued, but he couldn't quite get himself to meet Miriam. He asked her to send him her résumé, copies of filings she'd made with the

National Association of Securities Dealers, her social security number, and other information. Then he ordered David Rosse to do a security check on her.

Marty and Miriam finally met several months later. For Marty, the relationship was an eye-opener. Miriam was far more experienced than he, and she was a good teacher. She taught him about the psychology of S&M and encouraged him to practice it safely and cleanly.

"What's the most painful thing anyone's ever done to you?" Marty asked her. He considered the answer a challenge, and he soon outdid it. In his large bedroom upstairs and away from his trading room, he attached clips to her labia and banged at them with a stick. The pain was excruciating.

Marty's new conquest made for some serious new tension in the Greenwich household. Sonia was not exactly comfortable with the situation, and the tension escalated sharply when Marty insisted on taking both women out to dinner, together. Sonia's sexual tastes had always been pretty orthodox. With Schulte, her sex life had been downright traditional. But she was willing to go along on Marty's adventure, especially after Miriam arrived on the scene, in hopes of keeping his affection and attention. Once Marty coaxed both women into bed. Sonia performed oral sex on Marty while he beat her bare bottom with a whip. Miriam watched.

Marty also videotaped one of his sessions with Sonia, trying out a variety of newly acquired sex toys for the show. He made Sonia snap on nipple clamps and videotaped her using a vibrator. Shakily aiming the camera, he whipped her with leather straps and then spanked her with a paddle. There was only so much Sonia could take. She finally told him it was hurting her and asked him to lighten up. (Marty gave a copy of the tape to David Rosse. "I might need it sometime down the road," Marty explained, leading the bodyguard to believe Marty might use it to blackmail Sonia.)

Through some of his new contacts in the S&M world, Marty arranged to have two women flown in from Germany to entertain him. The women were fantasy role-playing professionals and it wasn't completely clear to those around him whether the gig entailed play-acting or sex or both. Basically, the two women were being paid to be kinky and then leave.

But before they arrived on the scene, Marty suddenly became self-conscious about his sparse furnishings. At the time, the house was still decorated with not much more than the recliners from Toledo and a number of strategically placed cardboard boxes. "Everything else hurts my back and I hate furniture," Marty whined. Even his bedroom needed an overhaul. His sheets, blankets, and pillows were, in a word, dreadful. But a new interest in interior decorating awoke within him as the time for the German women's arrival approached. He badly wanted to impress them.

Marty and Miriam went off to ABC Carpet & Home, an upscale home-furnishings store in Manhattan, for blankets and pillows and then picked out an oversize sofa and armchair. They placed an order, but then Marty had second thoughts about the furniture and they canceled the order. When he changed his mind again, it was too late to reinstate the order, so Miriam ended up ordering floor-model leather sofas from Maurice Villency to ensure that the furniture arrived on the scene before the Germans did.

Sonia, who'd wanted to decorate the house herself, was furious. David Rosse was also sulking. He didn't approve of importing women from Germany and, having put so much effort into guarding Sonia, he was none too fond of Miriam, either. Once the women arrived, Rosse thought they were horrible. They did a little kinky role-playing in the bedroom upstairs; then they were whisked away in a chauffeured limousine for a Manhattan shopping spree financed by Marty; then they were gone. The leather couches remained.

For Marty, the sex games had just begun. He started putting advertisements in the *Village Voice,* on a telephone personals service, and on Alt.com, a BDSM (bondage–discipline–sado-masochism) website that claimed that 18,000 new members joined a week. "Are you looking for a little kink in your nightlife?" the site asked.

Marty was. "Submissive Woman Wanted by Very Rich Man," he wrote in the notice he crafted. He adopted "marquisdenow" as his handle.

"I seek a woman who wants to give up complete control over her mind, will, and body, a woman who wants to be totally owned and controlled by her master. I seek a woman who will do anything to please her master. I seek a woman who will help her master be sexually satisfied in any way he desires. I seek a woman who wants to serve a truly kinky,

twisted, perverted master, a woman who views her master's sexual satisfaction as her highest goal in life. I am very, very rich and can make all
my and your dreams come true," the marquis wrote.

Marty portrayed himself as a sexual and intellectual powerhouse. He
said he enjoyed "24/7 (total power exchange)," and described himself as
"liberal," "assertive," with a "very long/very thick circumcised" penis.
The Marquis de Now was an atheist who had a Ph.D. and lived in New
York City.

As it turned out, there were plenty of women, from as far away as
western Canada and as close by as Manhattan, looking for what Marty
had to offer. His usual practice was to contact the women who responded to his advertisements and have long, rambling conversations
with them. They discussed sex, sadomasochism in particular, but also
talked about the woman's secret desires and hopes. In Marty they found
an attentive listener. More than one came away with the feeling that
Marty had a special understanding of their needs, wants, and interests.
He was a sensitive guy.

One woman who was not so enthusiastic about Marty's sampling of
this sexual smorgasbord was Sonia. The kinkiness of it all just wasn't her
cup of tea. While Marty said in his Alt.com profile that he thought about
alternative lifestyles "all the time," Sonia had other things to worry
about. At the top of her list were her two daughters, and her desire to
make sure she eluded John Schulte.

Sonia decided to start life anew. First she returned to California and
then she moved to Jupiter, Florida. Marty was not happy about this, but
he kept giving her money and she continued periodically to fly north to
help create the monthly statements for Marty to send to John Hackney.
After she had been living in Florida for a short time, Sonia met Stefan
Radencovici, a Romanian immigrant, at a nightclub near her home.
They got married just a few weeks later. Her few remaining friends in
Toledo were shocked, but Sonia clearly felt she had taken a giant step out
of Marty's world of silliness. Stefan had a son of his own, and Sonia felt
Stefan was very good with her own daughters. In fact, he quickly became
a surrogate father to them.

Sonia talked to John Hackney only occasionally, and they never met.
But he couldn't help but notice that the statements always got out more
easily, and the phones at the Greenwich mansion were answered more

efficiently, whenever she was around. One day when Sonia answered the phone she told him that she'd gotten married and that her relationship with Marty was over. She explained that she "couldn't stand it because he was too weird." Hackney, who knew a bit of Marty's recent sexual proclivities from their lengthy phone conversations, was not surprised. "Have you told him yet?" Hackney asked, dreading Marty's reaction.

"Not yet," she said, clearly not relishing the prospect either.

Already, Marty had been angry and bitter about Sonia's withdrawal from his closed little world in Greenwich. He told the growing number of women around him that he wanted to marry her. But at the same time he would savagely call her a "bitch."

"She won't even come back and fuck me," he complained.

The conversation in which she broke the news of her marriage remained privy only to the two of them, and perhaps to Stefan Radencovici. But in the wake of Sonia's marriage, Marty increasingly blamed his life as a sadist, with which he was not entirely comfortable, on Sonia. When one of the women he'd met through a personal advertisement asked how he had gotten into sadomasochism, he said it was because of Sonia.

"You mean you wouldn't be a sexual sadist?" the woman asked.

"Exactly," Marty replied. "I wouldn't be as perverted." Sonia, he said, was "controlling and domineering." He felt badly treated by women generally. And, he explained, as he "met more sadistic, domineering bitches," his own sadism intensified.

Miriam kept having to order more blankets and sheets, because Marty kept adding women. Through a *Village Voice* advertisement in late 1993, he met Kaethe Schuchter, a German woman who lived with roommates in lower Manhattan.

Kaethe was an artist who scraped together a living as a cocktail waitress along with other jobs. The friends she partied with in the East Village thought her primitive-style artwork showed considerable talent, and she aggressively went about marketing herself. But by the time she met Marty she'd suffered a series of artistic disappointments. She put together a prototype for a children's book, but it didn't sell. Kaethe made her own clothes, painting directly on the fabric, and she wangled a meeting with a buyer for the ultra-chic department store Bergdorf Goodman. But even though the buyer liked her work, nothing came of the meeting. And although she aspired to the social world of the Upper East Side, she seemed stuck in semipoverty downtown.

Marty's taste in women was changing. Sonia had gained some weight in the time before she'd left Greenwich; Miriam was a touch chunky, as well. Increasingly Marty realized that the look that really excited him was more waiflike. Kaethe was petite, with a delicious foreign accent, occasionally reddish hair, and taste in clothes that ran to the punkish and sometimes trampy. She had few, if any, sexual hang-ups. Soon she had him wrapped around her little finger. With Marty's money at her disposal, her taste eventually ran more toward Versace.

Marty was enthralled. He bought Kaethe an expensive baby grand piano, which assumed a prominent position in the hallway of the mansion's upper level. It was rarely, if ever, played, but became a symbol within the household of the power Kaethe wielded over the boss. Kaethe wanted her own office, and Marty presented her with a small room that had been assigned to a former bedmate. Kaethe liked ducks; she drew them and incorporated them into her designs. Marty started calling her his "ducky," and even obsessed about her on the phone with Hackney, an avid hunter. Hackney joked that Marty "liked ducks and I liked to kill them."

One night Marty took Kaethe and Miriam to a private party at an S&M club, given by people Miriam knew. The two women began to bicker. Then Miriam lost her temper and a fight erupted. Miriam pulled Kaethe's hair. Marty loved it.

No longer Marty's lover, Miriam was relegated to a sort of big-sister status. He would call her and ask her advice on his entanglements with other women, but she plummeted in the pecking order of the women around him. Kaethe's status went way up in the wake of the fight, even though Marty's sexual interest in her was already cooling as he moved on to yet another woman, Adriana, an elegant Brazilian he'd met through another *Voice* ad.

Marty dumped Kaethe and told her she had to go home. But Kaethe informed Marty that she had already given up her apartment. The Greenwich compound was now her home. Rather than send her packing, he let her stay. For one thing, he was positively titillated by a new, and more vicious, battle, one brewing between her and Adriana. The growing number of current or former girlfriends in the house, and other staffers, referred to the fights as the Kaethe/Adriana Wars, or sometimes as the Limo Wars. Kaethe and Adriana fought over who had the better car or the more attentive chauffeur service. They bickered over who was getting more money out of Marty.

The goal was to be Marty's favorite, in and out of bed, and although Kaethe was no longer his sexual playmate she always managed to claw her way to the top of the heap of bickering women. To one woman, Kaethe was "the personification of evil," to others she was "the bitch," and many tried to stay clear of her. For the most part, she treated the other women in the house as though they were not worthy of her attention, or even, as one woman put it, like "dirt." She refused to sit in the kitchen and eat with them. She dined alone, or with Marty.

Marty whined about Kaethe's behavior around the house. She was "a bitch," he told Hackney, David Rosse, and others—she drank too much, she fought too much, she was spoiled. Still, time and again he gave in to her demands. When Kaethe insisted on having her own place in Manhattan, Marty shelled out roughly $6,000 a month for an apartment for her in the ritzy Metropolitan Tower, on West Fifty-seventh Street. Of course, Adriana needed a nice place, too.

"You're giving everyone so much, why not give me some?" Miriam was heard to whine. Marty gave her an allowance, but he called her "a hooker."

They were all hookers, he said.

By 1996, Marty had quite a staff on his hands. There were a multitude of women whom Marty had collected through personal ads. Marty told some that he wanted a harem, but many of the women didn't excite him sexually, or didn't excite him for very long. Many were lost souls, former strippers, refugees from bad marriages and abuse, women who for one reason or another answered ads seeking "a woman who wants to be totally owned as a sexual slave," as one of Marty's personals put it. One woman walked around the house veiled, and everyone assumed she was Muslim.

Marty happily agreed to employ many of the women, some of whom moved into a house, also on Lake Avenue, he rented for $15,000 a month. (He later bought a house for them, again with Franklin American's money.) Others moved into apartments he paid for with wire transfers from his Swiss bank account to their landlords.

The endless stream of money helped the women forget that Marty was not exactly a hunk. He was skinny and stooped, pasty-faced and disheveled. He was ugly. But even beyond the money he had his attractions. He listened to them, and for the most part they were women who had rarely found a man so attentive to their special needs. And he gossiped. Gossiped madly, pitting one woman against another until they couldn't give up the fight for his affection.

For the most part, the women made lousy office workers. The bitterness felt by those who did not make the sexual cut frequently bubbled over into full-fledged fights. They were inefficient. They pried open doors that were meant to be locked, so alarms sounded constantly, competing with the phones that were always ringing. In general, they were far more interested in sabotaging each other's work than in the mundane clerical tasks Marty assigned them.

In the midst of one not otherwise memorable skirmish, one woman reached into her underwear, extracted a soiled tampon, and threw it at her antagonist. The incident took place right outside Marty's trading room; the resulting screams from assorted women roused him from his work. Completely unnerved, he summoned David Rosse to break up the fight. On his orders, gloves were dispensed to staffers and the area was quickly sanitized.

"Crazy screaming domineering bitches," Marty was heard to mutter as he walked through the house. The bickering, he complained, was unbearable. "I need everybody to be quiet. Because I'm so distracted I can't trade. You're all making it worse, because you're not isolating me and I have trader's block," he told the women. A sign was put up to warn the women that if they talked to Marty they'd be fined $1,000. After a week one of them took it down and no more was said about it.

The more women he had, the more fearful he became about sexually transmitted diseases. There was open chatter about Marty's fear that his penis would simply fall off one day. He worried about penile and prostate cancer, and about AIDS. He talked for hours with one woman about how it was possible for a man to get AIDS even if he used a condom. He became an expert on the human papillomavirus, or HPV, which can cause cervical cancer. He sent his sexmates for frequent testing and put some of them in quarantine before he took them to bed. As a prophylactic measure, he dispatched one young man to buy the dried peas he believed would prevent prostate cancer, if regular ejaculations did not do the trick. The staffer spent a week scouring southern Connecticut and Westchester for the proper peas, and a health food store in Greenwich kept his beeper number on file so that he could be alerted as soon as the peas were in stock.

Whether a woman made it into Marty's bed was an important measure of where she stood in the household pecking order, but there were drawbacks to being a favorite as the scene upstairs in Marty's bedroom grew continually stranger. He had a potty installed in his walk-in closet, which was not very large, so he could lock women inside, and he dispatched a young aide to Manhattan to buy a large cage. Everyone knew about his favorite sex stunt, "clipping and whipping," the trick he'd learned in his early experiments with S&M in which clips were placed on a woman's genitals and then savagely knocked off.

For their part, the women were happy to do what he wanted. They called him "the Marty God," "the Boss," or sometimes a "shit stirrer" because "he was always trying to get a reaction," as one woman put it. Those who didn't ascend to the coveted position of mistress, girlfriend, or sex slave never gave up hope. One woman teased him by walking around in a teensy skirt with nothing underneath and flashing him when he walked by.

Hackney got used to a revolving set of voices on the other end of the line in Greenwich. He saw how frustrated Marty was with the women and suggested that he get someone with an M.B.A. to help run the business. But Marty, of course, wanted to keep outside meddling to a minimum. In fact, he trusted very few of the women who worked for him. Only a small number were allowed to touch line 12, the telephone line for Liberty National Securities. Few helped handle the wire transfers from Hackney's growing empire into Marty's private accounts. Assignments kept changing as women moved in and out of favor. There was a lot of busywork, and many of the women were not involved in Marty's real business but in managing the household.

There was a lot to manage. There was a man to take care of the cars, and that man had an assistant. There were limousine drivers to schedule and pay. David Rosse had his own assistant, too, and commanded his own little security force of off-duty police officers from Westchester. At least two people were kept on staff to deal with the computer system. Although Marty ate very simply, preferring plain fish, salads, and bottled water, a chef was kept on staff to cook for the household.

They all had to be paid, and although regular staffers were often paid with checks and on a schedule, the women were not. They received cash as they needed it; often, they were handed fistfuls of blank traveler's checks to pay their expenses. They all had "accounts," by which Marty kept track of the cash they were using, and someone, of course, had to be assigned to keep tallies.

Most of the women knew precious little about what Marty was doing and how he did it, but there were a few exceptions. First there was Kaethe. Beyond her bickering with Adriana, she caught Marty's attention by making herself useful. She started cataloguing Marty's many magazine subscriptions and organizing them. While he had to beg Sonia to return every so often to do what some women in the house called "secure accounting," Kaethe seemed more than willing to work. Marty soon began using her for his most sensitive missions.

He even taught her about the market. For Kaethe, pulling the trigger was no problem at all. Soon she was hunkered over a keyboard, executing trades. There were no secrets in Marty's world and the news swept through the house, creating yet more jealousy. "Are you crazy?" one of the women bellowed at Marty, after one of the chauffeurs told her that Kaethe was trading. He insisted that Kaethe was trading only her own money.

Another woman Marty increasingly relied upon was Karen Timmins. Marty met her through a personal advertisement in 1996, and she became the closest thing the mansion had to an office manager. Almost as soon as she showed up in Greenwich, Marty realized that he was not sexually attracted to her, partly because in his opinion she was overweight. But he offered to bring her on as an office assistant, and she readily agreed. He relied on her to keep the oddball crew of sexual acolytes and clerical workers in some semblance of order.

At the same time, he continued to lead her on romantically. Karen had a touch of bitterness. She had little life outside the house, although she had an extended family in Westchester, and like Marty she seemed to revel in the masochistic machinations of the household.

Karen told the others that Marty wanted to marry her. And Marty told everyone that Karen was in love with him and wanted to get married. But that, he told many of them, was not going to happen. Karen is a "stupid, stupid, stupid person," he told one of the women. Marty explained that Karen had a problem "intellectually grasping" things. He had a hard time believing she'd gone to college, he said.

Karen morosely took it in stride. "I'm the stupid one," she said around the house. "Kaethe's the bitch and I'm the stupid one." Nevertheless, Karen had important responsibilities in the house, including the distribution of blank traveler's checks, and she became a link in Marty's convoluted laundering of the assets of Franklin American and its sister insurance companies.

The traveler's checks were the final leg in the long trip that the insurers' money took to Europe and back again. Typically, Hackney, Atnip or one of their employees transferred the money to a Dreyfus Cash Management Plus Account, usually held at the Bank of New York. Marty then had that money wired to his accounts at Banque SCS Alliance in Switzerland. Then the trick was to get the money back to the United States. Sometimes, the money was simply wired back to the United States to pay Marty's—or the women's—big bills directly.

But much of the cash spent by Marty and his minions came back from Switzerland in the form of traveler's checks. Several $50,000 batches of the checks, usually issued by American Express, were sent to Kaethe and Karen at home.

Marty also turned to David Rosse for help. Rosse had a relative, Phil Miller, who owned Highland Industrial Park in nearby Peekskill, New York. Using that as his address, Rosse received bundles of traveler's checks from Switzerland almost weekly and then turned them over to Marty.

After a while, Marty began to worry that all those traveler's checks floating around would arouse suspicion. (Indeed, unbeknownst to him, in 1997 American Express filed a report with the U.S. government alerting it to suspicious money transfers and possible money laundering. Nothing, apparently, came of the report.) Finally he prevailed upon Miller, Rosse's relative, to allow Banque SCS to wire money directly into Miller's account, which he would then turn over to Marty. A special enticement was dangled in front of Miller. Marty told him that he could keep $500 to $800 per cash infusion for his trouble. Over about nine months, $10,000 a week was shipped back to the United States by this route. Marty would simply dispatch an employee from Greenwich to pick up a "package" from Highland Industrial Park. Over time, these couriers picked up some $330,000 from Miller.

Karen also became, to some degree, Marty's aide for managing broken hearts at the two-mansion compound. The stickiest situation involved a young woman named Frances Burge. Marty had met her through a personal advertisement he'd placed in the *Village Voice* in the summer of 1996. After they had talked on the phone, Marty dispatched a limousine to pick her up at her dad's house in Shirley, Long Island. Frances and Marty had a romantic dinner, prepared by Claude, Marty's chef. They talked for hours, and then Marty asked Frances to take off her clothes. Marty was disappointed. Frances was overweight and he simply was not turned on.

Still, they kept in touch by phone. Marty found the story of Frances's sad life moving. Having suffered though her parents' bitter divorce, she had lived for a time in a homeless shelter with her mother. She'd gotten pregnant at sixteen, and had given the baby up for adoption. She never quite got over it. Suffering periodic bouts of deep depression, she was hospitalized. When Marty met her she was working as a clerk in a Long Island video shop.

In the fall, Marty invited Frances to come live and work at the compound. Her tasks were menial. Sometimes she received strange packages, which Marty told her were cash. But Frances could not quite empty her mind of the possibility that she would someday have a romantic relationship with her elusive boss. And, ever interested in stirring the pot of female emotion in his household, Marty sent what could be construed as mixed signals. Finally, he ordered Karen to have a talk with Frances. She told Frances in no uncertain terms that Marty did not want to have sex with her.

Even so, Frances began to study S&M, which she knew to be close to her boss's heart. She acquired a video and literature that taught bondage techniques, and she got a riding crop. She even contemplated placing her own personal advertisement and wrote out a draft:

"Young woman looking for a special relationship with that special kinky fun erotic person. You must be attractive, attentive and hold [sic] to acquire my attentions. If you feel that your qualifications meet my standards left [sic] a message and I might respond to you."

But the person she really wanted was Marty, and everyone in the house knew it. He called her into his trading room for a talk. She was there for a long time, and confided that she'd in the past been depressed and had attempted suicide several times. As usual, Marty seemed to give himself over completely to her story. He was attentive and concerned.

Afterwards, he called Karen into the room and told her what Frances had said. They decided that Frances needed help; Karen encouraged her to see a psychiatrist, who prescribed antidepressants. Although Marty and Frances didn't often cross paths in the extended household, he continued to be gracious and solicitous when he saw her, once even complimenting "her nice-looking hair ribbon."

The other women in Marty's orbit, however, feared that Frances was a disaster waiting to happen. She started hiding in her room. Frances's concerned mother called Karen because her daughter hadn't been visiting or even calling home.

On the afternoon of August 6, 1997, Mona Kim, who worked for Marty, arrived at the house Marty rented for his women, to see if Frances was going to keep their date to go to the Six Flags Great Adventure amusement park in New Jersey. The front door of 881 Lake Avenue was unlocked, as usual, and Mona went into the kitchen and dialed extension 33, which rang in Frances's bedroom. No one answered; Mona went downstairs and knocked loudly on the bedroom door. Again, no one answered the door, and when Mona cautiously opened it she found the room empty.

Mona was alarmed. The car assigned to Frances was outside, and it was no secret in the household that she was depressed. Mona called over to the big house and spoke to Mary Ann, another woman who worked for Marty and lived at 881 Lake. Mary Ann told Mona that she had to check the bathroom. Mona was afraid, but Mary Ann promised to stay on the phone. After finding the bathroom empty, Mona ventured outside, through the sliding doors in Frances's room that led to the pool area.

She saw Frances' body hanging from underneath an elevated deck. A white clothesline-type rope had been fashioned into a slipknot. A chair was nearby, as was something that looked like a leather riding crop.

Mona began screaming and could not make herself stop. She ran back into the house and spoke to Mary Ann. Karen and Claude, the chef, quickly drove over from the main house. Claude took out his pocket-knife and cut Frances down. Karen began screaming and ran into the house. Claude did his best to administer CPR, but it was hard, because Frances's tongue was sticking out of her mouth. Screaming out from the house, Karen ordered Claude to continue. But clearly, Frances was dead and had been for a while.

There remained the question of what to do next. The answer, of course, had to come from Marty. Still extremely upset, Karen called him. He told her to call an ambulance and the police.

The episode shattered the complete privacy in which Marty had cloaked himself. Police swarmed into the compound and interviewed Mona, Mary Ann, Claude, and Karen. David Rosse told them that the house Frances had died in was leased by Sundew International, and that he and Marty were Sundew's employees. In Frances' bedroom, the cops found half-eaten food on the floor and a bondage tape in the VCR.

Finally, the Greenwich detectives investigating the death invited Marty to police headquarters to give a statement. He arrived carrying several bottles of water. To Detective Scott McConnell, he seemed strange. He was pasty and it was somehow inappropriate to carry all that water to a police interview. Marty explained how he'd met Frances and hadn't wanted to have sex with her because she was overweight. "I want to tell you about the situation with Frances Burge and the other females that live at 881 Lake Avenue," he told McConnell. "The females are mostly my ex-girlfriends that I met through personal advertisements. I date a lot of women and these girls are special to me. I care about these girls." He explained that the four women who lived in the house had all answered his personal ads, but that he'd had a relationship with only one of them, Adriana. Claude, the chef, and a handyman also lived in the house, he said.

"Some of these girls think that they might be my girlfriend someday," Marty told the detective. "I trust all these girls. The girls do not get paid a salary but I give them money as they need it."

Even before the medical examiner's report was complete, it was clear that Frances's tragic death had been a suicide. But to Detective Mc-Connell and his partner, Edward Zack, it was equally clear that something was not right at 889 and 881 Lake Avenue. Zack did some computer research on Sundew and found precious little. "Things were not falling into place," McConnell later recalled. He and Zack decided to go back and try to "get our foot in the door" of Marty's house.

Marty allowed them into the house, and the two detectives staged a sort of buddy act. Trying hard to act like "one of the boys," Marty fell for it. He said he was a trader, and explained that he did all of the trading for a Swiss bank. The two detectives tried to keep him talking by pointing at his screens and asking him to explain things. Marty described the various market-data features on his computer setup. Throughout the whole conversation, he stood, holding his bottled water.

The detectives were about to leave when their friendly chat was interrupted by the arrival of Sonia. "Stop talking to them," she ordered Marty under her breath, giving him a withering look. Marty got the message.

"Thanks a lot; maybe you can help us with investing," one of the detectives said on his way out.

"I'll help you guys out whenever you want. Anytime," Marty answered.

Just a few hours later, McConnell got a phone call from Mickey Sherman, a well-known criminal lawyer, who had a simple message for the Greenwich Police Department: "You're not to speak to my client unless you go through me first."

McConnell and Zack had nothing to pin on Frankel other than general weirdness. Still, they believed something was up. They contacted the IRS, supplying Marty's real name and the fact that he was supposedly a trader. On New Year's Eve day, they drove an IRS agent around, showing the agent as much of the compound as they could see from the road. The two detectives also alerted Greenwich's zoning department, in case Frankel was violating zoning rules by operating a business out of his home. Nothing came of either contact.

Meanwhile, David Rosse decided to beef up his relationship with the Greenwich Police Department. He had Marty make nice donations to the police union. Rosse also took two officers—one was Steve Carlo, who was then a detective—on a golf extravaganza. They visited several courses, including one in Myrtle Beach in South Carolina, flying in a 1995 Gulfstream Turbo Commander, bought by Marty and piloted by Rosse himself.

Another potential threat to Marty's world came from inside the household itself. Marty met Cynthia Allison over the phone in 1997, through a tele-personal advertisement. She was living in California, where she was trying to put her life together in the wake of a divorce. She flew East to see him.

Looking her over, Marty was not pleased. Cynthia was yet another overweight sex candidate. She was in her thirties, with unruly red hair and blue eyes. One of her hands trembled slightly, the result of some childhood trauma. Still, Marty offered her a clerical position, which she accepted.

The Greenwich compound was never an oasis of tranquility. But Cynthia was someone almost everyone agreed on. They didn't like her. Considered by all to be volatile, she flew off the handle easily at those around her. Word around the house was that she'd had a hard life and had been orphaned young. Perhaps she was neurologically or emotionally impaired, the women speculated. At least one of the young men who worked around the house called her Shaky Red. Soon she was relegated to working weekend shifts, when the population of the house was relatively sparse.

The group became more alarmed when it became clear to everyone that Cynthia had a crush on Marty, and that it was deepening. She was hanging around the house as much as she could. True, many of the women aspired to Marty's bed. But to the other women, Cynthia's obsession seemed particularly pathetic, certainly more so than their own. She started to get her hair done every two or three days, and offered to act as "nanny"—that was Marty-speak for "guard"—to Marty's favorite of the moment, a Russian named Oksana who arrived at the mansion while still a teenager. Marty declined Cynthia's offer.

Then, one day, someone heard Cynthia blurt out a threat.

"I would like to take a gun and blow his brains out!" she said. There was no question in anyone's mind that she was talking about Marty. Although no one had ever seen Cynthia with a gun, or do anything that was physically violent, many in the household felt uneasy, believing that her behavior was becoming too unpredictable.

The news quickly got back to Marty. He was frightened and decided to ban Cynthia from the compound. But when she was given the edict she became hysterical and it looked as if she wasn't going to budge from the house. It was evening, and Marty was afraid to emerge from the trading room. Rosse dispatched his assistant, a young man named Steve, to stand guard outside Marty's door.

Then Marty called Cynthia on the phone. They were only a few yards apart, so close that Steve could hear both sides of the conversation. They could almost have talked through Marty's closed door. For an hour and a half Marty tried to calm the weeping Cynthia. She begged him to change his mind and let her stay. He was trying to be nice. "I'm still going to take care of you," he crooned. "I can't have you here because you're upsetting other people."

Finally, Cynthia accepted that she had to get out. She got off the phone with Marty and told Steve that she was too upset to drive. He called her a cab, and Marty emerged from his trading room a free man. Cynthia's photograph was soon posted in the guardroom so that security guards would recognize her if she tried to sneak back into the compound.

Marty did not oust her completely from his life. He kept her in reserve, waiting on the sidelines for an important assignment in the future. Until that day came—and it would come—he sent her on minor assignments outside the compound. And he paid for her BMW, and for the rent of her apartment in Mount Kisco, New York, with wire transfers from Banque SCS.

In Oksana, Marty had finally found a woman who pleased him. She and Katia were recruited through an advertisement he placed in a Russian pornography magazine with the help of a jilted sex candidate. The two young women arrived in Greenwich, as one Frankel associate liked to put it, straight off the Russian breadlines and desperate to escape their homeland. Marty was developing an obsession with things Russian, perhaps because his Swiss banker, with whom he chatted with by phone, was doing business in Moscow and had ties with government officials there.

When one of the older women in Marty's circle asked him about his interest in the Russian girls, he summed it up this way: "I love you, hon, and I'll always take care of you, but I'd rather trade in a forty-year-old for two twenty-year-olds."

The two young Russians' English was only sketchy. To help them understand their benefactor's sexual preferences, Marty's other women collaborated on a videotape illustrating Marty's favorite S&M feat, clipping and whipping. (In the tape, Marty was played by a woman.)

First Marty bedded Katia, an aspiring rock-and-roll star. As one of Marty's other women put it, Katia was a Leo and really thought she would make it to the top of the music world. She was pretty when she smiled, but Marty's sexual interest in her flagged relatively quickly. Even after they stopped having sex, however, Marty would listen to her music, sometimes over the phone late into the night. Eventually, Katia found an American to marry.

Marty then started to sleep with Oksana. She was more to his taste than any other woman in his orbit, though she was a bit scruffy when she arrived. Her hair was scraggly and her skin needed work. But she had the kind of childlike body Marty now craved.

Oksana was none too enthusiastic about Marty's kinks, and although she did participate, he agreed to keep the S&M to a minimum. Meanwhile, she took advantage of her good fortune. Marty paid for skin treatments and language lessons, and Oksana even began to take courses at a nearby college. She convinced Marty to bring her mother and grandmother over from Russia. Marty complained about the difficulty of persuading the grandmother to leave behind her cat but agreed to pay for their housing and language lessons.

Some of the other women felt sorry for Oksana, but they believed she had made a choice—a business contract—to cater to the sometimes unorthodox sexual needs of her master in exchange for an opportunity to make it in the United States. Despite her childlike looks, they believed that when it came to men, Oksana was quite sophisticated. As the relationship persisted, the women discussed among themselves whether Marty had actually fallen in love.

Perhaps he had. She was, he said, his "little kitten." On one of his rare forays out of the house, he took her as his date to the wedding of Mark Burgess, the freelance software consultant. Miriam escorted her to Manhattan and bought her a Moschino Cheap & Chic dress and a heart-shaped handbag. Oksana wished the dress were tighter, but everyone thought she looked gorgeous as she plopped down on a clearly delighted Marty's lap at the wedding.

Marty obsessed endlessly about whether his devotion to Oksana was reciprocated. He worried incessantly that other men would lure her into their beds. A succession of "nannies" accompanied Oksana everywhere, from shopping expeditions around downtown Greenwich to college, where they sometimes sat in the classroom with her and other times stood guard in the corridor.

In fact, one of the nannies later said, "Marty did have something to worry about." Oksana was a little on the promiscuous side, and was sleeping with at least one of the men who served the household. Her special friend was Greg, in his early twenties, who was employed to help with the array of computers in the house. Greg "was a very immature young guy," the nanny later said. "To have a woman or a girl like Oksana was a big deal for him."

Marty's suspicions about Oksana and Greg drove him to distraction. But Greg also solved a problem. Oksana, of course, did not have a green card—a resident alien permit—so she would not be able to stay in the country indefinitely. This was a problem Marty had encountered before. Kaethe, who continued to be a favorite despite the end of their sexual relationship, also had had immigration problems. She married Jeff Moreau, a gay artist who in his paintings used "various pharmaceuticals glued directly to the canvas, making these works of art incredibly valuable, not to mention—illegal," as he put it on a website displaying his work. Kaethe told friends that Marty had paid her groom $10,000. Moreau steadfastly denied it, insisting that he was in love with his bride and that they were very compatible.

Marty made a deal with Greg. He promised him money and a Lexus if he agreed to marry Oksana. Implicit in the arrangement was that Marty would still have rights to her. Certainly most of the women understood that the marriage was, in the words of the nanny, "a sham." But they also knew—better than Marty did—that there was genuine affection between Oksana and her intended.

Without much fanfare, the wedding was performed, with a nanny as a witness.

Once, Oksana left Marty, telling him she wanted to be with her husband. But after a short time, Marty lured her back, and she continued to be the only woman with a bedroom in the main house. For well over a year, Oksana maintained two very different kinds of relationships. She was Greg's wife, but she indulged Marty in his fantasies.

Meanwhile Marty's first love, Sonia Howe Schulte Radencovici, continued to help him propagate the fiction that he was a master trader, earning remarkable profits. Each month, or sometimes a little less often if she could manage it, Sonia arrived on the scene to work on the statements and confirmation slips that were then sent down to Franklin, Tennessee. In 1996, she, Stefan, and the girls had moved to Charlotte, North Carolina. She would board a plane, and a chauffeured car would pick her up at the airport. The car would take a circuitous route to the Greenwich mansion in case they were being tailed by John Schulte or one of his spies. Over time, Marty pumped hundreds of thousands of dollars into Sonia's life, but increasingly she viewed her trips north as a chore she wished she could get rid of.

One day, David Rosse drove her to Greenwich from the airport. To some degree, they were in the same boat: like it or not, they were privy to too many of Marty's secrets. On the way to the mansion, Sonia confessed to Rosse that she really wanted out of Marty's empire. But, she said, she couldn't quit. He just had too much on her.

Chapter Seven

Mounting Pressure

Sitting in his trading room with his computers blinking at him, Marty forced himself to try a few trades. It was 1998, and he had just acquired First National Life Insurance Company and was liquidating its portfolio. Shaky, fearful, and choked with anxiety, he managed to execute some twenty to thirty trades of government and corporate bonds through Prudential Securities. The trades were small, worth about $25,000 each, and not especially risky. But for Marty, they were absolute agony.

After one small purchase he kept a woman on the phone with him as he tracked price fluctuations on his computer screens and tried to quell an escalating anxiety attack. He refused to let her hang up. About an hour after he'd made the trade, the price edged slightly downward and he became so agitated he couldn't think straight.

"I have to be out of these. I have to be out of these. I have to be out of these," he moaned again and again. The price popped back up, and he quickly sold the bonds at exactly the same price at which he'd bought them.

The good news was that he actually had made a trade. The bad news was that the emotional toll on him was enormous. And he hadn't made a penny.

Marty never gave up hope that he would conquer the trader's block. He had accounts at Bear Stearns, Merrill Lynch, and Prudential and often negotiated the trading and commission terms in meticulous detail. But once he opened the accounts, precious little would happen. "He would put millions of dollars in and freak out," one of the women

113

said. When it came to trading, he had endless emotional roadblocks to overcome. He worried that he would execute trades "under the wrong star," or that the government would freeze the account he was trying to trade in.

Distraught, he went into therapy, visiting his counselors in Manhattan on Saturdays, because he was unwilling to travel to the city when the market was open. (He usually saw his medical doctors at night, after the market closed.) He visited one therapist in her downtown loft, where she practiced hypnosis. Back home he doggedly listened to the tapes she gave him as homework. He tried Ari Kiev, a therapist who had carved out a specialty working with traders and also advised Olympic athletes on performance issues. (Kiev in 1998 published a book called *Trading to Win: The Psychology of Mastering the Markets*.)

But mastering his demons was beyond him. Nothing helped. "I need you to help me," he begged one of his women. "I need you to isolate me because then I can trade." Anyone who wanted to enter the trading room had to call and seek permission first. But on any given day, the sounds of the Federal Express or UPS trucks pulling up to the mansion would disturb him. Or the perfume one of the women was wearing would irritate him and a day's work would be interrupted.

He hated the rectangular earpieces on modern telephones and couldn't focus properly on the market until David Rosse finally located the more old-fashioned round ones. The little red light on his phone's console drove him crazy. When he sat down at his desk he had to cover the light with a napkin. He constantly had to have his mineral water or a soda. He'd call in a woman with the beverage but he couldn't open the can himself for fear he would injure his wrist. In the words of one woman who helped coddle him, "He wouldn't let himself be isolated. It was a living hell that he created for himself."

And when it all got to be too much for him, he would lash out at the women around him. "You cost me fifteen million dollars today!" he screeched at one who had distracted him from trading.

Finally, the brokerage firms lost patience with him. At Prudential, managers were excited about Marty because he talked up his intentions and prowess and they expected him to be an active trader. When he stopped making transactions altogether, they were disappointed. At Merrill Lynch, executives also became annoyed when Marty opened an account in early 1998, borrowing David Rosse's name as an alias, but left it largely dormant. He closed the account later that year.

At Bear Stearns, Marty usually just put money into his accounts and switched it out again. Finally the firm informed him it was considering closing the accounts.

"My God! They think I'm laundering money!" Marty exclaimed to members of his household. He set up a meeting with Bear Stearns representatives and persuaded them to continue working with him. The firm assigned him a new broker, and Marty quickly acquainted himself with the details of her life. He soon earned her loyalty by buying her lover's artwork.

Marty's renewed efforts to trade came at a time when he was feeling some heavy financial pressure. He was going through mountains of cash. He had finally bought the house he was living in, plunking down $3 million in Franklin American's cash. His payroll in Greenwich, if it could be called that, numbered well over twenty people, including sex partners and other women, techies, security guards, maintenance men, chefs, maids, and nannies. Over time, the denizens of Marty's compound went through some $9 million in traveler's checks.

Each time he bought an insurance company, "cars would bloom like spring flowers," as one of the women put it. Marty's favorites drove around in $1.8 million worth of cars, courtesy of the folks buying burial policies down south. There were Mercedeses for himself and his special sex mates. There were BMWs, Lexuses, and Chevrolet Tahoes. Once Marty had a new limo chopped in half so that a few extra inches could be added to accommodate his six-foot frame.

Then there was the tribe's American Express bill, which at least once hit the $600,000 mark. The account was in Kaethe's name, although several of Marty's close associates, including Karen Timmins and David Rosse, had cards. In one month in 1998, for which the total was a modest $306,954, there were Amex charges for chartered jets totaling $22,300. The tab for cell phones and beepers—which almost everyone in the house carried—topped $6,000. On the same bill there were charges at Hermès, in both Paris and New York, and Frette, the expensive linens store in Rome. More than $1,135 was spent on sheets. There was a $4,808 bill for the Hôtel de Crillon in Paris and a $8,851 bill for a Howard Johnson's hotel in Connecticut. More than $7,500 was spent on stereo equipment. An auction house specializing in horology—clock-making and watchmaking, charged $18,400. Buccellati, the exclusive silver and jewelry shop, charged $2,684. Even though Marty owned cars and employed drivers, the tab for limousines that month was more than $12,000.

The bills were beginning to add up, and Marty had to find a way to seriously up his cash flow. Barring trading, that meant putting pressure on John Hackney to step up the pace at which he bought insurance companies and, more significantly, acquired the pools of ready cash that came along with them, so that Marty could replenish his personal bank account. Marty developed a new vision for his empire. He wanted Franklin American to be a billion-dollar company, he told Hackney over the phone. Previously, they had talked endlessly about Marty's admiration for Warren Buffett and Bill Gates. Now he added to his list of idols Sandy Weill, who had made the Travelers Group into an insurance power-house. He wanted to be just like Sandy Weill, he told Hackney.

But for John Hackney, turning Marty into the next Sandy Weill was not a priority. To Marty's dismay, he kept turning down suitors. He rejected possible acquisitions in North Carolina, Mississippi, Florida, and Texas. When Marty called him on the carpet, Hackney explained that there were business problems with the companies or that the price wasn't right.

Marty kept pushing. "Just go on and get it done," he said. Usually Hackney would talk him out of it. It took time to absorb a new insurer into the company, he explained. There were concerns about policies, accounting, and marketing, not to mention regulatory matters. "That's your problem. You take care of it," Marty snapped. He was increasingly frustrated.

He was also worried. He had a string of insurance companies down south, and a cultlike string of followers up north: somebody might notice and suspect something. Within the household, there were some bizarre clues that Marty might not be operating on the right side of the law. But most of the women seemed not to realize it, or at least not to care—so long as the money and loving kept flowing. When Marty started talking about moving the whole operation to an ocean-bound yacht for security's sake, his paranoia was brushed off by the women as just another one of his strange—even sick—personality traits.

For almost a decade Marty Frankel passed himself off as an eccentric multi-millionaire with a knack for playing the financial markets. In fact, he rarely could bring himself to execute trades. He confided to friends and lovers that he suffered from "trader's block." *AP/Wide World Photos*

Leon and Tillie Frankel took pride in the high intelligence of their son Marty. They taught their children that money was not very important, and that they should place more value on social justice and learning. *The Toledo Blade*

Frankel lived with his parents in their middle-class Toledo home until he was in his thirties. He ran his investment business out of his bedroom.

Convinced of Frankel's talent, Ted Bitter (pictured with his wife, Sharon) tried hard to coax Frankel out of his trader's block. But Ted lost his life savings when he invested in the Frankel Fund.
Steve Liss/Timepix

Lawyers Terrance K. Davis, Jeffrey S. Creamer, and Stephen A. Rothschild were so incensed at the way Frankel had conned two Frankel Fund investors that they agreed to take their case, even though they knew it would not be a big moneymaker for their large Toledo law firm.

Frankel fell deeply in love with the wife of John Schulte, his arch-enemy, who had fired him from a brokerage job. Attached to this postcard of the Schulte family, sent to voters when John was running for state senate, was a letter from Sonia Schulte calling her husband "a very special person." Exactly one year later she left him for Frankel.

Sonia and Frankel accused John Schulte of molesting his two small daughters, but he was acquitted of criminal charges and proclaimed his victory in front of his brokerage office.

Frankel and Sonia Schulte wanted to set up house together and considered buying this large home in Ottawa Hills, a Toledo suburb.

Instead, Frankel bought this more modest home for $70,000 in cash. It was across the street from his parents' house.

Unemployed and desperate, John Hackney was convinced by Frankel to help him build an empire of burial insurance companies based in Tennessee. Hackney knew Frankel by at least three names and worked for him for about eight years before actually meeting him.

As a bonus for acquiring new insurance companies, Frankel bought Hackney the Blackburn House, built in 1874, with $515,000 wired from his Swiss bank accounts. *Courtesy Comas Montgomery Auctioneers, Charlie Montgomery Agent*

His insurance empire growing rapidly, Frankel moved to Greenwich, Connecticut, where he bought a stone mansion with $3 million stolen from his companies. He later bought another house for the women he met through personal advertisements, in which he called himself "a truly kinky, twisted, perverted master." *The Toledo Blade*

Sonia Schulte was turned off by Frankel's pursuit of other women and his budding interest in sadomasochism. She broke off their relationship but continued to work with him, visiting the Greenwich mansion on a regular basis.

Through a girlfriend, Frankel met a mysterious and well-connected business consultant named Thomas Corbally. He promised to introduce Frankel to people with money and power.

Corbally introduced Frankel to Robert Strauss, former U.S. Ambassador to Russia and a Democratic Party powerbroker. Frankel impressed Strauss, who agreed to have his law firm represent Frankel's interests.
AP/Wide World Photos

Frankel also enlisted lawyer Tom Bolan (*right*), a close associate of the late Roy Cohn (*left*), chief counsel to Senator Joseph McCarthy during his Communist-hunting years. Bolan negotiated with Vatican officials on behalf of Frankel, who wanted to set up a Catholic foundation to buy insurance companies. *AP/Wide World Photos*

In one unsuccessful attempt to enlist Church-related organizations to act as his front, Frankel sent a former girlfriend to the famed Church of San Miniato al Monte in Florence, Italy, to meet the prior of its monastery. She arrived in a halter top, hot pants, and reptile-skin stiletto heels.
G. E. Kidder Smith/Corbis

Father Peter Jacobs, a controversial priest who partied with New York's social and literary elite, agreed to become president of Frankel's Saint Francis of Assisi Foundation, to Serve and Protect the Poor.
AP/Wide World Photos

Frankel hoped to curry favor with Pope John Paul II by trying to arrange for the pontiff to visit Russia. Those efforts were ultimately unsuccessful.
AP/Wide World Photos

Frankel lavishly entertained Dewi Sukarno, the socialite widow of Indonesia's first president, and tried to impress her with his financial savvy. But, after listening to his pitch, she declined to invest with him.
B.D.V./Corbis

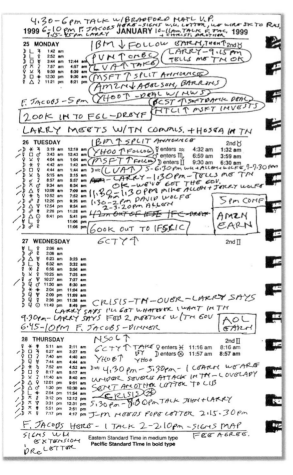

As state officials grew suspicious of Frankel's insurance empire, and as he began to worry that his associates were trying to blackmail him, Marty Frankel poured out his fears in the diary he kept in an astrological calendar.

Frankel's associates pummeled Mississippi Insurance Commissioner George Dale with phone calls in an effort to convince him to let Frankel operate as he pleased in the state.

Mississippi Special Assistant Attorney General Lee Harrell thought something about Frankel's operation smelled funny. He convinced Commissioner Dale to put Frankel's Mississippi insurance companies under state supervision.
Shepard G. Montgomery

Feeling himself cornered, Frankel fled to Rome and then to Hamburg, Germany, where he made the Hotel Prem his home. *AP/Wide World Photos*

He was accompanied to Germany by Cynthia Allison (photographed in shadow), a woman he had met through a personal advertisement and later banned from his mansion. She was the only woman willing to accompany him on the lam. *Ted Thai/Timepix*

Captured at the Hotel Prem with a cache of diamonds, Frankel was put in a Hamburg jail, where he soon became a celebrity among his fellow inmates.

Frankel, pictured with Dirk Meinicke, his German lawyer, argued that he should be allowed to stay in Germany because the long prison sentence he faced in the United States was tantamount to life in prison. *AP/Wide World Photos*

Two young federal prosecutors in Connecticut, Kari Dooley and Mark Califano, got Frankel indicted and began pursuing many of his associates.
AP/Wide World Photos

John Hackney was one of many Frankel associates to plead guilty to criminal charges.
AP/Wide World Photos

His assets frozen and seized, Frankel had no money to defend himself. Jeremiah Donovan and his wife, Terry Donovan, were appointed by the court to represent him.
AP/Wide World Photos

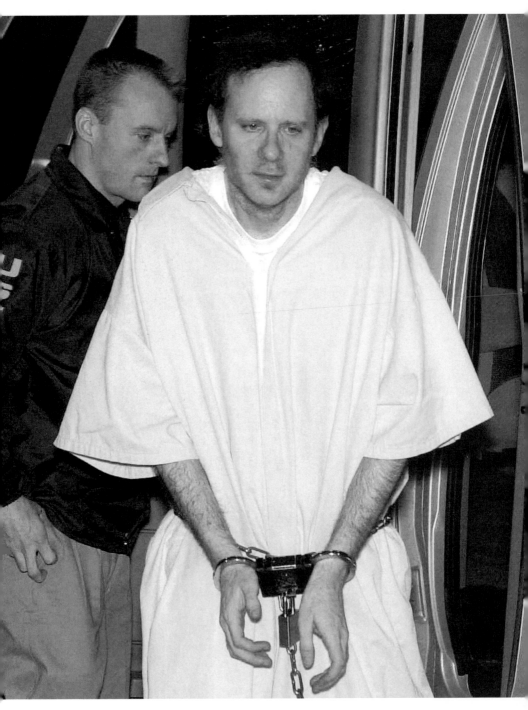

Despite his efforts to remain in Germany, a heavily guarded Martin Frankel was returned to the United States in March 2001 to face charges that he had bilked his insurance companies out of more than $200 million. *AP/Wide World Photos*

He asked Mona Kim to order him a Harley-Davidson motorcycle so he could "shoot out" of the compound if he was ever in trouble. The idea was that he would have a driver on call and that he would just leap on the back of the bike and take off if necessary. This seemed an odd request from a man who got motion sickness in elevators and sometimes felt uncomfortable above the second floor. Mona, whom Marty had met through the telepersonals before rejecting her as a sex mate, told him that she'd get right on it. In fact, she ignored him. About two weeks later, he looked at her and remembered his order. "How's the motorcycle search going on?" he asked. It was soon forgotten.

One day a woman walked into the room where Sonia did what was called secure accounting. Usually the room was locked, so the woman took the rare opportunity to do some snooping around. On Sonia's desk was what appeared to be confirmation slips and trading tickets. "Great," the woman said to herself, "at least he's doing some trading."

Suddenly, Sonia arrived. She called Marty and reported the indiscretion. Marty had "a shit fit," the woman later said. That afternoon, he called her into the trading room. "Did you notice anything?" he asked. She hadn't seen anything she thought was suspect, just some Liberty National Securities statements of insurance company accounts and some confirmation and trading slips.

"Good," Marty replied.

A week or so afterward, Marty drifted into the woman's work area after the market closed, and sat down. "I want to tell you a story," he said. "I want to tell you the truth and the funny thing is it started with $40,000." He bragged about the successful trade he'd done for Ted Bitter so long ago, launched into his diatribe about Doug Maxwell, and ended with the theft of the insurance company's assets. He told her that he would regain his trading powers, make money, and put the money back.

The woman was horrified. Marty was surprised too. He thought she'd figured out the situation after spying the phony trading slips on Sonia's desk. His plan to put the money back, the woman feared, was "maybe a lie." She quickly withdrew from the Greenwich scene. However, she continued to take Marty's money.

By 1998, Marty also had told Karen Timmins and Kaethe Schuchter at least something about the way he ran his business. Karen Timmins used the information to enrich herself—and to try to develop a more intimate relationship with Marty. She was soon living in a Manhattan apartment on Fifty-fifth street, just a few blocks from Kaethe, and a rumor circulated among her jealous colleagues that she was earning between $20,000 and $25,000 a month.

Karen also helped Marty indulge in his most dangerous sexual fantasy. A visitor to the house once joked that the weight of the women in the house ranged from fifty to four hundred pounds, but Marty was most interested in the mere wisps among them, like Oksana. Finally, he confessed to a few of the women that he fantasized about having sex with children. He meant it to be a secret, but of course the news quickly spread through the house. When one of the women who heard the gossip broached the topic with Marty, he got extremely agitated and upset. "I know," he said. "It's so terrible you can't even say it out loud." Even he was horrified.

Soon some of the women in the house embarked on what they called "special projects," or sometimes "mergers and acquisitions": the quest to find Marty tiny sex partners. The ideal, Miriam explained to some of them, was to find a shiksa, a small, non-Jewish girl, who looked like Jon-Benet Ramsey, preferably with blond hair, blue eyes, and tiny features. Oddly, the women most interested in helping Marty stage his fantasy were those he was least sexual interested in.

It was Karen Timmins who went furthest to fulfill his new wishes. Working through an agency in California (according to its literature, it was founded and operated on the basis of "Christian values") Karen got donors to supply eggs and sperm to create a baby, and then a surrogate to carry it. Over $40,000 in bills for the "special project" were paid with stolen money wired directly from Marty's Swiss bank accounts.

The baby was a girl. Her birth in California and arrival on the East Coast at around the beginning of 1998 sent Marty into a tizzy of conflicting emotions. On one hand he was completely titillated, and on the other hand he was scared, even repulsed, by his own impulses. As soon as the baby was born, he said he didn't want her. Nevertheless, almost at once he was doing astrological charts to figure out how he would relate to the child. One chart showed that their future sex life together would be "wonderful."

As Marty tussled with his inner conflicts, Karen tortured him with them. She hoped that having the child would draw her closer to Marty, that they'd become a sort of family. She spent $1,500 on professional portraits of the child. Some were mother-and-daughter shots but others showed the child naked, draped in pearls. She put them in a prominent spot in the dining room so that Marty was likely to see them. He refused to pick them up and she refused to take them away. Every time he walked through the room the portraits were a bitter reminder of just how perverted he had become.

Finally, he couldn't take it anymore. His fantasies terrified him too much. Plus, he worried obsessively that Karen had substituted her own eggs when the baby was conceived in its petri dish, and that he would end up having sex with her biological child. He demanded that Karen give the child back. Karen refused, and the two had a row that lasted for days. Karen quit, saying that she would never give her baby away. Soon, of course, she was back.

The child, often in the care of nannies, thrived happy and unharmed. Marty completely rejected her, but he did pay some of her bills. She even had her own account in the household ledger.

To the other women in the house, Marty's sick whims were rich blackmail material. They respected and feared Karen because she had so much leverage over him. They watched jealously as she got jobs at the Greenwich mansion for her sister and brother and a Volvo for her mother. Other women also threw themselves into "special projects." Satisfying their boss's fantasy became a way to get closer to him, and for some women his fantasy became their own.

One woman began to dream about being artificially inseminated so that she could give birth to a sex slave for Marty. Then, deciding to adopt a young Russian child, she took Russian-language classes at Berlitz and started the adoption process. She got as far as the stage where a social worker was to make a "home visit" meant to ascertain whether a prospective adopter can provide an acceptable home.

Another woman, Jodi, together with Marty hatched a plot to kidnap a nineteen- or twenty-year-old to be Marty's sex slave. The plan, which included the purchase of a van to put the victim in, was kept secret for an unusually long time. There was much resentment in the house as Marty paid for Jodi's trips to concerts by the rock group Phish, her special favorite. Eventually many of the women realized that the idea was to stage a kidnapping at a Phish concert, and the furor died down. The plans never came to fruition.

Marty also became increasingly beholden to Kaethe Schuchter. By late 1998 she was integral to his plan to find new ways to expand his insurance empire. Marty had decided that he couldn't afford to rely solely on John Hackney, who was just too poky for his needs. He began telling people that he was funding Kaethe's lavish lifestyle so that she could meet rich people and connect him with new investors. The Greek chorus of women in the household gossiped that Marty was looking for investors for a new hedge fund. Meanwhile, Marty told John Hackney that Kaethe's high-class hobnobbing would lead him to people who wanted to invest in insurance companies.

With Marty as her backer, Kaethe poured her heart into the New York social scene. She indulged in her hankering for $500 Manolo Blahnik stilettos. She wore outfits by Versace. She dined at Jean Georges, one of New York's most exclusive eateries. Marty made sure that she had what the household called "hot and cold" limousine service—'round-the-clock car and drivers—and the sophisticated and money-conscious people she met on the party circuit took note.

Then there was wine. Kaethe started collecting it, sometimes charging it on the American Express account paid for by wire transfers from Banque SCS. Eventually, her collection included some 574 bottles and was worth about $53,000. Among her holdings were a 1995 C. Dugat Charmes-Chambertin, worth $350; twelve bottles of 1994 Tinto Pesquera Reserve, worth in all about $840; and a 1996 O. Leflaive Bâtard-Montrachet worth $300. (One Riesling was worth only $20, and there was a Merlot worth $10.)

By day, in Greenwich, Kaethe increasingly closeted herself with her computer and her trading. She wouldn't, as one woman later put it, "condescend to fuck with you." By night in Manhattan, though no Blaine Trump or Nan Kempner, she was having a measure of success with a certain social circle she aspired to. She threw parties for as many as twenty or thirty people at her two-bedroom apartment in the Metropolitan Tower, where Vera, Marty's personal maid, helped out.

And, slowly, Kaethe started introducing some monied folk to her boss, although her first efforts had far from the desired effect. First, she introduced him to George Roberts, a real estate investor and frequent visitor to international social hot spots from London to New York to Palm Beach. Kaethe and Roberts were dating, although more for convenience than for love; it was not an exclusive relationship. She'd showed him her paintings and he thought she was "very talented."

She didn't tell Roberts much about her day job and seemed very protective of her boss, whom she called David Rosse. Roberts met "Rosse" on a Saturday afternoon when the trader was in Manhattan buying books. Dressed in blue jeans, he seemed upbeat, almost jolly, "a little nerd." On several occasions, Roberts called Greenwich to speak to Kaethe, and "Rosse" got on the phone to chat instead. But Roberts was not interested in pursing a friendship.

Next Kaethe introduced Marty to Dewi Sukarno, who was a little closer to what he was looking for. The widow of Achmad Sukarno, Indonesia's first president, she was sometimes referred to delicately in the press as a "former bar hostess" from Tokyo. Madame Sukarno had evolved into a legendary partier on a global scale. Almost forty years younger than her husband, she was his third official wife; she made headlines after his death by posing naked for a book that was banned in Indonesia in 1993, and for her romances with fellow jet-setters.

Kaethe and Madame Sukarno became pals after meeting at a party. "A little kiss for my little angel," Kaethe wrote her new friend on a card depicting angels.

Soon Kaethe invited Madame Sukarno up to dine with her boss, "David Rosse," in Greenwich. Kaethe warned her that "Rosse" was very eccentric, and that he would not shake hands for fear of germs. A car and driver was dispatched to pick Madame Sukarno up at her Park Avenue apartment.

In Greenwich, Madame Sukarno was seriously underimpressed. Accustomed to visiting some of the most sumptuous houses in the world, she immediately saw that this was not one of them. There were no paintings on the wall. There was no furniture to speak of. There were no bouquets of flowers. Kaethe had told her that "Rosse" had $20 billion; Madame Sukarno had not believed that figure to begin with, and now she began to wonder whether he was even rich. Plus, he was ugly.

At dinner, "Rosse" ate only poached salmon and fresh salad. He used no salt. Kaethe and Madame Sukarno tucked into steaks. Madame Sukarno loved champagne, and Kaethe had made sure the chef had Dom Pérignon on hand. But the former first lady was aghast when it was served not in champagne flutes, but in ordinary wineglasses.

Then came the pitch. "Rosse" wanted Madame Sukarno to invest in his Columbus Investment Fund. One share was $1,000, and clearly a large investment was expected. "Rosse" said he'd wanted to name the fund Jupiter, but had deferred to Kaethe who liked the name Columbus better.

A few days later "Rosse" followed up with a prospectus sent to Dewi Sukarno at home. She was wary. First, shares suddenly cost $100,000. The minimum investment was $1 million. Also, she saw that the fund was based in Tortola, in the British Virgin Islands. She didn't understand why "Rosse" wouldn't have a New York address.

Kaethe tried to calm Dewi's fears. She told her friend that "Rosse" was very much like Howard Hughes. He considered New York too dirty and too noisy to work in. The air quality was poor. Why, he was even considering purchasing a large tract of land in New Jersey, the size of two golf courses, so that he could put a large glass or plastic bubble over it and work there.

Madame Sukarno dined in Greenwich once more and also met Kaethe and "Rosse" at La Grenouille, a fashionable Manhattan restaurant. Again he ate poached salmon and eschewed alcohol. The two women indulged in foie gras, another favorite of Madame Sukarno's, and sipped an excellent wine. Madame Sukarno asked Marty how, if he was so fearful of germs, "you make love to a lady?" "Rosse" got as red as a *homard,* Madame Sukarno later recalled.

Madame Sukarno didn't like the looks of the whole thing. Eventually, she decided to pass on the investment opportunity and she and Kaethe had a falling out. Soon after, in late 1997, at a party at Doubles, a club frequented by playful upper East Siders, the tension between the two ladies erupted in what appeared to be violence. Kaethe claimed that Madame Sukarno crept up behind her and pulled her hair. Madame Sukarno vigorously denied it.

The whole matter would have drifted into obscurity had not Madame Sukarno already been famous for that sort of thing. In 1992 she'd served thirty-six days of a sixty-day jail sentence for slashing a fellow socialite with a champagne flute at a party in Aspen. As news of this new incident traveled, it caught the ear of George Rush, a gossip columnist for the New York *Daily News*. He called Madame Sukarno, who in a panic called "David Rosse."

Clumsily, Marty attempted to mediate between the two strong-willed women. Negotiations went on long into the night. Fearful that the little skirmish would become much too public for his taste, he led Madame Sukarno to believe that he could persuade Kaethe to call the *Daily News* and say the incident had never happened.

But Kaethe was not as malleable as he thought. She had no desire to help her former friend save face, and the gossip item was printed, and reprinted, in newspapers as far away as Australia.

Several months later, in 1998, Madame Sukarno sued Kaethe for spreading the hair-pulling tale. Kaethe refused to back down, and had a fellow attendee at the Doubles event file an affidavit swearing that "It was an explosive situation every time the two were on the same premises. . . . Mrs. Sukarno tore at Mrs. [sic] Schuchter's hair, yanking her head backwards, ruining the pretty party hairdo."

Madame Sukarno demanded $10 million in damages. But to Marty much more was at stake. Referring to him as "Rosse," chairman of Columbus Investment Fund Limited, her lawsuit claimed he'd threatened to "expose Mrs. Sukarno's allegedly invalid immigration status" and file a criminal complaint against her. The document described "Rosse" as Kaethe's "employer and patron, overseeing and funding [her] obtaining of U.S. immigration status to remain in this country and legal defense of this case."

It turned out that Sukarno had the whole story of Marty's paying for a husband for Kaethe. She spelled it all out in litigation documents, including a private detective's report showing that Kaethe's husband was gay and did not live with her.

The litigation dragged on and on, with Marty paying Kaethe's legal fees and consulting with her lawyers. It continued to threaten to put a very public spotlight on the mysterious "Rosse," the unknown Columbus Investment Fund, and the question whether he'd violated the law by buying a husband for the woman who'd made an enemy of a world-renowned socialite.

But as he waited to see whether Madame Sukarno's caper would be his undoing, he was distracted by a new development in Kaethe's social life. In spring 1998, she introduced him to Tom Corbally, a debonair man in his late seventies known for his way with women and, more to the point, for his extensive business contacts around the world. For Marty, it was yet another new beginning.

Chapter Eight

Mr. Corbally and Mr. Strauss

Tom Corbally had worked for over half a century to cultivate an air of mystery about himself. He had been largely successful. Over the years it was not always clear on what continent he lived, what he did for a living, or sometimes even whom he was married to.

The one thing that people knew for sure about Tom Corbally was that he knew everyone, everywhere. Barbara Walters, Rita Hayworth, Lee Iacocca, Henry Kissinger, Larry Tisch, Roy Cohn, Heidi Fleiss . . . he'd hobnobbed with them all.

Given Marty's goal of building a billion-dollar business empire and meeting people who could help make that happen, Corbally was exactly the kind of man he needed on his team. Kaethe met Corbally on the social circuit through her friend George Roberts and immediately saw that he had potential. Likewise, he saw the potential in her. To him, it looked as though she were rolling in money. She always had a limousine waiting; her apartment had an excellent address; and she knew some of the same people he did, including Dewi Sukarno. Over time Corbally and Kaethe traveled together, enjoying the comforts of some of Europe's finest hotels, the Hôtel Plaza Athénée in Paris and Claridge's in London. And when he was clearly in her thrall, she began to regale him with tales of her boss.

He was a recluse, she said, and an extraordinarily rich stock trader with a seemingly magic touch. Exactly as Kaethe had hoped, Corbally was tantalized, and a meeting was arranged.

Corbally's arrival in Greenwich excited the gaggle of women who played at working in Marty's offices. He looked a little like Jason Robards, but with an impressive head of silver hair. His suit was custom tailored in London and looked it. He wore expensive jewelry, and his gravelly voice made "Johnny Cash sound like a soprano," in the words of one of his old friends. Preceding him into every room he entered was an odor all his own—a combination of smoke and a cologne that seemed to incorporate the fragrance of lavender. To him, every woman he encountered was a great beauty. The word "charm" did not do justice to this skill. The women in Marty's mansion had no idea who he was or why he was there. They only knew what Marty had told them: that he was Kaethe's new boyfriend.

Kaethe escorted Corbally into the trading room and introduced him to "David Rosse." His host received him unshaven, in stocking feet. To Corbally, the man who stood before him was like a Howard Hughes for the nineties. The stacks of computer screens filled with data in which Corbally had no interest gave the place the feel of a spaceship's bridge. He prided himself on being something of a man of the world, and so Corbally was not surprised that a man as rich as this "David Rosse" would be, well, unusual.

Marty began to talk. He insinuated that he was much wealthier than Kaethe had led Corbally to believe. Years before, Marty told Corbally, he had bought some insurance companies over the phone. He didn't have much time to really deal with them, he explained, and had never met any of the people who ran the companies day to day. He wasn't even sure how many he actually owned. These companies, he suggested, were really the smallest part of his holdings. With his left hand behind his back, he made enormous trades of U.S. Treasury bonds for the insurance companies, he said, and he was able to earn profits of more than 19 percent.

Still, Corbally thought, Marty appeared to be a modest man. He pointed out that Warren Buffett earned 21 or 22 percent on his portfolio, and that some people did even better than that.

Marty told Corbally that he had decided to pay a little more attention to his insurance business, really for the first time. His plan, he said, was to make between $100 billion and $150 billion in acquisitions over the next twelve to fifteen months. But the purpose was not simply to make money for the sake of making money.

"I've been all over the world," Marty said. "I've seen everything, done everything. Been in Palm Beach—lived down there." Now all he wanted to do was trade every day and devote his wealth to finding cures for cancer and helping the world.

Marty had a proposition. He had heard about Tom Corbally's connections around the world. He wanted Corbally to join his team, and help put together a group of professionals to make his dream happen. For this, Corbally would claim one percent of the value of the acquisitions as his own.

Corbally saw that the man sitting before him lived a life of luxury. He conjured up an image of the mansion Marty had once owned in Palm Beach. He didn't need a calculator to figure out that if Marty made just $100 billion in acquisitions, $1 billion would be his. He signed on.

For Corbally, Marty Frankel—or "David Rosse"—couldn't have come along at a better time. Corbally had money on his mind. He was seventy-seven years old and his wife, Renee, was a few decades younger. His health was not good: he suffered from emphysema and at times had to suck from an oxygen tank to relieve his breathing difficulties. To be sure, he still spent time in bars in London and New York, paying for the drinks of old and new friends. But he knew those times might soon be curtailed by his inability to get around.

Also the closest thing Corbally had ever had to a real job was drying up. For many years, he had had a close relationship with Jules Kroll, the founder of perhaps the world's best-known private detective agency. Part of what Corbally did was steer business to Kroll Associates, for which he received a commission of roughly 5 to 10 percent. Because he knew so many people on both sides of the Atlantic, he was also used as a resource by Kroll employees the world over, putting them in touch with high-placed informants who otherwise would not have returned their phone calls. Corbally even engaged in the occasional sting. One story in circulation around the time he met Marty was that recently, while working as a Kroll operative, he'd posed as a producer of pornographic films in an effort to set up the estranged wife of a famous artist.

But times had changed at Kroll Associates. Now the firm was managed by seasoned professionals like Michael Cherkasky, a former prosecutor, who looked at Corbally as "a character" out of the firm's deep past.

"We are a very straitlaced firm," Cherkasky said much later. "You looked at him and said, Who is this guy?"

In early 1998, Corbally brought Kroll a case that proved, for a variety of reasons, to be messy. Kroll didn't need the business in the first place: it had plenty of corporate clients willing to pay hefty retainers. Corbally's expenses, Cherkasky said, were "unbelievable . . . ridiculous." Furthermore, office space was in short supply at the firm's Manhattan office and Corbally was occupying precious square feet.

It fell to Jules Kroll to tell Corbally to vacate his office. Although Kroll told Cherkasky and others that he'd had that delicate conversation with his old friend, nothing happened. As of May 1998, when Tom Corbally walked into Marty Frankel's trading room, he still had his office, but he knew it was just a matter of time before he was cut off.

It was the end of a long career that almost defied description.

The first Thomas J. Corbally, Tom's grandfather, immigrated to the United States from Ireland in 1879 and rose to the level of inspector in the police department of Newark, New Jersey. In 1908 and 1909 he was indicted for nonfeasance and malfeasance and arrested on charges of suborning perjury. His trial made headlines, but the jury hung, and he remained a senior member of the police department, becoming what the local newspaper in 1943 called the "arch foe of horse thieves."

Corbally's uncle was also a cop, but it was his grandfather who made a bigger impression on young Thomas Corbally, who was born in 1921. He later told friends that as an elderly gent, the retired inspector took him on a little field trip so he could watch people being beaten up with nightsticks.

Young Tom, it turned out, was not cut out for the family profession. As a teenager he had a brush with the law; a kindly judge who knew the family suggested that the young man might escape punishment if he agreed to join the military. Corbally joined the Royal Canadian Air Force, serving as a rear gunner, and after World War II ended up in London, where his street-smart American swagger was a hit in the upscale bars and clubs of Mayfair. There he met some illustrious contemporaries—Lord White, Lord Hanson, and Sir Jimmy Goldsmith—friends whom he would parlay into business contacts in the future.

He partied with a younger member of the wealthy Mellon family and was well connected in London's social and political scene. In 1963, he did a little snooping around—at the behest, he later said, of U.S. Ambassador David Bruce—and learned that Christine Keeler, a young London call girl, was involved simultaneously with British war minister John Profumo and a Soviet naval attaché. Keeler and her pal and fellow party girl Mandy Rice-Davies had sold their list of contacts to a British newspaper, which had not yet published a story. Corbally passed on that information to Bruce's office, along with the luscious tidbit that the two young women had skinnydipped at a party attended by Profumo at Lord Astor's Cliveden estate. But the embassy neglected to alert the U.S. State Department. The story evolved into the international scandal dubbed the Profumo affair, and there was a fuss in Washington, D.C., about why the embassy had not relayed Corbally's tale. The issue became fodder for the FBI, which in secret files described Corbally as an American businessman "who reportedly ran sex orgies in his London flat."

When in New York, Corbally could be found at El Morocco every night, except when he was at the Stork Club instead. Headwaiters "all liked Tom, which is a sign that he is a true gentleman," said his friend Taki, the international partier and columnist. A story circulated about a time when Corbally, hard up for cash, hit up a wealthy New York friend for $1,000. Half an hour after Corbally left his friend's apartment, the friend encountered a bellboy who worked in the building. "Great guy, that Mr. Corbally," the bellboy said. The friend asked why he thought so. "He just tipped me five hundred bucks," replied the youth. Or so the story went.

Women liked Corbally even better than headwaiters and bellmen did. One former business associate called him the "world's greatest ladies' man," and few would disagree. First he married Gertrude "Gorgeous Gussie" Moran, a tennis star who played at Wimbledon but became notorious for scandalizing the sports world by wearing lace-trimmed knickers under her tennis dresses. The rumor was that the couple was stone drunk when they tied the knot, and the marriage was dissolved in December 1956, not long after the nuptials. (He told friends he'd been hospitalized for alcoholism and apparently had stopped drinking.) Afterward, Corbally was seen with many attractive ladies, so many of whom he introduced as "the future Mrs. Corbally" that fellow revelers didn't know how many former Mrs. Corballys there actually were. In the 1950s he had been a real looker, a truly handsome bon vivant, and he'd lost none of his sexual confidence. At Kroll, where he arrived each day with a six-pack or two of Diet Coke, he was known for flirting with secretaries and even with his colleagues' mothers. While he was dining with some associates one day, a woman approached the table to say hello. Corbally drew a blank. "I suppose you don't recognize me with my clothes on," she said. When it came to women to young or old, Tom Corbally simply could not help himself.

Corbally arranged introductions and did a little minor-league snooping for a variety of clients, ranging from Shearman & Sterling, the law firm known for its representation of Citicorp, to Roy Cohn, the notorious New York power broker who had been counsel to Senator Joe McCarthy during his Communist-hunting years.

He also became pals with a notorious and briefly jailed wiretapper, Steve Brody, who worked for many illustrious businessmen and firms. He introduced Corbally to Jules Kroll, who was just setting out in the investigations business, needed people with contacts like Corbally's, and found the duo endlessly amusing.

But Corbally truly came into his own in the 1980s, as the Kroll office moved away from the traditionally shadowy world of investigations into high-end corporate work. Jules Kroll made a business out of representing corporations in the flurry of takeovers that marked that era. It turned out that Thomas Corbally was an important asset in cultivating that kind of work. All he had to do was tap into the pool of British peers and assorted business types he'd been cavorting with for all those years. When necessary he would roll up his sleeves and jump into the investigatory fray; and it was believed by more than one of his friends that he made love to the wives of Kroll targets, sopping up litigation strategy and corporate secrets all the while. Even as a senior citizen "he was fucking wives," one friend recalled.

Kroll helped finance Tom Corbally's lifestyle. It paid for his account at the "21" Club. He was such a frequent passenger on the Concorde that he had a favorite seat—on the aisle and near the bathroom. He preferred not to cross the Atlantic any other way and rarely, if ever, paid the tab himself. He made the trip so often that he kept a set of clothes at Claridge's. In New York he lived at the Delmonico Hotel on Park Avenue.

None of his compatriots thought Tom Corbally was a man of extreme wealth. But the source of his funds remained partly mysterious. There was talk that he was a gun dealer, but there was no evidence to support it. Other rumors linked him with the Mob but, as his friend Taki put it, "he spread them himself and people who are involved in the Mob never do."

In fact, Corbally did have some questionable contacts. The most notorious was Thomas F. Quinn, a disbarred lawyer who was to play a role in Marty's career later on.

All of this Marty Frankel found very appealing. Kaethe had painted a larger-than-life picture of Corbally and the man lived up to expectations. Corbally was all charm, and his confident demeanor betrayed none of his own worries. Still, Marty was nervous about throwing his lot in with this new character; he asked the real David Rosse to check him out.

Rosse shortly afterward caught up with Corbally in Geneva, where he was camped out in a $1,000-plus-a-night suite, complete with Jacuzzi, at the Noga Hilton Genève, one of the largest deluxe hotels in Switzerland. Chain-smoking cigars and passing out $10 and $20 tips with dramatic flourishes, Corbally met with Rosse, suggesting that they have dinner the next day.

Dinner, it turned out, would be a plane flight away. The next morning Corbally picked up Rosse in a limousine and the two flew to Nice in a private jet. They lunched and took a stroll. Then they got into a Mercedes-Benz limousine, again arranged for by Corbally, and drove the hour or so to Monte Carlo. Along the way Corbally talked almost nonstop, dropping names Rosse had never heard of and hinting that he had been a CIA operative.

After yet another meal, Corbally headed for Monte Carlo's famed green, copper-domed casino, not even pausing as he headed through the entrance for favored gamblers. He was stopped by a guards and directed to the casino's manager.

The manager checked Corbally's passport and politely asked him to leave the premises. Corbally, it turned out, had been banned from the casino. He did not take his ejection gracefully. He start ranting about a conspiracy against him but the management remained unmoved.

Rosse flew home, was granted permission to enter the inner sanctum of the Greenwich trading room, and issued his report: "Stay away from this guy. He's a con artist." The routine check of Corbally had found little, Rosse told Marty, but he emphatically pronounced his boss's new associate "a bullshitter and con artist. This guy's been barred from casinos."

Sitting behind his desk, television and computer monitors turned on behind him, Marty was beside himself. "Oh my God!" he exclaimed. "Oh, no. I can't believe it. I can't believe it. Are you positive?" He pointed out to Rosse that Kaethe had given Corbally a favorable report.

That didn't impress Rosse, who detested Kaethe, called her Horse Face behind her back, and had made it clear to her boss that he thought she had an alcohol problem. "Anyone who's a CIA agent doesn't tell you," he told Marty. (In fact, Corbally never was a CIA agent, though he had friends who had worked for the OSS.)

Marty's gut told him that Corbally was okay, and that he could trust him. Urged on by Kaethe, he ignored David Rosse's advice and began talking with Corbally almost daily. Rosse was annoyed, but it was not the first time his views had been solicited and then ignored by his boss. Frequently he had been asked to investigate Marty's romantic conquests, and though he often came back to him using words like "skanky" and "bad news," his advice was usually discarded if Marty wanted the woman in question badly enough.

Marty's sense that Corbally was the right man to jump-start his efforts to expand his business proved quickly to be correct. Shortly after their meeting, in the spring of 1998, Corbally announced that he had talked to his friend Robert Strauss, and that he would be happy to meet Marty. Marty had finally hit the big time.

Even for a man like Corbally, Robert S. Strauss was an A-list contact. He was one of the most powerful lawyers in Washington, D.C. Nearly eighty, he'd been U.S. ambassador to the Soviet Union and then Russia, and a member of Jimmy Carter's cabinet. But his real clout came from his position in the Democratic Party. He'd served as chairman of the Democratic National Committee in the 1970s and knew everybody and everybody's secrets. He'd also built one of the most prestigious law firms in the country, Akin, Gump, Strauss, Hauer & Feld, which had almost a thousand lawyers.

Strauss had pretty much given up the practice of law, but he remained one of his firm's preeminent rainmakers, or generators of business. To receive his blessing gave any client or associate the same credibility he wielded himself.

Having met Corbally at social functions, Strauss did not know him well, though well enough to return his phone calls. He thought of Corbally as a man who knew a lot of people in trouble. And for a law firm like Akin, Gump, trouble inevitably translated into dollars.

Marty actually donned one of his very few suits for his meeting with Strauss, and conquered his fear of flying long enough to get to Washington. It was Memorial Day weekend, little business was being transacted anywhere, and Strauss had invited Corbally and Marty to join him at his apartment in the Watergate complex.

Corbally introduced his friend as "David Rosse," even though having met the real David Rosse he must have known that the financier had borrowed his security chief's name. Marty told Strauss that he owned insurance companies and planned on buying more. Because he expected that these would be high-profile transactions, he wanted a large law firm to deal with competitive and regulatory issues.

Quietly and quickly, he talked about his trading philosophy, his high-velocity trading of U.S. Treasuries, and his "enormous yields." Strauss was intrigued and the two talked stocks and bonds awhile, as Corbally watched in satisfaction. Strauss even asked Marty for a little investment advice, which his visitor supplied with aplomb.

They all agreed that Marty's lieutenants should meet with an Akin, Gump partner as soon as possible. Everybody shook hands, and Corbally and Marty left the Watergate triumphant.

On the way home, he and Corbally moved on to the next question— who should represent Marty at Akin, Gump a few days hence. Since the insurance companies were involved, Marty decided that John Hackney should be trotted out to make an appearance, for credibility's sake. Corbally would also attend, as the group's connection to Strauss. So would Kaethe, as "David Rosse" 's personal representative.

It was right after Memorial Day when L. Kay Tatum, a partner at Akin, Gump who specialized in corporate transactions, got a call from Bob Strauss asking her to meet with some prospective clients. Akin, Gump was a big firm, and she certainly did not talk with Strauss often. She happily agreed.

Meanwhile, Marty had called John Hackney and ordered him to fly to Washington to meet Bob Strauss. "Strauss wants me to start working on some of his investments for him," Marty bragged to Hackney over the phone.

Hackney's plane was late into Washington. He took a taxi to the small luxury hotel where Corbally was staying, and called up to his room from the lobby. Kaethe answered the phone and the duo came down to meet Hackney for the short trip to the Robert S. Strauss Building, Akin, Gump's Washington headquarters.

Hackney thought Corbally seemed nervous. He had never met the man before, but he'd been briefed by Marty, who told him that Corbally was an ex-CIA agent and that he was "a weird, kinky old guy who likes to go out with young women."

"You're dressed nice," said Kaethe, whom Hackney had heard about from Marty but had never met. Hackney was wearing a conservative suit, a white shirt, and a tie. Kaethe was wearing a slinky outfit in red that barely covered her rear. To Hackney she looked "just so tacky."

The little group was ushered into a hushed conference room at the law firm, and Strauss walked in to introduce everyone and get the ball rolling. Hackney was worrying about Kaethe's "cheesy" outfit, but if Strauss noticed, he didn't react. Neither did the other Akin, Gump staffers in the room, although afterward they talked among themselves about how she looked like a hooker.

Strauss turned the meeting over to Kay Tatum, said his good-byes, and left. The little group discussed the plans for the acquisitions and Tatum was led to believe that Franklin American would be her client. "David Rosse," Marty's emissaries told her, invested Franklin American's assets. He was devoted to the notion of giving to charity and had ties to the Vatican as well. Hackney explained how his family of insurers kept their investments in bonds, tried to contain expenses, and had grown through acquisitions. Marty's team agreed to pay Akin, Gump a $100,000 retainer.

Hackney returned home to Franklin that night, and the next day received a phone call from a buoyant Marty Frankel. Tom Corbally, in on the conference call, was filled with good cheer; he glowingly reported to

Marty on Hackney's stellar performance in Washington. "Bob [Strauss] really liked you and thought you were a nice guy," Corbally told Hackney. "If I were trying to typecast the CEO of an insurance company it would have been you." The conversation gave Hackney a strange feeling, because in his view he hadn't been play-acting at all. It was "no big deal," Hackney told Marty—after all, he knew his companies well.

Marty was thrilled. He ordered Hackney to send the firm a check from Franklin American's account. (The check's arrival so soon after the meeting in Washington was proof to the Akin, Gump lawyers that their new client was flush with cash, more of which might come their way.) Having Akin, Gump at his side as he embarked on his new expansion strategy was invaluable to Marty. Few sophisticated businesspeople would question the integrity of a person, or the soundness of a company, represented by the likes of Bob Strauss and Akin, Gump.

For Corbally, things were looking up, too. To reward his first efforts, Marty had made some pretty grand gestures. He'd supplied Corbally with a car, a Mercedes 600 SL. He'd also agreed to buy an apartment for his use. Corbally chose a three-thousand-square-foot, three-bedroom, four-bath apartment at 515 Park Avenue, practically across Park Avenue from the Delmonico. The not-yet-completed building was the first new luxury residential tower to be built on the street in many years, and the apartment's price tag was $5.8 million. If all went as planned there would be more riches to come, Corbally believed, and he set out to forge the connections that would make it happen.

Chapter Nine

Getting Religion

Marty called Mona Kim into his trading room and gave her an assignment. He wanted her to start buying books about Catholicism. Lots of them. In particular, he wanted her to acquire books about St. Francis of Assisi, who back in the thirteenth century had abandoned all his possessions and founded an order of friars to preach simplicity and poverty. Mona and a few of the other women got to work ordering books, mostly over the Internet. By the summer of 1998, the bookshelves of the Greenwich mansion, especially those outside the trading room where visitors awaited permission to enter the inner sanctum, were lined with books about the Catholic Church.

Marty was concocting a new scheme. His thought was to set up a charity and have it acquire insurance companies. The charity would be Catholic, he decided, with ties to the Vatican itself. That way he'd be screened from the probing eyes of government regulators. After all, who would question the motives of the Church? And everyone knew the Vatican had gobs of money.

The new plan would solve several nagging problems. To acquire bigger and richer insurance companies, Marty would need more cover than John Hackney's little conglomerate in Tennessee could provide. So far, Hackney had relied on the track record and financial statements of the Thunor Trust and its Franklin American Corporation when making bids for new companies. But Marty knew he would need more impressive financial muscle behind him on his quest to build a billion-dollar company.

Also Marty was nervous about pesky questions that insurance regulators, especially in Tennessee, occasionally asked about Liberty National Securities, Marty's "brokerage firm," which of course they'd never heard of. Under Tennessee rules, insurance company assets had to be held by a bank, or by a clearing corporation through a custodial bank. At one point Hackney had urged regulators that Franklin should be exempt from this holding requirement so that it could act on its philosophy of trading frequently. Hackney pointed out that the trading strategy was completely legal.

That seemed to satisfy state auditors, who for the most part knew far less about securities than they did about insurance, and who usually lost interest after their periodic reviews. They had other, bigger insurance companies to worry about. Franklin American, after all, looked pretty much okay. Its financial statements for 1997 and 1998 showed that its reserves exceeded minimum requirements.

While Marty wanted to become the next Bill Gates, Warren Buffett, or, more lately, Sandy Weill, he also flattered himself that he was at heart a do-gooder and champion of the disenfranchised. Way back at Whitmer High School in Toledo, he'd been deeply interested in public policy, both domestic and foreign. John Schulte and later John Hackney, both conservatives, had him pegged as an unrepentant, old-fashioned liberal. Marty could still talk the talk, and starting a charity suited his self-image.

Again, Marty turned to Tom Corbally for help. Some sixty or seventy years before, Corbally had been an altar boy, he told Marty. And he was ideally suited to Marty's project, because he knew people with strong ties to the Vatican, both in New York and in Rome. Given Corbally's recent performance with Bob Strauss in Washington, there was no reason not to believe him.

Corbally put in a call to an old friend with the improbable name of Fausto Fausti. An international business consultant in Rome, Fausto was a former pilot with ties to the aerospace industry. He had, at times, been a Kroll Associates source and had hosted Jules Kroll's son while the young man studied in Italy. Corbally informed Fausti that he had a client who wanted to make a large donation to the church. For Fausti, then in his sixties, this was an ordinary business proposition, for which he expected to get a fee.

After a few conference calls, the group decided to set up a foundation in Assisi, the magnificent hilltop town in Umbria. For Marty the timing was lucky. A year earlier, Assisi, known for its basilica with ceiling frescos attributed if not to Giotto himself then to his followers, had suffered a devastating earthquake. Fausti began preliminary negotiations with a priest whose monastery had been badly damaged. The idea was that Marty would pay to build a new chapter house; architectural drawings were quickly drafted. But then, suddenly, the priest got cold feet and Marty's hopes for a foothold in the city that had been close to his favorite saint's heart were dashed.

The Assisi caper, however, spawned a development that would ultimately create yet more domestic chaos in Greenwich: Kaethe apparently fell in love. During a delicate point in the negotiations, a group of Marty's emissaries had converged on Assisi. Kaethe had come to Umbria on the arm of Tom Corbally. But upon her arrival in Assisi, she almost immediately became romantically entangled with Fausto Fausti's son, Alfredo, who was in his twenties. Alfredo, who aspired to the practice of law, often worked on projects with his father.

The smitten couple pursued their romance in Italy. Corbally returned to New York to regroup and make another run at the Catholic Church. This time he turned to Thomas A. Bolan, a seventy-four-year-old New York lawyer whose major claim to fame was that he had been a close friend and colleague of the controversial lawyer Roy Cohn. For many years, Cohn had lived and worked at an East Side townhouse owned by his and Bolan's law firm. The law firm paid many of Cohn's expenses and allowed him to live rent free, in part because Cohn was in hot water with the IRS and he didn't want to hold property in his own name. During the many years when Cohn was in and out of trouble, Bolan was his staunch defender, once telling a bar association panel seeking to disbar Cohn that his friend was "a man who loves people, loves animals. He once jumped into a river to save a dog in trouble."

From Marty's point of view, Corbally had made a brilliant pick. Bolan was a devout Catholic and had a sheen of establishment credibility. A Knight of Malta and a trustee of St. John's University, Bolan was active in other Catholic organizations as well. He was the New York finance co-chairman of Ronald Reagan's first presidential campaign, and the New York co-chairman of his second presidential campaign. Reagan had appointed him to serve as one of his personal representatives to greet Pope John Paul II when the latter visited the United States in 1981.

Corbally and Bolan had known each other for several decades, going back to the time when Corbally did business with Cohn. They had run into each other at Cohn's legendary parties, which had been chock-full of celebrities and power brokers. Although Bolan and Corbally had never been especially close—years went by in which they didn't see each other—Cohn remained a bond between the two aging men. Now, suddenly, Bolan was hearing from Corbally quite a lot. First Corbally had asked Bolan to do some legal work in connection with an apartment that someone—Bolan wasn't told who—was buying for him. Then Corbally called seeking help for Kaethe Schuchter, whom he called a "very good friend," in the wake of the nasty hair-pulling incident. Corbally asked Bolan if he knew Madame Sukarno and whether he could intervene before the spat grew even uglier and more public. Bolan did indeed know the former first lady and he had made a valiant, though ultimately unsuccessful, effort to mediate the dispute. In the course of his shuttle diplomacy between the two formidable women, he had learned that Kaethe was employed by "David Rosse," a very wealthy man who paid her generously. At one point, he had been supposed to speak by phone with Kaethe's benefactor, but the phone call never happened.

Now Corbally called Bolan and asked him to lunch at Harry Cipriani, an expensive Venetian restaurant with astonishingly low ceilings. It was popular with power-broker types and was conveniently located at the Sherry Netherland, just a few blocks from Corbally's Park Avenue hotel where he still resided. Harry Cipriani was Corbally's favorite lunch hangout, and he hosted Bolan at his regular table. "David Rosse," Corbally told Bolan over lunch, was a "most selfless" man, who for "the rest of his life wanted to help the poor and the needy" and was anxious to work through the Catholic Church. "Rosse" would need to approach the Vatican. Corbally said that he knew Bolan was involved in church matters and wondered if he was interested in helping "Rosse" accomplish these goals.

Bolan did indeed know a priest with Vatican connections. His name was Peter Jacobs and he had moved from New York to Rome in 1990.

Corbally said that he, too, remembered Jacobs from their Roy Cohn days.

It was early August, and warm, when Corbally escorted Bolan up to Greenwich in a chauffeured Mercedes. They were to have a late lunch with Marty. As they drove through the front gates of the compound Bolan took note of the fleet of expensive cars parked outside. The two elderly men entered the mansion's long foyer, lined with what seemed to Bolan to be thousands of books. Corbally entered the "trading room" to confer alone with Marty, and Bolan took a few minutes to scan the bookshelves. He saw that virtually all the books were about the Catholic Church and that there were many about the saints and popes.

Finally, he was ushered into Marty's presence. The man sat in a dimly lit room, with fifty or so computers lit up behind him. To Bolan, it was a scene out of *Star Wars*. When his eyes adjusted to the gloom, he saw Marty, almost in silhouette, clad in a T-shirt and jeans and unshaven. Bolan and Corbally, both of course in business suits, took seats and Marty began to talk.

He had amassed a fortune, he began, and wanted to help the poor, build hospitals and aide "the most unfortunate creatures in the world." Though he was Jewish, he told Bolan, his number-one hero was St. Francis of Assisi. His obsession began after he saw *Brother Sun, Sister Moon*, Franco Zeffirelli's movie about the saint. He was so enthralled with Francis's life that he sat through the film six or eight times. Once he looked up after a screening to realize it was just him and some nuns riveted to their seats in the movie theater. He'd gone on to read everything he could find about St. Francis, and as he talked on and on Bolan saw that Marty knew a great deal about the Vatican, church history, and the lives of the popes, past and present. Marty explained that every night before he slept he read about the lives of the saints. That really hit home with Bolan. The man was clearly very spiritual, he thought.

Marty said that he could make billions of dollars for the Church. His plan was this. He would donate $55 million to a Church entity. The bulk of that money, $50 million, he would use to acquire insurance companies in the charity's name. The other $5 million, the charity would keep to use as it saw fit.

Bolan suggested that Marty consider just giving the $55 million to St. John's University. But Marty preferred to deal more directly with the

Vatican and the Pope, although he said he would not insert himself into decisions about how the profits of his investments were to be spent. "If you can't trust the Pope and the Catholic Church, who can you trust?" Marty asked.

Bolan was anxious to help. Marty, he thought, was as eccentric as Corbally had made him out to be. Nevertheless he saw him as "a likable man, a sincere man, a shy man." He almost felt sorry for him. Certainly, Bolan thought, the man's concern for the poor was "heartfelt."

The car and driver took Bolan back to New York. A day or so later, he received an urgent phone call from Tom Corbally. Was Bolan available to fly to Rome? "Rosse" had a deal pending with a Catholic charity in Italy, and if all went according to plan he wanted Bolan to take a look at the papers in his capacity as a lawyer. Bolan reluctantly agreed, although he'd been given less than seventy-two hours' notice. Corbally told him not to worry about any of the arrangements and mentioned that he would also be in Europe to work on the matter.

One of Marty's minions had arranged for Bolan to be greeted by a special representative of Delta Air Lines at Kennedy Airport in New York. He then flew to Italy on prepaid tickets and was driven to the Hotel Hassler Villa Medici, one of Rome's oldest and most elegant hotels. He was escorted into a huge suite that seemed to take up half a floor, and there he took a nap.

While Corbally and Marty had been chatting up Bolan in New York, Fausto Fausti was busily courting clerics in Italy. He had approached Father Christopher Maria Zielinski, prior of the monastery at San Miniato al Monte, one of Florence's oldest churches, and spiritual director of the Genesis Center, also in Florence. Fausto talked with Father Christopher about "Rosse"'s interest in making a donation, and mentioned Jules Kroll as his associate and "David Rosse"'s.

The Kroll name meant something to the Genesis Center's director, an American lawyer named Michele Spike who had worked in New York. She conferred with Fausti in Italy, who told her that "Rosse," an eccentric and very wealthy investor, wanted to donate $50 million to her foundation, that the money would be invested in insurance companies and that the profits would go to her organization. Kroll, Lee Iacocca, and Bill

Fugazy, a well-known New York businessman (convicted of perjury for lying in a bankruptcy case and later pardoned by President Bill Clinton), were all on "Rosse" 's board, he told her.

Intrigued, Spike faxed corporate, bank, and IRS information to Corbally in London. Soon afterward she heard from Corbally, who explained the deal but expressed a little worry about the fact that the Genesis Center, which devotes itself to promoting interreligious dialogue, was so small. Would a $50 million donation to a tiny charity attract unwanted attention?

"Well, we hope that this sort of large influx of cash won't raise the eyebrows of the IRS," he told Spike.

"I'm not worried about that as long as what we're doing is legal," she responded. But the remark made her a little uncomfortable.

Another meeting was set up for a few days later to discuss the donation. There was some talk of Corbally representing Marty at the meeting, but he was in London and said he couldn't make it. Then there was a discussion of what Bolan's role should be. But at the last minute, in a flurry of transatlantic phone calls, it was decided that Kaethe would represent Marty's interests at the meeting in Florence. Corbally called Spike and told her that Kaethe was wonderful and would handle everything. Spike couldn't help note the lilt in the old man's gravelly voice when he talked about her.

On the day of the meeting, Spike lunched with Fausto Fausti. Though they barely knew each other, Fausti went on at some length about how upset he was that his son Alfredo was having an affair with the more sophisticated Kaethe. "He's so in love with her. She's Mr. Rosse's girlfriend, and he's going to get hurt," he said.

It was late afternoon when Kaethe's Mercedes stretch pulled into the courtyard of the church, which is one of Florence's finest examples of Romanesque architecture, and features the symbols of the zodiac on its eleventh-century floor. Dressed in lavender hot pants, a silk halter top in chartreuse, and reptile-skin stilettos, also in lavender, Kaethe tumbled out of the back of the car with Alfredo in tow. She was rumpled and he was flushed and they left the indelible impression that they had very much enjoyed their trip.

Spike and Father Christopher invited them all into a church office, and Kaethe handed Spike a Federal Express package that she said had been sent from New York to Bolan in Rome. Inside were documents, she explained, and if Spike had questions she could give Bolan a call in Rome.

Spike was accustomed to legal documents, but these raised an unusual number of questions. In fact, she was alarmed. One was a brokerage agreement. The other was a fuzzy power of attorney that seemed to protect Marty while leaving the Genesis Center totally exposed. "Oh my God," she thought. "This is not for us."

Everything was bizarrely vague. The documents didn't even specifically mention that Marty would make a $50 million donation, although that was the understanding of everyone in the room. Spike asked Kaethe where the money would come from. "I can't tell you that," Kaethe replied. "I'm not telling you where the money is coming from."

Spike put in a call to Bolan in Rome. She was left with the impression that he was familiar with the documents, but all he promised was that he would check out the matter with "Rosse." The meeting had now gone on for hours. Father Christopher had taken a break in order to officiate at mass in the church's ornate nave, and when he returned to the meeting, Spike informed him that she could not sign the documents. "I'm not going to next year have widows lining up outside here saying they've lost their five hundred dollars on burial policies. How can I do that? We're a church," she told him.

In a desperate attempt to salvage the situation, Kaethe grabbed the church phone and called Greenwich. Marty's voice emanated from the speakerphone. For about an hour he rambled on in his whiny voice, spouting New Age "philosophy" about St. Francis and explaining his desire to do good and help the poor.

To Spike, it was all very strange. While Corbally had sounded like a professional, Marty struck her as particularly unassertive for an experienced businessman. She told him that the paperwork was utterly unacceptable.

"Don't worry about that," he said. "My lawyers probably didn't understand what I meant, and we'll get you other documents that are more acceptable."

The meeting came to an abrupt end. Spike said she wanted to hold on to the documents, but with barely a pause Kaethe plucked them out of her hands. "Oh, no, you won't," she said, impressing Spike with her command of the situation.

Shortly afterward Bolan, who was in Rome awaiting further instructions, got a phone call from Corbally informing him that the deal had fallen through. He got on a plane and flew back to New York.

Referring to what she called this "curious experience," Spike fired off a letter to Jules Kroll in New York. She had taken her visitors' use of his name "as an indication of their serious intentions," she wrote, and she wanted to make Kroll "aware of the deceptive means they used to present their proposal and that we firmly rejected it. If however you are not involved in business with these particular people, then you should be aware that they are trading off your good name and reputation and in the process tarnishing it."

Jules Kroll was none too pleased. Confronted by a Kroll Associates senior staffer, Corbally, who'd been mentioned in the letter, insisted he didn't know a thing about the episode in Florence. He promised to find out about it, but never did get back to his associates at Kroll with an explanation.

Spike also sent Marty a copy of the letter, which complained that "no one ever offered to reimburse us for our time" or "offered us a minimum donation." Almost immediately, Spike received a phone call from Kaethe, who was in Rome. She offered Spike $2,000 to compensate her for her time. "When do you want the money?" Kaethe said. "I can be there in two hours." But there was a snafu. Spike didn't want cash, and Kaethe said she didn't have a check. Kaethe was clearly annoyed, as though she couldn't be bothered to deal with such a piddling sum. The problem was solved when Fausto arrived with a check for $2,000 and an IBM ThinkPad for the Genesis Center. Spike never heard from any of them again.

Back in New York, Bolan tried another course of action on behalf of Marty. He contacted Father Peter Jacobs about what could be done to help this extraordinary rich Jewish man make a donation in the manner he preferred.

Father Peter Jacobs, then seventy-two, had been flirting with controversy for almost forty years. Called alternatively Father Jake, the Junkie Priest, the Jewish Priest, and the Reverend to the Stars, he had survived numerous scraps with his superiors over his long career in the Church. His most famous transgression was running the Palantine, a glitzy restaurant he opened in New York's theater district in the early eighties, with the notion of giving the profits to the needy. The plan was embraced by the literati and celebrities who frequented the place, including Bianca Jagger and Yoko Ono. But it was frowned upon by the District of Columbia archdiocese, to which Father Jacobs officially reported. He was suspended in 1982, and although the suspension was reversed five years later, after he finally closed the restaurant, he had never regained his authority to perform certain priestly functions, such as marriage and the annointing of the sick.

But that was only Father Jacob's most famous brush with trouble. The balding pixie of a priest had, in the words of a friend, "a very simple view of his ministry," and that was to help the city's most downtrodden. For about four years in the 1960s he supplemented his income by loading trucks at Bloomingdale's so he could spend the rest of his time in Harlem, where he earned seventy-five dollars a month plus room and board. He spent time downtown with junkies and whores and generally refused to take orders from anyone.

That didn't sit well with New York City's legendary cardinal Francis Spellman, who wasn't fond of unmanageable priests and who was always looking for an excuse to kick Father Jacobs out. Whenever it looked as if the cardinal might be coming close to that goal, Father Jacobs—who persisted in calling the cardinal "Spellie"—would turn to Roy Cohn, a friend of Spellman's, for cover.

Somehow, despite his many misadventures, Father Jacobs always managed to curry favor in Rome. For years he worked at Rice High School, at 124th Street and Lenox Avenue in Harlem. When Pope Paul VI visited the United States in 1965, his motorcade made an unscheduled stop at the school to see Father Jacobs. The priest wasn't there at the time—he was in Greenwich Village visiting with junkies—but the visit made the newspapers.

Father Jacobs also had another and very different life. When he wasn't ministering to New York's low life he was living the high life, hobnobbing with the city's rich and famous. Some of these pals called him "the

Jewish Priest," because his father had been a Jew. He knew Jackie Kennedy and Walter Cronkite and Grace Kelly. He partied with the writer Norman Mailer and the agent Swifty Lazar and the newspaper columnists Pete Hamill and Sidney Zion.

Upon his retirement, Father Jacobs gave his townhouse in the West Village, where he was sometimes seen walking his pet Dalmatians, to a church-related organization in Italy. The understanding was that the church would provide him with a percentage of the investment income to live on. He moved to Rome, where he tooled about on a blue motor scooter and chatted in his good—though American-accented—Italian. He visited New York regularly, but was in Rome during the summer of 1998, when Bolan tracked him down. The two men, who of course knew each other from the Cohn era, hadn't laid eyes on each other for many, many years.

Father Jacobs was keen to aid Bolan in his mission. It would not be the first time he'd helped a wealthy donor choose charities. He had also helped the late retailing mogul Milton Petrie—another Jew—disperse some of his millions to charities, something the priest loved to chat about on the party circuit.

After hearing from Bolan that Marty wanted to hook up with the Vatican, Father Jacobs decided to bring his friend Monsignor Emilio Colagiovanni into the circle of aging Roy Cohn acolytes advising Marty.

Colagiovanni ran the Monitor Ecclesiasticus Foundation, which, published a review of canon law. A round man, with dark strands of hair pulled over his balding pate, Colagiovanni in his prime had sat on the Roman Rota, a Vatican's court of appeals. Now, using an aging computer, a jar of rubber cement, and scissors, he put together his law review in the small, dark Roman town house where he lived and worked. *Monitor Ecclesiasticus* was not officially part of the Vatican, but it had been blessed by a previous pope, and perhaps more significant from Marty Frankel's point of view, it had a Vatican bank account.

It just so happened that Monsignor Colagiovanni was in the United States, vacationing in Cleveland where he was visiting his sister and a bishop. Father Jacobs gave him a call and asked him to come to New York to meet "David Rosse." On August 8, 1998, just a few days after the debacle at San Miniato al Monte, a chauffeured car was dispatched from Greenwich to La Guardia Airport to pick him up. Bolan and Father Jacobs in from Rome, were driven up separately. Marty reprised for the newcomers the show he'd put on for Bolan less than two weeks before, displaying his knowledge of the life of St. Francis. Fresh from his recent disappointments in Italy, Marty stressed that he wanted to give away $50 million through a foundation formed in the Vatican or through an existing foundation with Vatican ties.

To bring that kind of money into the Church would certainly attract favorable attention from the Vatican, and Colagiovanni was game. He responded with a recitation of his unique qualifications for the task. He knew just who to go to within the Vatican, he told the little group sitting in Marty's trading room; he was pals with the Vatican's secretary of state and other high Church dignitaries. He knew exactly how to make Marty's dream happen.

The priests then launched into an enthusiastic discussion of where Marty's first donation of $5 million would go. Monsignor Colagiovanni clearly hoped his foundation would benefit. And Father Jacobs badly wanted some of the money to go to a charity close to his own heart, the Boys Town of Italy. After some discussion, the three old men had carved up the $5 million among them: $3.5 million would go to Monitor Ecclesiasticus, $1.1 to Father Jacob's charities, and $400,000 to Bolan's.

That their benefactor had agreed to donate $55 million, but to hand over the control of only $5 million up front, did not seem to trouble anyone in the room, even though the plan certainly was unusual.

It was a very jolly group that traveled back to New York, again in a car provided by Marty. On the way back to La Guardia, where they dropped off the monsignor, the group chatted about how much good the money would do and what a splendid man "David" was.

Back in Cleveland, Monsignor Colagiovanni hit the phones, arranging for Bolan and Father Jacobs to have the access they needed at the Vatican. On August 22, Bolan once again left for the Hotel Hassler in Rome. "Please don't get me a ballroom," he had pleaded with Marty, "a little room will be fine." He was put in a smaller room that, nevertheless, was very nice.

On the same day that Bolan departed, Marty drafted a fax to him spelling out the terms of the deal he was hoping to make with the Vatican. "A secret set of bylaws" would detail the agreement between himself and the Vatican, "spelling out exactly my control of the $50 million, that

I am the original Grantor of the funds, and spelling out the Vatican's control of the extra $5 million." He went on to say that he would use the $50 million to buy insurance companies and that, "In each case of every purchase, the Vatican must be prepared to state, if necessary, that the Vatican is the source of funds." Bolan later said he never read the letter and doubts having received it.

In Rome, Father Jacobs had booked Bolan solid. After napping for several hours, Bolan and Father Jacobs sipped tea at an outdoor café on the Via Veneto. Then they headed for Boys Town to meet the priests who ran it. All treated Father Jacobs like a long-lost brother. Dinner was at a long wooden table outdoors, and although Marty's plan was supposed to be confidential, Father Jacobs let "Rosse's" name slip out, much to Bolan's dismay.

The next day, a Monday, Father Jacobs took Bolan on his own personal tour of Vatican City and the Basilica of St. Peter. He showed him a secret entrance to the basilica that only cardinals used. From the Swiss Guards to personnel at the Vatican Bank, everyone knew the American priest. Then it was on to an appointment with Bishop Francesco Salerno, the secretary of the prefecture for the Holy See's economic affairs.

While Father Jacobs waited outside, Bolan met with Bishop Salerno and explained the plan to set up and finance a Vatican foundation. Bishop Salerno told Bolan that he thought the idea was an excellent one, and that he should prepare bylaws for the proposed charity. Bolan returned to his hotel in Rome and called his office in New York, asking assistants to fax over model bylaws for nonprofit organizations. With those in hand he got to work drafting bylaws, which Father Jacobs then arranged to have typed.

But as soon as the bylaws had been drafted and fiddled with, Father Jacobs had a disturbing conversation with Bishop Salerno. It turned out that the office of the Vatican's secretary of state had a difficulty with the proposal. Father Jacobs negotiated an appointment for Bolan with Monsignor Gianfranco Piovano, an assistant in the office of the secretary of state for the Vatican. The meeting was complicated by the fact that Bolan spoke precious little Italian and Piovano's English was no better. But with the help of a translator, the message finally became clear.

Although the secretary of state's office thought the general idea was "wonderful," there was one little element that was not going to pass muster. And that was the notion that this foundation would be running insurance companies, which was clearly not the vatican's usual line of work. In no uncertain terms, Monsignor Piovano told Bolan that he'd have to find another way. "I never thought it would be so difficult to give away fifty million dollars," Bolan told the Monsignor.

Bolan reported to Marty by phone and then flew back to New York. The following Sunday, he and Corbally drove up to Greenwich to discuss the trip to the Vatican. It was a sunny, warm day and they met outdoors. Marty put in a call to Robert Strauss, explaining what had happened. Strauss told Marty that he knew Zbigniew Brzezinski, the former national security advisor under President Jimmy Carter; Brzezinski, in turn, knew the Pope's secretary, who like Brzezinski's family was Polish. Marty put Bolan on the phone so that he and Strauss could talk lawyer to lawyer. Strauss explained that Brzezinski was very meticulous and that it was important to spell out the proposal and send it to him in a letter. The letter never was sent. Through a spokesman Strauss denied that he referred Marty to Brzezinski.

What followed was a bit of a muddle. Bolan received a letter from Monsignor Colagiovanni saying that he had talked to Vatican officials and that they were agreeable to setting up a foundation. There was good cheer all around, and Bolan began to make plans to return to Rome yet again to complete the deal. But it turned out that Colagiovanni had been unaware of Bolan's second Vatican meeting. When that misunderstanding was cleared up, Colagiovanni came up with a new proposal.

He suggested that his foundation, Monitor Ecclesiasticus, receive the money and, in turn, donate it to a non-Vatican charitable foundation. Once more Bolan flew to Rome. There were discussions among Bolan, Colagiovanni, and Jacobs, and many phone conversations with Marty back in Connecticut. Monsignor Colagiovanni said that he had talked with a Vatican official and that his foundation was authorized to receive Marty's money. Father Jacobs then asked what account the money would go into at the Vatican bank. That focused Marty's attention on a new fear. What would happen, he began to worry, if the Vatican changed its mind once the $55 million was in its bank? What would happen if the

Vatican took control of the money? He proposed that he put the $50 million in a Swiss bank, and $5 million in the Vatican bank. The larger sum would be passed through Monitor Ecclesiasticus to a new foundation, to be named after his hero, St. Francis of Assisi. The $5 million, Monitor Ecclesiasticus could keep for itself.

The latter was at the insistence of Monsignor Colagiovanni. For his troubles, he wanted the full $5 million. Father Jacobs and his charities were cut out. And—only grudgingly—Colagiovanni agreed to consider giving $250,000 to the Human Life Foundation, an antiabortion organization in New York, Bolan's choice.

Marty cautioned his small group of associates that his plan might take five years or longer to yield results, but he promised that ultimately his purchase of insurance companies would yield billions of dollars for charity in the name of his beloved saint.

He now needed some time to mull the situation. He agonized over what to do—make a deal with Monitor Ecclesiasticus, or make another run at the Vatican using some other vehicle or connection.

Meanwhile he had the dueling egos of Monsignor Colagiovanni and Father Jacobs to massage. Father Jacobs felt a bit put upon, with none of the $5 million destined to go to his pet charities. He tried to persuade Marty to find another religious order to funnel the money through; Marty did look at one of Father Jacobs's favorites, the Sons of Divine Providence, whose members take vows of poverty and perpetuate the charitable work of the order's founder, Don Luigi Orione, who'd been declared blessed by Pope John Paul II in 1980. After some study Marty was almost as much of an expert on Don Orione, who'd called himself the "porter of God," as on St. Francis.

Marty and Father Jacobs had long, rambling discussions, and the priest soon began to feel that he had become "David's shrink." Father Jacobs could tell that the multimillionaire was troubled merely by looking at him. There was something mentally wrong, some kind of nervousness, he thought. He wasn't quite sure what the difficulty was, but he certainly wanted to help "David." Marty, for his part, wanted to keep Father Jacobs happy. He promised him he'd be the international spokesman for St. Francis, a role suitable for a man with such extensive social and celebrity contacts. And he did as much as he could to satisfy Father Jacobs's strong desire to get money to the deserving as quickly as possible.

"Is there anything I could do right now?" "David" asked one day, while the details of his $55 million donation were still in flux.

Father Jacobs reported that Cardinal Pio Laghi, a Vatican official who had once been the Pope's representative to the United States, was very interested in a hospital in Albania.

"Would a hundred thousand be okay?" Marty asked.

"That would be wonderful," Father Jacobs gushed. "David" said that he would take care of it, and $100,000 was transferred from Banque SCS to Father Jacobs's bank account. Jacobs forwarded the money to the fund for Our Lady of Good Counsel Hospital in Tirana, Albania.

In December, Father Jacobs received a letter from Cardinal Laghi thanking him "for the donation made by your Foundation" to the hospital, "a cause very close to the heart of Mother Teresa . . . your help to the poor sick is greatly appreciated."

It appeared to be a form letter, but the cardinal had taken note of Father Jacobs's and "David Rosse' "s interest in the poor—and in the money "Rosse" clearly had at his disposal. While the Vatican hierarchy was contemplating how to handle the mysterious benefactor and his possible contributions, Cardinal Laghi intervened and requested that all necessary assistance be given to Marty.

Back in Greenwich, Marty also promised Father Jacobs that he would send $50,000 to some priest friends of Jacobs's, members of the Sons of Divine Providence, who were aiding a group of children living on a garbage dump in Manila. Soon, a letter arrived thanking "Rosse" for the donation. Father Jacobs brought one of his Manila friends up to Greenwich to meet his benefactor, and the visiting priest suggested that he and Father Jacobs pray for their host. (As always, Marty was on his best behavior in Father Jacobs's presence and treated his visitors with respect, if not actual reverence. But some days later, on the phone with Hackney, he laughed with glee as he told the story of Father Jacobs praying for his soul.)

Marty took other steps, too, to strengthen his relationship with Father Jacobs. When Marty learned that the priest tooled around Rome on a "motorina"—a motor scooter—he became terrified that Jacobs would have a fatal accident. He insisted on buying him a car. Father Jacobs had previously driven Volkswagens bought for him by Milton Petrie and by John Revson, a member of the family that once owned Revlon, so he suggested a Volkswagen. "We'll get a Mercedes engine and put it in the Volkswagen to make it stronger," Marty said. But the priest said he was "crazy," and agreed to accept a dark blue Volkswagen, with the motor it came with. He refused to give up the scooter altogether.

In November 1998, and continuing for five months, Marty also began sending Father Jacobs $3,300 a month after the priest suddenly had to vacate his apartment.

As he wrestled with his indecision, Marty also worked hard to keep Monsignor Colagiovanni's allegiance. He wrote the monsignor two letters, on the same day. "I was so glad you gave me a copy of your 'Global Approach to the Poverty Problem,' when you were so gracious to visit with me recently," he wrote. "You are right; the solution, as you have stated, must be to educate social workers, so that these social workers can teach poor people skills, so that they can become self supporting." He went on to call for a "Marshall Plan to fight world poverty. Such a plan would start with your mission. . . . I have no words to express how grateful I am to you and the Church for helping me to help others."

In his second missive he laid out his life story, borrowing heavily from the life of the real David Steven Rosse. He said he was born in Mount Kisco, New York (the real Rosse's birthplace), had done a stint in the army (as had Rosse), and that he had become a private investigator. His paternal great-grandfather, he said, "was a very orthodox rabbi in Poland/Ukraine" and was a direct descendant of the Talmudist Rashi, who in turn was a direct descendant of King David.

He went on to claim that his insurance companies' bond portfolio had returned 19.13 percent in the previous year, and that if "our portfolio had been a publicly traded mutual fund," it "would have earned us recognition by 'Money Magazine' as the 6th best performing bond fund in the country in 1997."

In October, "Rosse" summoned Monsignor Colagiovanni and Tom Bolan to a meeting in Greenwich. He had finally decided to go with the plan to funnel his $55 million through Monitor Ecclesiasticus, with the understanding that $50 million would be donated to "The St. Francis of Assisi Foundation, to Serve and Help the Poor and Alleviate Suffering," which would buy insurance companies.

The foundation was set up in the British Virgin Islands with a retroactive date of formation. Although Marty hadn't really made up his mind until October, the official launch date was August 10, which he thought was astrologically advantageous.

Soon after the October meeting, Bolan received a phone call from Tom Corbally. "David wants you to send a bill," he said, adding that "Rosse" thought he'd done "a great job." Bolan sent Sundew International a bill for $50,000. Marty wired him $100,000. (He later sent him an additional $75,000 in fees.)

No timetable was set for the $55 million transfer to Monitor Ecclesiasticus.

Bolan and Marty continued to have periodic talks about getting St. Francis off the ground. Marty always answered the phone with the salutation, "What can I do for you?"—a way to avoid confusion since he now was known to so many people by so many different names. Although Bolan liked his client, he came to dread their talks, which would drag on for hours. During one conversation, Bolan mentioned his son, who was dying of multiple sclerosis. His son had reached the point where he was totally helpless and was fed through a tube. During the day, an assistant helped the Bolans, who were both in their seventies, take care of their son.

Marty told Bolan that his son should have 'round-the-clock care by a registered nurse. "I want to help," he said. "I'm not going to take no for an answer."

Bolan got off the phone, deeply moved, and told his wife. She broke down and wept. Every day from then on, a chauffeured car picked up a nurse and delivered her to the Bolans' to care for the stricken man from four P.M. to ten P.M.

Marty now spent considerable time thinking about whom to put on St. Francis' board to give it the greatest possible credibility on its quest to buy bigger and better insurance companies. One possibility was Lee Iacocca, to whom Corbally had been close for many years. The former chairman of Chrysler Corporation was not inclined to lend his name to the new foundation, but Marty and Corbally kept trying to convince him, and Iacocca was intrigued with Corbally's tales of "Rosse" 's prowess as an investor. Finally Marty offered Iacocca the use of a private jet for a trip to Italy. Iacocca, who after his retirement from Chrysler had started a company to market electric bicycles, accepted the offer and spent about ten days traveling around in a Gulfstream jet, courtesy of Marty.

When Marty asked Father Jacobs if he knew anyone with a sterling reputation for the foundation's board, the priest suggested the former CBS anchorman Walter Cronkite.

"Do you really know him?" Marty asked in wonderment.

"Sure," answered Father Jacobs. This was true: he actually was a friend of Cronkite, and shortly afterward, he attended a birthday party for the newsman. Father Jacobs told Cronkite he had a billionaire friend who wanted to give $50 million in charity; he compared "Rosse" to Milton Petrie, whom Cronkite had also known. Cronkite congratulated his friend on finding such a benefactor.

"Will you give some advice on the charities?" Father Jacobs asked. He assured him that he would not have to go to meetings—"you are not a real official." Father Jacobs later recalled that Cronkite agreed.

But Cronkite thought that he had committed himself only to a little friendly phone conversation, and that he'd made clear to Father Jacobs that he didn't want to be on any board. So when an associate of the priest's wrote him soon afterward saying that Father Jacobs had said he would be helpful on foundation matters, Cronkite was annoyed. He called Father Jacobs and told him in no uncertain terms not to use his name.

Around the time that Jacobs approached Cronkite, Marty received a visit from Ed Krauss, his old friend from Toledo. The two had spoken only sporadically in recent years, but Marty called Krauss in the fall of 1998 because even he was beginning to see that the chaos in his office was threatening to paralyze his business. He hoped Krauss could advise him on how to handle his clerical needs.

Much of the advice Marty ignored. Krauss told him that everybody had to pay taxes and that many of the women's benefits were in reality taxable income. Marty worried that these sort of tax details would bring him down, but he told Krauss that the women simply didn't want to pay taxes. Noting the fights between the women and their occasional refusal to accept assignments, Krauss suggested that some of them be fired. Marty balked. "I've got secrets and I trust my people," he told Krauss.

Some of them, he said, knew his "system," and he was sure they would not reveal it to anyone.

On the evening of Krauss's visit, Marty had Father Jacobs over for dinner. His chef served the priest and Krauss gravlax and truffles and sushi. Marty dined on low-fat chicken-vegetable soup and sipped bottled water. Much of the conversation centered on Catholic charities and the good Marty could do with his investing.

Father Jacobs relished the conversation but sometimes steered the talk to his busy social life, mentioning in passing the famous people he knew, including Walter Cronkite. He reported that he had been invited to a party given by Alice Mason, a New York real estate broker known for her star-studded dinner parties, and said that Jimmy and Rosalynn Carter would be there.

Krauss was much impressed. He turned to Marty and suggested that he, Marty, go to parties like that so he could meet contacts for his business. Marty was reluctant. "I know if I do that they'd be wanting to invest and there'd be more information of where I was," he said, ever worried that John Schulte would find him.

Still, Jimmy Carter's name struck a chord in him, and soon afterward Jacobs made contact with the development office of the Carter Center, the former president's human rights organization, in Atlanta. He explained that he represented someone interested in making a large contribution to the center, but that he was not yet prepared to reveal the man's name. The potential donor, he explained, wanted to help the poor all over the world. Father Jacobs's talks with the Center continued for many months.

Marty had been keeping John Hackney and Gary Atnip informed about his development of the St. Francis Foundation, even toying with the idea that once it was up and running St. Francis would acquire the whole insurance empire. Marty told Hackney that Corbally knew Lee Iacocca and that he would be on the foundation's board or its advisory board. Walter Cronkite would be on the advisory board, too, he said, and "we're going to get Jimmy Carter."

After so many years, Hackney and Atnip were used to Marty talking big and they were not so impressed. Why, they asked him, do you need all these people?

"You need name recognition," Marty responded. "Lee Iaccoca will help with stuff."

Of course, Marty had no commitment from Iaccoca, Cronkite, or Carter. Finally, he solved that problem himself. Using a different type-face on his computer, he drafted, or had drafted, a document, under Akin, Gump's name, entitled "Memorandum Summarizing The Saint Francis of Assisi Foundation, to Serve and Help the Poor and Alleviate Suffering."

"The Foundation has instituted an Advisory Board which will render advice to the Foundation with respect to a variety of matters relating to the management of hospitals and insurance companies, general busi-ness management issues, and charitable giving activities," the document said. "The Advisory Board members include, among others, Walter Cronkite and Lee Iacocca, who have graciously agreed to serve in such capacity."

Chapter Ten

Enter the Consultants

Marty arrived in Toledo for his father's funeral with Adriana as his date. Lovely in an understated way, she was the most presentable of his many women. Sonia, of course, couldn't return with him to Toledo for security reasons. Oksana was too young and not socially adept enough to handle the Toledo crowd of aging family members and old friends. Kaethe's wardrobe alone would have stunned them all into their graves.

It was fall of 1998, and Leon Frankel had died of a heart attack the day before he would have turned eighty-eight. Quoting Marty's brother, Robert, extensively, the obituary in the *Toledo Blade* hailed Leon as a lawyer devoted to his profession, an athlete, and an enthusiastic volunteer. "By word and deed, he taught his children integrity," the obituary stated. "The family requests tributes to a charity of the donor's choice."

Marty pulled up to the house on Stanhope with a small motorcade of rented cars. He was attended by three bodyguards—the real David Rosse, Rosse's sidekick Steve, and a freelancer, an off-duty police officer.

Greatly grieved by his father's death, Marty was almost overwhelmed by the fears that always accompanied his infrequent trips back to Toledo. Although it had been years since he'd heard from John Schulte, he remained terrified of running into him in Toledo. He worried that Sonia's former husband would somehow figure out where he was living. And he was certain the man wanted to kill him.

In fact, Marty Frankel was still very much on John Schulte's mind. Schulte had finished his federal prison term and was trying to put his life together. He was renting a house for $250 a month in a working-class section of east Toledo and was soon to move back to the house on his family's farm, which was still worked by his cousin. Financially he was just scraping by, making about $20,000 a year. He had rented an office in Oregon, Ohio, an area that had once been farmland but was now a desolate patch of vacant lots dotted with industrial and commercial properties. There he brokered mortgages, although business was not exactly booming. On the side, he advised old clients on their stock market investments. That was all informal, of course, as Schulte had been banned from the securities industry for life.

Schulte read about Leon Frankel's death in the *Blade* on Sunday, November 1, with much interest. He figured that Marty Frankel would emerge from whatever hole he'd buried himself in, and attend the funeral. Schulte reasoned that if Frankel was in Toledo, it was likely that his "ex-spouse," as he often called Sonia, was too. In that case, he thought, his daughters also might be in town. He set out to find out for sure, picking up his girlfriend, Judy, on his way to the Frankel house.

Marty's small security force had theorized that if Schulte put in an appearance, it would be during the funeral, which was held at a local synagogue. So they relaxed a bit when family and friends returned to the Stanhope house after the service. Steve and the freelancer had been staking out the front of the house for hours when Rosse came to relieve them. They drove around the corner to a Wendy's restaurant for a bite to eat. It was sometime after five P.M. when suddenly the radio crackled a report from Rosse: he had Schulte in his sights.

Schulte was driving slowly by the Stanhope house when he spotted Rosse, whom he recognized, standing outside. (Rosse had guarded Sonia and her children when Schulte visited them in California.) Rosse jumped into his car and started chasing Schulte, who then turned off Stanhope with Rosse close behind. Communicating with Rosse by radio, Steve and the freelancer slid to the back of the line of cars. Quickly Rosse and Steve hatched a plan over their two-way radios to box Schulte in. Rosse pulled to the side of Schulte's green Taurus. Then he swerved in front of Schulte at a four-way-stop, blocking him off. Rosse jumped out of his car and leaped onto the hood of the Taurus. Schulte veered around the stopped car and roared off. Rosse rolled off the windshield on the passenger side of the vehicle, narrowly escaping injury.

The whole thing was just like a *Hawaii Five-O* stunt, Schulte thought.

He was scared. As he sped away, driving over a few front lawns, the passenger door flew open and it looked as if Judy was contemplating leaping from the moving car. Schulte decided to head for Ottawa Hills, the nearby town where Sonia had lived in the early days of her romance with Marty. His goal was to head for the town's police station, and for three miles Rosse and his associates followed behind.

Schulte stopped in front of the Ottawa Hills police headquarters, while Rosse and his cohorts continued on. The police escorted Schulte to the town line, where a Toledo police car waited, and Schulte and Judy made their way back to Stanhope under police escort. There the police tried to sort things out. Rosse told the police that Schulte had hit him with his car. Schulte responded that he'd just been looking for his kids. He parked in front of the Frankel's house and waited for the police to investigate.

Meanwhile Steve went into the house and told Marty that the police were outside on the street talking to Schulte. He turned away briefly, turned back, and found that Marty had vanished. Tillie Frankel didn't know what had become of her son and Steve searched the small house, calling his boss' name. Finally, in a darkened back room, he found Marty cowering in a closet. Steve stifled a laugh and coaxed him out.

Eventually, the police came to the house and spoke briefly with Tillie and Marty. The officers then told Schulte that his children weren't in the house, and warned all the parties to stay away from one another. The crisis was over. Schulte withdrew to his lair in east Toledo, without gaining any intelligence about Marty or about his ex-wife's new stomping grounds.

Marty returned to Greenwich greatly saddened and with his fears of Schulte renewed. He felt that he'd had a close call. Still, once safely home again in the trading room of his guarded mansion, he immersed himself in his plan to go global. St. Francis was largely in place; Monsignor Colagiovanni and Father Jacobs, who was to be the foundation's president, were firmly on board. Now it was time to start targeting insurance companies to buy.

That, of course, was way beyond the expertise or interest of his in-house churchmen. Marty grew more and more sure that Hackney could not be relied on to make a play for a big insurer. He was increasingly frustrated with his loyal puppet, who he still had not met. Hackney kept talking about the need to check the viability of potential acquisitions and to carefully absorb each new company that entered the Franklin American family.

Marty confided to some of his intimates that Hackney couldn't move fast enough and was not thinking creatively about new businesses. In 1998, when he had decided to get into the annuity business, which he figured would be a lucrative sideline for his existing insurers, he felt he had to drag Hackney into the project and had hired someone near Greenwich to do the groundwork for the program and get regulatory approval in the states where Franklin already operated.

So he turned to Tom Corbally again. Corbally knew nothing about insurance. But he told Marty he knew people who did, and he promised to recruit them into Marty's circle. Truth be told, Corbally's black book was not exactly overflowing with insurance contacts, but he did not tell Marty that. Instead, he called Larry Martin, a businessman he believed could summon the expertise needed to carry out Marty's plan.

Larry Martin was a former patent lawyer, trained also as a civil engineer, who had left the mundane world of law behind for the entrepreneurial life. He now spent his time as an investment banker on large commercial real estate deals. When he wasn't flying around the country, he drove the green hills of upper Westchester in a chauffeur-driven Jaguar. He and Corbally had met in the early 1990s, when Larry Martin visited Kroll Associates to discuss a possible investigation. The case had never materialized but Martin and Corbally, who shared an appetite for Cuban cigars, had kept in touch.

Corbally saw Larry Martin as the kind of no-nonsense guy who was good at structuring deals, could get things done, and was almost neurotically organized. Corbally asked Martin whether he would be willing to meet "David Rosse," the "Howard Hughes of the nineties." He described "Rosse" as a strange recluse who wouldn't leave the house and made millions of dollars a day trading.

Martin was intrigued and asked who else was in on "Rosse" 's game. Corbally mentioned Robert Strauss, and said that Akin, Gump was "Rosse" 's law firm. He also listed Lee Iacocca, Walter Cronkite, and Edgar Bronfman, Jr. (Bronfman, then the chief executive of Seagram, had never met Marty, but Father Jacobs had helped officiate at his wedding.)

There was a fleet of Mercedeses outside the Greenwich mansion when Martin drove up soon after his conversation with Corbally. The women milling around the outer offices of this "Howard Hughes of the nineties" seemed to vary dramatically from the waiflike to the obese. Marty also seemed to have some sort of weight-related emotional issue. On his scrawny frame hung jeans with what appeared to be a forty-inch waist. Larry Martin's unkempt host sat in his overstuffed desk chair, surrounded by computer and television screens. Martin, who was usually meticulously and expensively turned out, thought he was a messy nerd.

Impatiently calling out to his bevy of women for something to drink, Marty described himself as the best bond trader in the world. He owned insurance companies, he said, and had audited statements to prove how well they'd done over the years. He said that a substantial portion of the profits from the acquisitions he planned to make would go to charity. Marty told Martin that he wanted him to put together a team that could structure an investment fund to acquire the insurance companies. He urged his visitor to check him out with Akin, Gump.

Larry Martin did indeed call Akin, Gump. A lawyer there told him that, yes, the firm was representing the man they knew as "Rosse," and that "Rosse" and Corbally had met with Strauss. They were considering an acquisition of an insurance company in Colorado, and there was a substantial amount of money on the table.

Satisfied by this conversation, Martin agreed to take on the assignment. Marty asked him for his birthdate, to be sure he and his new consultant were astrologically in sync, and agreed to pay him $100,000 a month for his services. The idea was that Martin would negotiate other fees when the plan was up and running. It was clear to the consultant that this gig was going to be a financial bonanza.

Some of the money for his new scheme, Marty told Martin, would come from European investors. And since the Catholic Church also was involved, a European bank was needed to hold funds and to verify the sources of money.

The truth was that the "European money" would be coming from Marty's own Swiss bank account. And, although Larry Martin did not know it, Marty had become obsessed with the need for additional overseas banks for his funds. Not only was he slowly growing afraid that Banque SCS Alliance was not confidential enough, but also he had begun to think that down the line he'd need some sort of international escape plan.

With the European flavor of the plan in mind, Martin decided to bring in Thomas F. Quinn to help out. Quinn, who was also one of Tom Corbally's shadier associates, had been convicted of securities crimes both in the United States and abroad. Corbally also used him as a source at Kroll. When in the States he lived in rented houses in Westchester County and Connecticut. Once, when a house he was renting in Salem, New York, burned down, he had moved in briefly with Martin. In New York, he stayed at the Delmonico, Corbally's Manhattan haunt. But he spent much of his time on the Côte d'Azur, on the hills above Cannes and the Mediterranean. The town where he lived, Mougins, was once the home of Pablo Picasso and was made famous by the sojourn of the exiled Haitian dictator, Jean-Claude "Baby Doc" Duvalier. Quinn had a sumptuous villa on a hilltop—the better, a former U.S. federal agent once joked, to see enemies if they came his way.

Quinn had plenty of enemies, many if not most of whom were government officials in the United States and France. Embarking on a series of illegal schemes after he graduated from law school in the early 1960s, within a dozen years he had been disbarred as a lawyer and banned from the securities industry, and had served a federal prison sentence for securities fraud. SEC and FBI officials considered him to be mob connected. In the 1980s he ran a boiler room stockbrokerage, which sold about $500 million in worthless stock to investors in some twenty countries. Quinn was sentenced in 1991 to four years in jail in France, and in the United States he was ordered in 1994 to disgorge $25.9 million in illegal profits in an SEC case involving the sale of stock in two companies. Hence his habit of renting rather than owning houses in the United States.

Martin knew, of course, that Quinn had had his share of troubles. But he also had been told that Jules Kroll was prepared to write a letter saying that Quinn was a reformed man. Quinn was a very smart guy, Martin believed; he later told a confidant that he believed Quinn would be able to spot anything in the operation that didn't look legit.

Martin told Marty that Quinn was "retired," and largely left it up to

Corbally to tell him about the ex-con's background. When Marty asked Corbally whether he knew Quinn, Corbally responded that he'd known him for twenty-five years. "He's very smart. I trust him," Corbally told Frankel, admitting, however, that Quinn had had some "problems." Marty asked whether Quinn had ever been arrested or been in jail and Corbally told him as much about his friend's legal problems as he knew. At the present time, Corbally said, he didn't believe that Quinn was up to anything. Marty was intrigued and voiced no objections to Quinn coming aboard.

Like Corbally, Larry Martin had no particular knowledge of insurance, but unlike Corbally he knew some insurance consultants. He proceeded to put a team in place. Most of Martin's contacts came through a friend, who put him in touch with Larry Brotzge, an insurance consultant. Brotzge had worked for Providian Corporation, a large financial services company acquired by a Dutch firm in 1997, and for the accounting firm that eventually became known as Ernst & Young.

Martin convened an organizational meeting at the Trump International Hotel, in a private suite complete with a dining room and spectacular views of Manhattan. Everything was first class. A meal was sent up from Jean Georges, the exclusive Manhattan restaurant downstairs that Kaethe favored. Corbally called down to the maître d' to complain that one waiter was not enough. He was so agitated he spilled his cola all over himself. When he calmed down, he entertained the group with stories about Roy Cohn, and how Cohn was so close to the Vatican that he knew who was going to be appointed archbishop of New York before the city's mayor did.

He called the man they knew as "Rosse" "the next George Soros . . . an investment guru." Quinn sat by quietly. He was cordial, very confident, and very polished, but the other consultants were not sure what he was doing there.

Late in the evening, about ten, the consultants rang up Marty and put him on the speaker phone. It seemed to some in the room that Larry Martin badly wanted to impress his new boss. Marty implied that he was still at his desk working. He explained that he could earn 18 percent a year trading U.S. Treasury bonds and that he wanted to acquire insurance companies so that he could manage their assets. "I've been trying to buy insurance companies for years," he complained to the group over the speaker phone. "Everybody tells me they're going to make it happen. Go make it happen."

The next day, Larry Martin, Larry Brotzge, and Corbally lunched at Harry Cipriani. Father Jacobs was dining two tables away, and Corbally introduced him to the group.

Before returning to Pennsylvania, where he lived, Brotzge made some important arrangements for the new venture. First he made the proper introductions so that Larry Martin could retain LeBoeuf, Lamb, Greene & MacRae, a prominent New York law firm known for its insurance work. Briefly, a LeBoeuf lawyer spoke on the phone with Marty. With Brotzge vouching for him, Martin also retained Ernst & Young as the group's accountants.

For a short time, Marty's new operation was referred to as Opportunity Fund # 1, but soon it was renamed American Life Acquisitions, and preliminary incorporation papers were filed in Delaware on a date that he deemed astrologically correct. Within Marty's circle, the organization was simply called ALA.

Over the phone, Marty told Hackney that ALA would help acquire insurance companies. Hackney thought the whole thing sounded silly and superfluous. Marty was a Jew, he pointed out, who had recently gotten involved in the Catholic Church. "Now you got Allah involved in this whole mess," he said.

Brotzge and John Yednock, another consultant Martin brought on board, began drafting a business plan with input from Martin and others. "The Fund's principal objective is to provide its investors with superior financial returns through active management of financial assets," the draft stated. "Insurance companies generally have a stable pool of financial assets with predictable cash flows . . . The Fund intends to raise $1 billion in 1999 and acquire up to $10 billion in assets during this year. The Fund intends to raise additional funds in the next several years and acquire additional assets of up to $50 billion over the next five years."

"The Fund consists of a general partner and a number of limited partners. The limited partners are required to invest a minimum of $25 million each. . . . A substantial number of investors have already been identified by the Fund's management group," the document stated.

Who these investors were remained murky. ALA listed as references the Jupiter Fund; "David Rosse" as president; Karen Timmins as vice president and treasurer; LeBoeuf, Lamb, Greene & MacRae; and Ernst & Young. Attached to the draft was a missive, obviously written by Marty, entitled "Franklin American Bond Portfolio Outperforms the Number One Public Bond Fund for the Five-Year Period Ending December 1997." There was also a statement from Franklin American's auditors, which of course, was based at least in part on phony information about Marty's "trades."

The analysis of Franklin American Life Insurance Company's investment returns showed that in the nine months ending on September 30, 1998, the company had realized a 20.31 percent return on its portfolio, a gain of over $12 million. The value of the portfolio, which represented just a portion of the funds under Marty's management, was $59 million.

That the gains were all a fiction necessitated by his "trading block" did not mitigate a rapidly approaching problem: taxes.

Marty's insurance companies were going to have to pay taxes on non-existent gains, and the very thought pained him. There was, however, a legal remedy, and that was to buy the losses of another insurer along with the "book of business," or bundle of policies, that went along with it.

Hackney and Atnip didn't have much experience with such transactions, but with ALA in place, Marty now had the right expertise on hand. With the help of his consultants, he completed a tax-driven reinsurance deal at the end of 1998.

The consultant John Yednock flew to New York from Chicago on November 19, 1998, where he met members of Marty's team to discuss the tax issue. Larry Martin was obviously in control, but he kept asking for Quinn's opinion, even passing him Yednock's résumé for review. Yednock's first impression was that Quinn could have been cast as the Godfather. At first he thought that Quinn was Larry Martin's lawyer, but then he decided that maybe Quinn was an investor.

The initial plan was that three of Marty's companies would buy a total of $25 million in losses from Cologne Re, a reinsurer. But the amount of losses that Marty's companies could utilize for tax purposes kept dropping as negotiations proceeded. In part this was because Yednock kept getting conflicting numbers from Hackney and his chief lieutenant and accountant, Gary Atnip. Yednock would call with what he considered to be run-of-the-mill questions, such as "What's your capital gain so far this year?" and Atnip would not have a ready answer. "It just boggled my mind. It was pretty basic stuff I felt he should know," Yednock said later.

To Yednock, who had worked at the United Insurance Company of America in Chicago, and the LeBoeuf, Lamb lawyers, the deal was pretty routine. But Hackney and Atnip didn't like the very idea of it. They didn't like this Northern incursion into their territory. And they kept trying to derail it. Whenever he hit a roadblock with the two executives in Franklin, Yednock called Larry Martin for help. Larry Martin, in turn, would call Marty, who would then yell at Hackney to cooperate.

Sometimes when problems erupted there would be a conference call between Marty, Larry Martin, Yednock, Hackney, and Atnip. The calls started out calmly, with the deal being discussed in rational terms. But things usually got out of hand quickly and Marty would end up screaming at the top of his lungs, over fairly mundane business issues.

The taxable losses his companies would acquire kept shrinking as their needs were reevaluated. Finally, the amount of taxable losses stabilized at $11.6 million. The fee Marty would pay had been fixed at $850,000, so he felt he was getting less for his money. And he was.

People were trying to rip him off or "screw him," he constantly complained. They didn't believe what he was doing, he ranted. He was successful, he insisted, pointing to the growing portfolios of his companies. "That's proof! Warren Buffett would wish he was doing that well," he screamed.

For Yednock, who had never met Marty, the ranting came out of left field. "Don't worry about it. That's just the way he is," Larry Martin told a slightly shell-shocked Yednock after his first dose of Marty over the phone. Explaining that their boss was a hermit, he added, "He doesn't know how to deal with people and so when he gets going he doesn't know when to shut up." That much was already crystal clear to Yednock. He stuck with the job, but he and Brotzge would occasionally compare notes and try to figure out how Marty fit into the whole ALA/Thunor scheme. They knew he was the insurer's asset manager. And Larry Martin had told Brotzge that Marty, or "Rosse" as they knew him, managed Vatican money. But they also theorized that perhaps he was the head of the Thunor Trust, or had some role in it. Why else would everyone be taking orders from him? Why else would Hackney listen to no one but him?

Even after the details of the transaction were hammered out, Marty spent several weeks mired in a near hysterical state of procrastination, trying to decide whether he wanted to sign the contract. The deal—which, being tax driven, had to be completed before the end of 1998—finally closed at three P.M. on New Year's Eve.

About six weeks later, after Hackney and Atnip determined that they needed only $6.2 million in losses to offset taxable gains, Yednock was instructed to try to renegotiate. But nobody could figure out a way to revamp the deal retroactively and the idea was scuttled.

Meanwhile, as the ALA team began scouting for acquisitions, the tension between them and Hackney and Atnip escalated, especially when, on occasion, ALA looked at a company Hackney and Atnip had already considered and rejected. At one point, Brotzge told Hackney, "I don't work for you. I work for Larry Martin. I take my orders from him." For Hackney, a line had been drawn in the sand. By early 1999, he was determined to oppose almost anything the rival team suggested.

Yednock, Brotzge, and other ALA consultants were singularly unimpressed with Hackney and his colleagues in Franklin, and they reported their appraisals to Larry Martin. Without, apparently, telling Marty, Larry Martin asked Yednock to investigate how much money Hackney and Atnip made. He had a theory that Marty didn't realize how much the duo was taking out of the organization. But Yednock was not able to dig up any real dirt for Larry Martin to use against them.

However, Martin did tell Marty in no uncertain terms that he and the other consultants didn't think Hackney knew much about running insurance companies. Hackney should be replaced by a professional, he told Marty. The financier told Martin that he would put someone other than Hackney at the helm of the companies ALA acquired. But although he said he wasn't very happy with his longtime associate, he made no promise to get rid of him.

A seasoned executive might have kept Martin's complaints to himself while he mulled over his sticky management problems. Marty simply fanned the flames between his dueling associates by telling Hackney what Larry Martin had said.

"I've heard you really should have someone who is a lawyer be president of an insurance company," Marty told Hackney over the phone.

"Where'd you hear that—Larry Martin?" Hackney snapped.

It was not the only war being waged in Marty's world. Kaethe and Corbally, once fast friends, were now barely speaking. The lilt in Corbally's voice whenever he mentioned Kaethe was gone. Within the gossip network of the Greenwich mansion, there was much talk that Kaethe felt her position threatened by Corbally's rise in the boss's esteem. The more power Corbally grabbed, they reasoned, the less important Kaethe became.

Corbally worked at solidifying his vague position in Marty's empire. Worried about being edged out by Larry Martin, ostensibly his friend, he attended many meetings on subjects he had no interest in and could barely understand. His goal was simply to stand his ground when a deal eventually was made and the big bucks were finally handed out.

With a keen sense of how to exploit Marty's vulnerabilities, he began to chat with the financier about his security needs. He couldn't have timed it better. Fresh from his recent brush with Schulte, Marty was increasingly worried about just how impregnable his compound was. Egged on by Corbally, he decided to call in consultants to check it out.

The firm he chose, at Corbally's suggestion, Decision Strategies, was the archrival of Kroll Associates; having been snubbed by his old firm, Corbally was more than happy to send business to a competitor, especially one that had become a haven for other Kroll defectors over the years.

It was not a big job. For roughly $50,000, Decision Strategies, officially DSFX Inc., took a fairly routine look at Marty's security and made some recommendations. But Marty told a neighbor, who had complained about the large number of cars and gun-toting guards in the family neighborhood, that he had hired Decision Strategies to take control of his security. Someone identifying himself as working for Fairfax International, which had recently merged with Decision Strategies, even called the neighbor to allay his fears. They'd had Marty checked out, the person explained, and found he "was a very legitimate guy." He promised to make sure that in the future, the security would be "undetectable."

Getting wind of Corbally's maneuvering, Kaethe sought to undermine him. She and the real David Rosse had never been pals—Rosse thought Horse Face was bad news, and he believed her drinking would somehow lead to trouble for Marty—so he was astonished when Kaethe warned him of Corbally's incursion into his territory, the security of the house. "You better be careful," she told him. "Corbally's really working to get rid of you."

Ultimately Kaethe prevailed over Corbally, and David Rosse kept his job. The truth was that Marty probably could not have fired Rosse anyway, since he was integral to the movement of traveler's checks and knew some of Marty's most alarming secrets. In the end Marty fired Decision Strategies, explaining that he was doing so at Rosse's insistence.

Kaethe's next attempt to banish her rival for influence in the Frankel household was more aggressive: she tried to convince Marty that Corbally was abusing his generosity and costing him too much money. Certainly, Corbally was exquisitely high maintenance. He, Quinn, and Martin went flying off to Europe on a regular basis, supposedly on ALA business. Kaethe, the keeper of the clan's American Express account, knew the cost of these jaunts; the statements she read were dotted with $9,000-plus charges for Corbally's Concorde flights.

Behind closed doors, she confronted Marty with tales of Corbally's extravagance but, although he listened, he refused to cap Corbally's expenses. Her angry response was to cancel Corbally's credit card. Corbally appealed to Marty, and his traveling privileges were reinstated.

For Kaethe, it was a severe loss of face, one that she would not forget, and her relationship with Marty remained shaky for months to come.

Chapter Eleven

A Credibility Gap

The stack of binders that landed on John Hackney's desk in Franklin, Tennessee, sent the usually easygoing insurance executive into a fit of near apoplexy. The package, of course, came from Marty, and it was a color photo of the Pope, Father Jacobs, and the priest's elderly mother that drove Hackney absolutely wild.

The photo adorned the cover of a binder entitled "Father Peter Jacobs Information Package." Inside, the caption of another photo read, "Father Jacobs' mother leaving the papal apartments after a two-hour meeting with Pope John Paul II, January 14, 1988. Pope John Paul II's Christmas tree is in the background." There was also a picture of "Father Jacobs with his good friend Walter Cronkite at Jackie Onassis' 50th birthday party," and a blurred picture of Father Jacobs with Princess Grace and Prince Rainier of Monaco. One of the other two binders featured a photo of Mother Teresa leading Pope John Paul II down some stairs as its cover shot.

In the midst of closing the deal with Cologne Re and getting ALA up and going, Marty was trying to orchestrate St. Francis's first acquisitions. Hackney, whom Marty had put on the board of the St. Francis of Assisi Foundation, to Serve and Help the Poor and Alleviate Suffering, thought the documents were so nutty that they'd put the kibosh on acquisitions pending in Colorado and Washington. He grabbed the phone to try to persuade Marty not to send the binders to anybody else.

"I need audited statements," Hackney sputtered on the phone to

Marty. "Bios of officers. They need audited statements. These things coming in my office, these pictures of Father Jacobs and the Pope, that's not even remotely businesslike. . . . It's not needed."

"I know what I'm doing. I know these people. I know how to set this up. You just do what I say!" Marty screamed back.

Hackney wasn't the only one who did a double-take when the documents arrived. "What the hell is this?" asked Kay Tatum, the Akin, Gump lawyer working on the acquisitions, when she received the packages by Federal Express. But she apparently failed to notice that the binder devoted to the St. Francis Foundation included the phony document that Marty had crafted—listing Walter Cronkite and Lee Iacocca as advisory board members—under her own name as author. (Marty had attempted to mimic real Akin, Gump documents.)

"The Saint Francis of Assisi Foundation was founded in the Vatican by Monitor Ecclesiasticus Foundation to help fulfill the ideas of Saint Francis of Assisi, by giving aid to world charities," Marty had written in something called an "Acquisition Business Outline and Mission Statement." He referred to Monitor Ecclesiasticus as "a Vatican foundation," which was not true, rambled on about a plan to acquire and aid hospitals, and boasted, "Our companies can use the forces of the marketplace to aid in the search to cure disease. . . . As Archimides proclaimed, 'Give me a lever and I will move the world.' "

He expounded at length about the philosophy of Don Orione, touched on the career of Thomas Alva Edison, and loosely compared his insurance empire to Conseco, SunAmerica, and Aegon NV, three major players in the insurance world.

Marty had hoped that using St. Francis as an investment vehicle would allay the suspicions of regulators and executives. He'd hoped that he'd be able to snap up insurance companies quickly. But things were not going exactly as he'd planned. It turned out that the Catholic Church's involvement raised questions every time his people walked through a conference room door.

This was especially true of the two deals Marty wanted to make in late 1998 and early 1999. At first, Kay Tatum believed that John Hackney was her client when the Thunor companies tried to negotiate the $550,000 purchase of Capitol Life Insurance Company, a small, troubled insurer in Golden, Colorado. But then she was told by Marty that a Vatican-related foundation would replace the Thunor companies as the acquirer of Capitol Life.

The acquisition should have been fairly routine. But in November, things suddenly became complicated, and the snafu came from an unexpected source: the law firm Tatum had hired as local counsel in Denver. Alexander & Crabtree was to make regulatory filings with the state insurance department. In the process, partner Hugh Alexander decided he had to make routine inquiries into the identity of his client. He asked George Trapp, an investigator he worked with, to take a look. What Trapp found made Alexander a bit uncomfortable, to say the least. First, Trapp made some calls about Father Jacobs, who as St. Francis's president had signed the retention letter with Akin, Gump. The biographical material provided by Marty noted that Father Jacobs had presided over police department funerals in New York City, but when Trapp called the police chaplain's office, no one had heard of the priest.

The archdiocese in New York, Trapp's next call, did indeed remember Father Jacobs. Unofficially Trapp was told that he was something of a con artist. Even odder was an address for a Father Peter Jacobs in Texas. Alexander presented this disturbing information to Kay Tatum, and she responded with a fax of a Vatican directory of church personnel, which listed Father Jacobs as a priest. (In fact, there was no evidence that Father Jacobs had been involved in any scam; it turned out that someone in Texas had "borrowed" his social security number without his knowledge.)

Still, the more Trapp looked the more worrisome questions he came up with. For one thing, he had trouble ascertaining to his own satisfaction that St. Francis was a real foundation or that it had been blessed by the Vatican. When Alexander pointed this out to Kay Tatum, a law firm in Tortola wrote a brief letter to Capitol Life's chairman saying that St. Francis existed in "good standing under the laws of the British Virgin Islands."

It made Alexander uneasy that the deal kept being altered, with the acquiring entity changing several times. At one point, something called American Service Corporation was going to be the purchaser. A statement from Prudential Securities showed that the company had a touch under $50 million in its account. But when Alexander checked back later, the money had vanished. He raised the question with Akin, Gump, which told him that since the acquiring entity was now the St. Francis Foundation, that money was being used for something else.

Then Alexander got a copy of a statement from something called Jupiter Capital Growth Fund Ltd., at which St. Francis supposedly had an account worth a touch more than $50 million. Unlike the Prudential statement, the one from Jupiter looked as if it might have been generated on a personal computer. Alexander asked his investigator to check further. Jupiter, according to the statement, had a Tortola address, and the account was in the name of the St. Francis of Assisi Foundation, "c/o Reverend Father Peter Jacobs, Center Line, Vatican City." (In reality, neither the foundation nor Father Jacobs had a Vatican address.)

Alexander and Trapp retained an investigator in the Virgin Islands who noted that the stamps affixed to the official papers documenting Jupiter's existence were postage stamps. Even though Alexander was told that sometimes postage stamps are used on documents in Tortola, he was still worried about whether the document—and the Jupiter Fund itself—were legitimate.

When Alexander told Tatum that he had brought in a private investigator to check out their own client, she was none too pleased, perhaps feeling that her role as primary counsel had been usurped. How dare he hire an investigator without telling her first? she demanded. In essence, she informed her co-counsel that his job was to make sure that signatures were in the right place on documents that needed to be filed locally.

Still, whenever Alexander raised an objection, she checked it out. The answers she came up with satisfied her that everything was all right with her clients. Certainly, they were a difficult bunch. Losing his temper and yelling about delays, Marty, using the name "Rosse," often tried to take control of the direction of the deal during conference calls. Tatum would admonish him to stop butting in, and remind him that if he was in fact in control, she would have to name him along with Hackney on the regulatory documents filed with the state of Colorado. Quickly he would back off, calm down, and say that Hackney was the expert on the insurance side of things. He was only a financial adviser.

It was usually Hackney who informed Tatum about changes in the deal; he confided to her that his relationship with Marty was deteriorating and that he was tired of dealing with the "financial adviser."

Working with Marty was so difficult that he was considering leaving his job.

During a tense conference call in November, Tatum told Marty about Alexander's burgeoning list of suspicions. Marty blew up. He was particularly irked at the notion that he was being investigated by his own counsel. After hanging up, an increasingly weary Tatum decided to take an additional step to allay her own growing concerns.

She decided to have Monsignor Colagiovanni sign an affidavit testifying to the source of St. Francis's funding. She drafted an affidavit for him to sign and faxed it to Marty. In his trading room, using his signature large type, Marty redrafted the affidavit:

"I hearby certify and confirm to you that Monitor Ecclesiasticus Foundation is the settlor of the Saint Francis of Assisi Foundation, to Serve and Help the Poor and Alleviate Suffering," the affidavit read. "The funds that the Monitor Ecclesiasticus Foundation has contributed to the Saint Francis Foundation for the purchase of the common stock of CLICO Acquisition Corporation [Capitol Life] have come from funds of the Holy See that are dedicated to use for investment for charitable purposes." It was signed Monsignor Emilio Colagiovanni, Vatican City.

Monsignor Colagiovanni was uneasy. After all, Monitor Ecclesiasticus so far had contributed no funds to St. Francis. And the Pope had given no money to Monitor Ecclesiasticus for Marty's charitable projects. And Monitor Ecclesiasticus was not based in Vatican City, but in Rome.

But Marty badly wanted Colagiovanni's signature at the bottom of that declaration. And he was very persuasive. He told Colagiovanni that as soon as he signed on the dotted line, the promised $5 million would be transferred to Monitor Ecclesiasticus' account. Colagiovanni took up his pen.

Shortly afterward Tatum received the signed affidavit back from Marty, with the words "Have a Nice Day" stamped across the top by the Greenwich mansion's fax machine.

After almost months of negotiations and changes in structure, it seemed the Colorado deal might finally close. In December 1998, at roughly the same time as Marty and Hackney were dealing with the Cologne Re tax deal, so-called Form A filings were made with the state of Colorado in preparation for the change of control of Capitol Life.

Alexander, however, still was plagued with doubts. Finally, he went over to the state offices and withdrew the Form A filing, holding up the deal yet again. Although Alexander refiled, Marty was furious about the delays. He screamed at Alexander during a raucous conference call, insisting that he was doing a lousy job. He, "Rosse," was ready to make a deal, but Alexander kept holding things up, making objections, he ranted, speaking very fast and very loud.

Alexander told him that he was quitting the assignment. And Marty answered that that was okay by him: he'd have someone from another Denver firm pick up the file. Alexander laughed when he realized that Marty had already lined up a firm to replace him. It was the last time the two men spoke.

State regulators and Capitol Life officials weren't sure who they were dealing with. They bombarded the prospective buyers with questions about who they were and where the money would be coming from. The answers were not altogether satisfactory. Finally, the team assembled for Marty bowed out of the deal. Executives at Capitol Life never received an explanation as to why.

By then, it was late December. The disappointment along with the stress of the Cologne Re deal sent Marty into a tailspin.

He had several insurance brokers scouting deals for him, and they had told him about a possible deal in Spokane, Washington. Although 1998 was drawing to a close and he had a lot going on, he pursued the Spokane matter with a vengeance. The company, Western United Life Assurance Company, a unit of Metropolitan Mortgage & Securities Company, had $886 million in assets, which Marty was eager to get his hands on to "trade."

Over the phone, Marty told officials of Western United that he was an investment counselor to the Vatican. He talked and talked, so much and so rapidly that those on the other end of the line got the impression that he didn't want to have to stop and answer any questions. He said he had met the Pope more than once, and left them with the impression that he, in his capacity as a Vatican adviser, would fund the Franklin insurance companies so that they could acquire Western United.

It sounded pretty convoluted, but C. Paul Sandifur, Jr., the president of Metropolitan Mortgage, agreed to a preliminary meeting, and Marty and Larry Martin were anxious to pounce on any opening. They decided that Yednock, the ALA consultant; Father Jacobs; and John Hackney should fly to Spokane immediately.

It was shortly before Christmas, and when Marty called Hackney, the insurance executive balked. First off, he said, Franklin American was not interested in buying Western United. His understanding was that Metropolitan Mortgage wanted $90 to $100 million for the insurer, but he thought it was worth only about $70 or $80 million. Marty didn't care. He was willing to pay more because he could make up the difference by trading, he said.

The reasons for Hackney's reluctance went way beyond the business at hand. He was growing frustrated with Marty, and was furious that his boss wanted him to fly to the West Coast at Christmastime, when he wanted to focus on his family and the frenetic social scene in Franklin. "It's the holidays," he told Marty. "People aren't doing stuff."

Marty's retort was that he and Larry Martin had talked about that. They believed that if Christian people would simply work during the holidays and "not waste all your time," everyone would get more done and make more money, Marty explained, angering Hackney further by bringing his nemesis into the discussion.

Reluctantly, Hackney tried to book a flight, but couldn't get one that would reach Spokane on time. At Marty's insistence he chartered a plane, boarding at about three A.M. to make it to the meeting.

Yednock also was called at the last minute, by Larry Martin. His marching orders were to act as Father Jacobs's adviser since the priest knew nothing about insurance. He was assured that Hackney, with whom he had clashed on the Cologne Re deal, would not be there. He got on a plane the next day and flew to Spokane, traveling first class.

In Spokane he was surprised to find Hackney. Yednock thought that Hackney tried hard to be pleasant at the meeting but was considerably cooler when they were alone. Father Jacobs, meanwhile, provided the entertainment. He told Yednock, Hackney, and several executives from Metropolitan Mortgage stories from his life, managing to drop the names of Walter Cronkite and Lee Iacocca along the way. He passed around pictures of himself with several popes and Mother Teresa. In between, he took calls on his cell phone.

Sandifur of Metropolitan seemed less interested in Father Jacobs's life story than in where, exactly, the money to buy his company was going to come from. He wanted to assure himself that St. Francis was legit. Why, he wanted to know, was St. Francis going to be involved in the purchase, instead of the Thunor insurance companies on their own?

The meeting lasted only a few hours. Yednock returned to Chicago, and Hackney got back on the chartered plane waiting to return him to Nashville and his holiday festivities.

Before negotiating any further, Sandifur wrote a letter to the Vatican, asking seven simple questions and inquiring about St. Francis. The answer was alarming at best. A Vatican official, Archbishop Giovanni Battista Re, sent a cryptic, one-sentence note: "No such foundation has the approval of the Holy See or exists in the Vatican." Sandifur called Marty and confronted him with this news.

Marty sounded relaxed. In a conference call, he told Sandifur and other Metropolitan Mortgage executives not to worry: of course the Vatican wasn't going to say anything in writing about St. Francis, he explained, because the Vatican didn't want anyone to know how much money it had. The best way to ascertain the truth about St. Francis, Marty confidently told the group, was to travel to Rome and meet people directly.

Kay Tatum had been brought into the Western United deal only when it was already being negotiated. When she heard about the letter Sandifur had received from the Vatican she grew worried and called John Hackney, who also seemed disturbed. She had a talk with Marty, too, to try to straighten out the confusion about St. Francis, and now she realized that there clearly had been errors in the affidavit Monsignor Colagiovanni had signed.

She drafted a new one and faxed it to Greenwich, with the intention of sending the revised affidavit to Lynn Ciani, a staff lawyer for Metropolitan Mortgage. "David," she wrote, "If possible, I would like to be able to fax Monsignor Colagiovanni's directly to him and have him fax it back to me directly so I would have a record to show Ms. Ciani that I sent this to a number that could be verified as a Vatican number. I think that would help her get over the issues that she has. Thank you for your help."

But a fax to the Vatican was problematic because Marty had summoned Colagiovanni and Bolan to Greenwich for a meeting that lasted some four and a half hours. Recently, Bolan had received a disturbing letter from Colagiovanni, who had enclosed his first affidavit and spelled out the circumstances under which he had signed it. Despite his promises, Marty still had not coughed up the $5 million, and Colagiovanni pleaded with Bolan to exercise his "persuading softness in dealing with Mr. D ["David Rosse"]. May I ask that at least this amount be transferred so that from one side we can go on in implementing the program of the M.E. [Monitor Ecclesiasticus] . . . and from another side my declarations . . . that are really worrying us, could be partially remedied."

But what struck Bolan was just how misleading the affidavit was. He told Colagiovanni that he should find a way to fix the problem. But Colagiovanni worried about revealing the names of individual donors to the Church, which might violate Vatican rules. On the day of the threesome's meeting in Greenwich, while Bolan was not present, Marty asked Monsignor Colagiovanni to sign the new affidavit. He explained that this was necessary so that he could make his contributions to St. Francis anonymously, which was of paramount importance to him. Despite his own reservations about his "declarations," the monsignor agreed to sign, and Marty sent the document off to Tatum.

> *I hearby certify and confirm to you that MEF [Monitor Ecclesiasticus] is the grantor of funds to The Saint Francis of Assisi Foundation, to Serve and Help the Poor and Alleviate Suffering, a British Virgin Islands trust. . . . MEF has contributed approximately $1,000,000,000 (One Billion Dollars) to The Saint Francis Foundation since the creation of The Saint Francis Foundation on August 10, 1998. Such funds were received by MEF from various Roman Catholic tribunals and Roman Catholic charitable and cultural institutions for MEF's charitable purposes. These funds have been donated by MEF for use by The Saint Francis Foundation for The Saint Francis Foundation's charitable purposes.*

The truth was, of course, that the $1 billion did not exist. And the $50 million that Marty had promised to use to buy insurance companies for St. Francis appeared to have hopscotched from the Prudential account to the Jupiter account and had, for the moment, dropped out of the picture. In any case, that money actually belonged to Thunor Trust's insurance companies.

Less than two weeks later, Sandifur and a small contingent of Metropolitan Mortgage representatives flew to Rome, just as Marty had suggested. Monsignor Colagiovanni, who had flown back to Rome from his meeting in Greenwich, received them at the Vatican, and did his best to explain his and St. Francis's interest in buying U.S. insurance companies. The meeting apparently got the deal back on track—albeit not on a fast track—and the two sides continued talking for months to come, until the proposed deal came to the attention of a skeptical regulator the following spring.

In the wake of the Sandifur debacle, Bolan was again dispatched to Rome to meet with Vatican officials and ensure that no other potential sellers of insurance companies were put off by representatives of the Holy See. Scheduled to meet with Deputy Secretary of State Archbishop Giovanni Battista Re, Bolan met instead with Archbishop Agostino Cacciavillan, the president of the Administration of the Patrimony of the Holy See, which is in charge of Vatican investments. Cacciavillan received Bolan and Colagiovanni graciously and then gossiped at some length in Italian with the monsignor, with whom he seemed quite friendly. Then the archbishop suggested that there would be no further problems so long as St. Francis was not identified as a Vatican foundation.

As it became clear that the Metropolitan acquisition was not going to happen nearly as quickly as he'd hoped, Marty's interest in it began to flag. For one thing, John Hackney continued to lobby against it. He thought it was impractical for a company based in Franklin, Tennessee, to try to absorb a firm more than half a continent away. And he was dead set against almost anything that Larry Martin was for.

But also, Marty was increasingly distracted by more disturbing developments that began to confront him as he sat before his bank of computers in Greenwich. Suddenly, state regulators in Mississippi and Tennessee began to ask questions about his insurance companies. And those questions were not so easily answered or deflected.

Chapter Twelve

Unmasked in Greenwich

It was only a fender bender, but when a lady from an escort service hit a car in the cul-de-sac outside the Greenwich mansion, Marty's neighbors decided it was time to bring in outside help.

Eight eighty-nine Lake Avenue had other problems, of course. The guards with guns, the deliveries at all hours of the day and night, the dozen or so cars that were parked outside each day—the neighbors hated it all. Their kids, they feared, were at risk.

On a weekend in late 1998, three well-heeled neighbors met with two representatives from Sutton Associates, a small investigation firm based in Jericho, New York, run by former FBI agents. The neighbors talked about their neighbor, "Mike King," and the havoc he'd brought to the once-genteel neighborhood. They were worried about drugs, money laundering, and worse.

The case was taken by Michael Henehan, a Sutton vice president and twenty-five-year veteran of the FBI. For Henehan, it was a small matter, one his firm agreed to handle as an accommodation to an individual connected to one of the firm's lucrative corporate accounts. His mission: to dispose of the case quickly, without generating big bills.

Henehan started by collecting bits and pieces of information from people who lived in the neighborhood. One person had scribbled down the number of an Ohio license plate on a car once parked in the driveway. The car had been rented in the name of Leon Frankel. "King" had mentioned to someone else in the neighborhood that his father was a judge. It didn't take a lot of digging for Henehan to figure out that the man whose name was on the rental agreement for the car had been a court referee in Ohio. That was close enough to a judge, and Henehan knew he had picked up the scent.

Another neighbor had once heard a member of "King" 's household call him "Marty." Henehan talked to the angry landlord of a house "King" had rented nearby, before he bought the second residence for his women. It turned out he had left some papers behind when he'd moved out. They showed that "King" had accounts with the New York Stock Exchange, Dow Jones, and Telerate.

Sitting in his small office in New Jersey, Henehan did a computer search of media reports from Ohio. He found an article from April 24, 1993, headlined "Exonerated Stockbroker Seeks Custody." It was about John Schulte's quest to win his kids from Sonia, and the article mentioned that Schulte believed his wife was living with "former Toledo stockbroker Martin Frankel."

Henehan called some of the firms with which Marty had accounts. Then he did a database search and found that Martin Frankel of Toledo, Ohio, had been barred from the securities business. He also found out that Marty had told the detectives who investigated Frances Burge's suicide that he did "all the buying and selling for a Swiss bank."

Henehan realized that Marty had gone right back into business. When he called John Schulte, he found a man happy to confirm much of what he'd learned.

There was, of course, the question of what to do with all this information. Henehan attacked on several fronts. He got in touch with the SEC, but officials there didn't seem ready to jump on the problem. "The SEC seems overburdened, slow to react, and not overly enthusiastic," Henehan wrote in a report to his clients. "Prospect for decisive and effective action in this matter: Unlikely."

Officials of the New York Stock Exchange were "understanding and sympathetic," he wrote, but "no effective action will be forthcoming in their part." He noted that the NYSE would cooperate with other investigations.

Henehan talked to a zoning enforcement officer in Greenwich, explaining that it looked as though business was being conducted on a property zoned for residential use. The official, James F. Maloney, was sympathetic but noted that there was a feeling of permissiveness about home offices. He suggested that the neighbors call his office and complain anonymously about any construction being done on the property, and that he might be able to take some action if Marty's work permits were not in order.

The only significant interest in the matter came from Kari Pedersen, an assistant U.S. attorney in Connecticut, who asked an IRS investigator to look into the matter. Henehan told the investigator, from the IRS's Criminal Investigation division, that an IRS office in Ohio had been investigating Marty and Sonia but had lost track of them.

Henehan pretty much had cracked the case. He had Marty Frankel's name—his real one. He knew that he'd been banned from the securities industry and he'd figured out that Marty now was breaking the law.

It had taken him all of twenty-nine hours to figure it out.

As Ms. Pedersen and the IRS pursued the matter, the neighbors discussed whether they should report Marty to the zoning department. That option made Henehan uneasy. In his report to his clients, he wrote that "Frankel and his cult . . . have established a psychological if not physical stranglehold on the cul-de-sac." He told his clients that Marty would figure out who'd ratted him out even if the neighbors made the calls anonymously. The neighbors worried that Marty might be dangerous, and Henehan suggested they weight the consequences carefully.

"This is a strange guy," he told them. "I will not predict for you what he'll do if you upset his little world." Some of the people who worked for Marty, he added, "might be a little on the rough side."

Marty's neighbors decided to wait and see what the IRS turned up.

Chapter Thirteen

Trouble

When midnight struck on New Year's Eve, Marty Frankel was cavorting with a woman named Nancy Sue, a playmate he'd recruited through one of his personal advertisements. When he wasn't busy in bed, he checked in with Sonia and Tom Corbally by phone, and on Saturday night, January 2, 1999, he hosted an intimate dinner party for a mishmash of old and new lovers. Attending were Oksana and her mother and grandmother, whom Marty had helped bring over from Russia. Kaethe was there with Alfredo Fausti, who was anxious to sell Marty on an investment in Italy. Nancy Sue joined the fun as well.

Marty knew that 1999 was going to be a make-or-break year for his business empire. It had never been more vulnerable. He knew it had to get bigger or it would fall apart. But most of his immediate problems centered on two nerdy visitors who had been sitting in the offices of Franklin American for several months. They were state insurance examiners, one from Tennessee and the other from Mississippi, and they were doing routine, albeit lengthy, examinations of the books for the companies domiciled in their states.

The more tiresome of the two, from John Hackney and Marty Frankel's point of view, was Billy Lovelady, on the job for Tennessee. Poring through column after column of numbers, Lovelady had found a problem. He was having a hard time verifying the company's assets held by Liberty National Securities, Marty's "brokerage firm," which handled all of the Thunor companies' investments. And Liberty National itself was a problem, in Lovelady's eyes, because according to Tennessee law,

broker-dealers could not hold securities owned by insurance companies. That meant, according to the arcane state regulations, that Franklin
American's assets could not be officially recognized by Tennessee's insurance commissioner.

And that led to yet another sticky problem. If those assets were not included in Lovelady's audit, the company would have to be considered
insolvent. What made the situation even worse, if that was possible,
was that Lovelady had alerted Mississippi's examiner to the issue. Mississippi's rules were a little more flexible, but he'd begun to ask questions, too.

Lovelady ordered Hackney to put the Franklin American Life Insurance assets in a real bank, and Hackney passed that troubling message on
to Marty. He was not happy with the news but dutifully wire-transferred
$69 million to the Prudential Savings Bank in Atlanta, Georgia.

The money couldn't stay there forever. Marty had ripped through a
fortune of over $100 million in insurance company assets. He'd paid for
houses in Greenwich. He'd treated numerous women to plane flights
around the world. He'd paid their rents. He had a staff to meet his every
need and a security detail fit for a head of state. And then there were
Corbally, Martin, Quinn, and a raft of other consultants and insurance
brokers whom he had to keep happy for fear they would alert law enforcement to whatever suspicions they had. While these expenses didn't
seem very hefty for a man of tremendous means, they had certainly
taken a big chunk out of the Thunor companies' assets over the years,
and there wasn't a lot of new money coming in the door.

Marty's new plan was for St. Francis to buy his existing insurance empire, or at least for the foundation to become a "grantor" or investor in
the Thunor Trust. That, he felt, would take some of the heat off. After all,
his thinking went, who would dare question the credibility of Monsignor Colagiovanni and Father Jacobs, two elderly priests who seemed
so anxious to do good deeds and who told such charming old stories?

He still hoped that he would eventually gain more solid backing from
the Church. Marty talked of wanting what he called "a Pope letter," documenting, somehow, the pontiff's support. To curry favor with the folks
in the Vatican, he was trying to help facilitate a trip by Pope John Paul to
Russia, something the Pontiff badly wanted. The problem was that the
Russian Orthodox Church opposed any papal visit. Marty put his Swiss

banker, Jean-Marie Wery, on the case. Wery knew the mayor of Moscow, who in turn, was owed a big favor by a Russian Orthodox archbishop. Meanwhile, through Father Jacobs, Marty met a mysterious former general, Gianalfonso D'Avossa, who was also anxious for the Pope to realize his dream. D'Avossa, who had resigned from the Italian army in 1996 amid corruption allegations, had Vatican ties and a home in St. Petersburg. On one end, D'Avossa worked with Marty's Swiss banker. On the other, he communicated with Cardinal Angelo Sodano, the Vatican's secretary of state, going so far as to tell him of "David Rosse" 's efforts on behalf of the Pope. But even though Marty seemed to be only a few degrees of separation from the Pope himself, his crusade resulted in little but frustration.

In early January 1999, Marty spent many nights without sleep preparing documentation for the proposed takeover and coming up with the information the insurance examiners wanted. During the day he talked on the phone and tracked the performance of various stocks, especially technology and Internet companies like Amazon.com, Yahoo!, eBay, Allegheny Technologies, and Intuit.

To deal with the examiners' questions and convince the states to allow St. Francis to take over Thunor, Marty knew he was going to need some special talent, people well connected in political circles, so that he could circumvent bureaucrats and go right to the top if things got uncomfortably hot. Hackney thought lobbyists were completely unnecessary. His attitude was, If Tennessee wants the money in a bank, then put the money in a bank. He'd always dealt with regulators himself, sometimes with lawyers at his side.

"You don't need all that heavyweight stuff going on here," Hackney told Marty over the phone. "You don't need that because we have solid little companies."

Marty, of course, knew otherwise. He certainly couldn't just put the money back. The trading gains were faked and much of the cash was gone. And he couldn't afford to rely on a country bumpkin like John Hackney to vanquish the regulators. So once again, Marty asked Larry Martin to intervene. With a little research he was able to pinpoint some high-powered lawyers and politically connected operators for Marty to hire.

The new campaign got off to a good start. Marty got a favorable opinion issued by George Dale, Mississippi's commissioner of insurance. The letter was only two sentences long.

"In reference to your letter of December 30, 1998, this will confirm that the Mississippi Insurance Department authorizes domestic insurance companies to trade securities in street name on an electronic basis at approved brokerage houses. Approval of the entries will be on an individual basis and must comply with NAIC [National Association of Insurance Commissioners] eligible investment standards and Department procedures."

What the letter essentially meant to Marty was that he could trade the assets of his insurance companies based in Mississippi. But it also gave the commissioner plenty of wiggle room if he changed his mind or didn't like the way Marty was doing business.

The Tennessee situation remained at an impasse, with the $69 million still stuck in the Atlanta bank. Marty hoped that the letter from Commissioner Dale would encourage the Tennessee insurance bigwigs to loosen up.

To make that happen, Marty and Larry Martin turned to Thurston Little, a controversial Mississippi businessman with a keen sense of the political landscapes in his own state as well as in Tennessee. Thurston Little had an unusual past. Principally a real estate developer, he had dabbled in politics for years. He'd been a close associate of the late Mississippi senator James O. Eastland, a noted segregationist, but in the 1980s became a big booster of the Reverend Jesse Jackson. Little had several other credits to his name. He had been indicted twice, convicted once on federal charges, and served a prison term.

Little introduced Larry Martin to a Tennessee lawyer with the connections to ease Marty's way in Tennessee. That lawyer was Harlan Mathews, who had been appointed by the state's governor to finish out Al Gore's Senate term when Gore was elected vice president. A longtime political player in Tennessee, he had served as the state's treasurer for many years. He had exactly the credibility Thurston Little knew Marty needed for the job.

Former senator Mathews had known Little for over twenty-five years, so when Little called and asked him to meet some prospective clients with serious money in their pockets he readily agreed. Little arrived in Mathew's office in Nashville with Larry Martin and Brad Dye, a former lieutenant governor of Mississippi, who now practiced law and represented Marty's interests in that state. They handed Mathews the letter from Commissioner Dale, and said they wanted to have a similar arrangement in Tennessee.

Mathews said he wanted some time to check things out. Officials at the insurance department gave him a favorable report on the Franklin American family of companies. Franklin American's assets were growing and the department was generally pleased that a company that had once been so troubled was faring so nicely. The only thing that puzzled the folks at the department was how Franklin American was able to earn the kind of investment returns it was reporting. But in general, they told Mathews, the department was reluctant to do anything that would put a crimp in that kind of growth.

After talking with the department, Mathews set up another meeting with Larry Martin. This time, Martin brought along Thurston Little and Tom Quinn, the convicted securities fraudster. Martin explained that he and Mr. Quinn were consultants to Franklin American and that they worked for American Annuity and Life Acquisitions (the name seems to have been a variation on "American Life Acquisitions"). Mathews was particularly taken with Quinn, who was dressed with exquisite taste and looked like a Wall Street broker. To Mathews, he seemed like the "essence of success," charming, with a negotiator's gift for gab that set people at ease. Mathews really got the sense that he knew what he was talking about. Feeling comfortable with his new clients, he agreed to try to negotiate with the state insurance department on Franklin American's behalf.

With Mathews on board, Marty was much calmer. He had several erotic encounters with a woman named Debbie, who had flown down from Canada. For some reason, Marty was fearful about having sex with her, but in the days after the meeting with Harlan, when it looked as if the former senator might be the solution to his problems, Marty indulged himself a little. He spent hours at night watching her naked, and rubbing up against her genitals, although he insisted on wearing long underwear while he did it. A night later he watched Debbie perform oral sex on Oksana.

Marty's sense of comfort was short-lived. For one thing, Larry Martin learned that Marty had yet to pay the $850,000 fee he owed Cologne Re.

Perhaps more important, he hadn't paid Larry Martin's fee for the deal either. That fee was also $850,000, and however exorbitant it seemed, Marty had indeed promised to pay it if the tax-savings deal closed.

The situation was awkward, to say the least. As his negotiations with state regulators proceeded, he was relying on Larry Martin more and more. But meanwhile their relationship was growing increasingly tense as weeks went by and Larry Martin received no payment.

Marty paid Cologne Re, but he continued to procrastinate about paying Martin. By February they were out and out arguing. Exasperated, Larry Martin explained that he needed a minimum of $1 million a year to live on. If Marty didn't come up with the $850,000 soon, he said, he would have the Mississippi insurance commissioner rip up the crucial two-sentence letter allowing Liberty National Securities to hold on to the insurance assets.

"BLACKMAIL," Marty wrote in an astrological datebook he kept notes in. "He threatens to destroy me in MS. Wants 850K."

Corbally didn't completely understand the Cologne Re deal, but he was appalled that Marty seemed to be reneging on his agreements. After all, if he balked at those fees, he might ultimately refuse to pay Corbally as well.

"David," he reminded him, "you said you were going to do it."

"Tom," Marty answered, "you've got to understand. I have a psychological problem. I can't say no."

"Fuck," Corbally answered. "It's a fine time for me to hear this shit!"

Even John Hackney and Gary Atnip took Larry Martin's side. Marty told them both that Martin was stealing money from him and was not getting work done. But it was clear to both men on the other end of the line in Franklin that their boss was just trying to get out of paying what he owed his army of consultants.

"If you owe somebody money, just pay him," Hackney argued. "And if you don't like the way they're doing business, don't do business with them anymore."

"I'm not going to [pay]," Marty whined back. "He hasn't done anything."

"Pay the guy and tell him to go away," Hackney retorted.

That Larry Martin and his posse of consultants would disappear was a fervent hope of Hackney's, but he slowly realized it was never going to happen. For Hackney and Atnip, it was humiliating to have the ALA group running here and there trying to make insurance deals and throwing around the name Franklin American as if they owned it. Larry Martin and his team were making overtures to companies that Hackney had written off as poor acquisition candidates. They were talking to state officials without so much as a nod to the executive suite in Franklin. They would fly to Nashville on a private jet and not even drive the twenty or so minutes to Franklin for a courtesy call. Sometimes, Hackney didn't find out that Larry Martin had been on his turf until he was already gone.

For the first time, Hackney was really miserable in his job. He told Marty that he couldn't use Franklin American to buy any companies if Larry Martin ran the deal, but Larry Martin kept cropping up everywhere Hackney looked. Finally Ann Hackney, who knew very little about her husband's business, said, "You've got to get away from this guy." Even some of their friends thought the job was going to kill him, she told her husband.

"Ann, it's the only job I have right now," he wearily told her. "I gotta do it. I gotta take care of everybody."

But by early February 1999, Hackney and Atnip had had enough. As they fielded questions from the two examiners on site, it became increasingly clear to them that neither Tennessee or Mississippi was ultimately going to let insurance company assets remain in the control of a tiny, out-of-state brokerage firm they couldn't monitor properly. Hackney and Atnip both knew that their boss's only interest in the companies was trading their assets. If he couldn't do that, it made no sense for him to hold on to them.

In a conference call, Hackney and Atnip made it clear to Marty that they thought the companies should be sold. Hackney suggested that ALA buy the lot of them. The phone call ended without resolution.

Marty wasn't ready to jump at the suggestion that ALA buy the companies. These days, he wasn't all that high on the ALA contingent. Even aside from the fee dispute, other problems were percolating. Larry Martin had promised Marty that he would generate $100 million by February 2, but nothing had materialized. Although the ALA team looked into no fewer than twenty-five acquisition deals over time, none got past the preliminary stages.

Typical were the discussions with Grand Pacific Life Insurance Limited, a Honolulu company that oversaw $156 million in assets. Some of the ALA consultants thought Grand Pacific was a good bet, and a broker was dispatched to Hawaii with the message that his clients might be willing to shell out $30 million for the company. But James Fagan, Grand Pacific's president, was skeptical of the pitch. It was not completely clear who the buyer would be, although St. Francis was discussed as a possible investor and the broker mentioned that the Pope approved of St. Francis's investments in insurance companies.

But two issues kept Fagan from taking the proposal too seriously. For one, the emissaries—there were two over time—kept mentioning that they had private jets at their disposal. Amusing though he found that, Fagan saw it as a sign that the group courting him was a little too flashy. Flash didn't sit well with an executive who had toiled in small insurance companies his entire life. But more significant was the fact that when he asked to see the acquirer's financials, a reasonable request for a company being courted, nothing materialized.

The chartered jets and the lack of audited financial statements repeatedly appeared as obstacles as the ALA team crisscrossed the country trying to make deals. At one point, Larry Martin and his team decided to try to buy a brokerage firm or two because Marty thought he might need them to trade the burgeoning portfolios he expected to acquire. Such a purchase, of course, would have given him unlimited access to customer accounts.

One of the young consultants on ALA's team was David S. Wolfe, a broker who had until recently worked in Memphis and who was a longtime friend of Larry Martin. Wolfe suggested that Larry approach two small brokerage firms in Memphis, Carty & Company and Duncan-Williams. Wolfe, Martin and Quinn flew in on a private jet to see their senior executives.

The two executives they met with, Bill Carty of Carty & Company and James Pauline at Duncan-Williams, thought their visitors were an odd bunch. They were told that Quinn was a retired operations guy who had worked for brokerage firms, but nobody in Marty's group seemed to be asking the right kinds of questions. And the visitors seemed excessively slick. Jim Pauline suspected he was seeing what he called "Armani slippers" on one of his visitors' feet. Quinn's shirts, he thought, looked custom made. And everybody's watches seemed a little too expensive. A big limousine had picked the group up at the airport and they made sure Carty and Pauline understood that a Gulfstream jet was waiting to whisk them away again.

Pauline interpreted their message this way: "Tell us how much you want. We'll write out a check. We have deep pockets. We don't have to do a lot of due diligence." (Due diligence refers to checks done on prospective associates and signifies that one has entered into business arrangements with care.) He later joked, "The minute I met them I literally counted my fingers to make sure my fingers were all there."

Carty and Pauline sent the group back to their jet. If they wanted the talks to go further, the brokers said, they would have to see ALA's audited financial statements. The statements never arrived.

The lack of financial statements worried several of the ALA team, especially Yednock, Brotzge, and the lawyers at LeBoeuf, Lamb, who were used to doing business in a pretty traditional manner and knew it was unlikely that a deal actually would go through without such a statement. They kept pressing for one, and Brotzge, who worked out of his house in a Philadelphia suburb, began to feel like the not too welcome "voice of reality" in conference calls that sometimes included an increasingly short-tempered Marty.

"Damn it, I'm paying you," Marty said angrily during one of the phone calls. "You make it happen."

They kept trying.

When a block of insurance policies controlled by Provident American Corporation became available and Larry Martin heard about it, Brotzge agreed to open talks. He wasn't happy with what he found. The purchase would have put some $20 million in assets into Marty's coffers, but after some investigation Brotzge decided there were risks in the portfolio of policies that made the expected purchase price of $4 or $5 million too high. He though the price should be in the $1 million to $2 million range and, at Larry Martin's instructions, wrote a memo counseling against the deal. Within a day or two he heard from a livid Marty.

"Who the hell do you think you are?" he demanded. "I'm telling you to buy the company. I'm telling you it makes sense."

Brotzge was nonplussed. "Are you telling me to walk into the car dealership and pay sticker price for the car?" he asked incredulously.

At that, Marty hesitated. "No," he finally said.

"But you don't care if the price is a little high?" Brotzge asked, finally understanding where Marty was coming from.

"Exactly. Do it," Marty said.

After getting off the phone with Marty, Brotzge called Larry Martin. "David Rosse may be a great investor, but he has no business acumen whatsoever," he reported. "This guy's going to drive you crazy. If I were you I'd run away from him."

Provident American ended up taking the block of policies off the market, and Brotzge breathed a sigh of relief.

It was one of the last conversations Marty had with Larry Martin's contingent of consultants. Frustrated by not being paid, and fearful that the project was spiraling out of control, Larry Martin issued an edict: his consultants were not allowed to deal directly with the man they knew as "David Rosse."

"You guys work for me," Martin reminded them.

Soon after, Marty called Brotzge directly.

"I can't talk to you," Brotzge told him, explaining that Larry Martin had instructed him not to. Marty went ballistic, yelling uncontrollably.

"I'm paying you guys! What do you mean?" he shouted.

From Marty's perspective, Larry Martin simply had not earned the $850,000 fee they'd been bickering about for weeks. He still felt that the fee was blackmail, but he worried that until Martin was paid he would sabotage efforts to straighten out the difficulties in Mississippi and Tennessee.

"You are a liar!" Larry Martin screamed during one of their final negotiations, losing the cool with which he usually conducted business. Finally, he said he had to eat and abruptly got off the phone. But when Marty called back later, Larry Martin was still furious, and simply refused to talk to him.

On February 9, with Marty still holding out, the war between the two men grew even hotter. Marty had planned to appoint some of Larry Martin's team to the St. Francis board of directors. But that morning, Larry Martin's lawyer called to tell him he couldn't do it. To Marty, this seemed like an hostile act, meant to box him in and force him to pay the fee. He had wanted some insurance experts on the board to forestall questions from regulators when St. Francis took control of the Thunor-owned companies.

For almost two hours that morning, Hackney and Atnip tried again to convince the nearly hysterical Marty that he should simply pay Larry Martin and move on. Finally, at around noon, Marty ordered a wire transfer from his accounts at Banque SCS to Martin. Shortly afterward, he got a call from Hackney that provided the first comfort of the day. A letter had arrived from the Tennessee insurance department. The commissioner had decided to allow Franklin to continue to keep its assets at Liberty National Securities. Marty was greatly relieved. "Crisis Over," he wrote in his astrological appointment calendar.

But there was a dark side to the good news. When Thurston Little called later in the day to discuss the victory he'd helped achieve, he told Marty that Tom Quinn had wanted him to try to "hold back" the letter. For Thurston Little, working from his base in Mississippi, the meaning of that might have been obscure. But for Marty Frankel, the message was crystal clear: Larry Martin and Tom Quinn had been prepared to prevent Tennessee from giving Marty the relief he needed until he shelled out the $850,000. It was an ominous warning that the duo was prepared to play some pretty hard ball, and Marty took it seriously. He was scared.

The truth was that Marty's relief over the Tennessee letter was premature. Though it did indeed allow Franklin to trade its securities, the state insurance department extended the company's right to do so for only another sixty days. During that period, the letter noted, the department would study proposals by former senator Mathews and Tom Quinn to remedy the company's noncompliance with state regulations. Two of the proposals under consideration were that the commissioner would change the rules and that Franklin American simply would move to a more hospitable state.

Douglas Sizemore, the Tennessee insurance commissioner, had agreed to draft the letter after a meeting attended by several insurance department staffers and Mathews, who'd pointed out that the department had allowed Franklin to handle securities as it liked for seven years without objections. But Sizemore agreed to the sixty-day extension mostly because he was favorably disposed toward the former senator and knew he was a highly respected man. He assumed that Senator

Mathews would have looked into Franklin American and its relationship with Liberty before taking on the insurer as a client.

For his part, Mathews felt he had no obligation to check out Liberty National Securities. All he was trying to do was make the point that perhaps the insurance department should let insurers trade securities through a brokerage firm. His interpretation of the conversation with Sizemore was, Get Franklin into compliance and then we'll talk. From the former senator's perspective, things were moving in the right direction.

But toiling away quietly, and far down in the Tennessee insurance department pecking order, Billy Lovelady was still perplexed about Liberty National Securities. And the more the examiner poked around, the more questions he had. In mid-January, still working out of Franklin American's headquarters, he had asked Hackney and Atnip for a copy of Dun & Bradstreet's report on Liberty National Securities. He started writing to the brokerage firm asking questions. Liberty National had a fake address at a mail drop on Wall Street, but Lovelady used the address on the Dun & Bradstreet report, and so the letters went first to Bob Guyer, the ostensible head of Liberty National, the man who worked from his enclosed front porch in Dundee, Michigan.

For Marty, any communication with Lovelady propelled him to a higher level of hysteria. Larry Martin attempted to soothe him with reassurances that he was in contact with Tennessee officials and would even talk to the governor. (That apparently never happened.) Lovelady had been ordered to back off, he told Marty, and if Lovelady called Dundee again he should be referred to his own insurance commissioner. "RELIEF—BUT IS IT OVER?" Marty wrote in his diary on February 17.

It wasn't. Even Larry Martin grew concerned when Lovelady turned up the fact that Liberty National Securities had a capitalization of less than $60,000, a pittance for a firm that was supposedly trading hundreds of millions in insurance assets.

Larry Martin had other reasons to be concerned. He knew something that he had not shared with Mathews or the state officials with whom he was negotiating. Although, in December, Marty had moved Franklin American's $69 million to a bank in Atlanta, he had in fact moved it again. Unbeknownst to the Tennessee insurance department, Marty had transferred the money to Tennessee, then to an account at Dreyfus in New York, and then, on January 20, 1999, to Banque SCS in Geneva.

Marty had told Hackney that he was moving the money out of the bank in Atlanta and the insurance executive had strongly argued against it. But Marty told him that Larry Martin had said the move was okay, and that the Tennessee insurance commissioner didn't mind. But as soon as Lovelady realized that Liberty National was an insignificant operation, Larry Martin urged Marty to return the money back to the Atlanta bank before anyone discovered it was gone. Marty stalled. (He eventually brought the money back to the United States, but only after Lovelady discovered it had been removed from the bank.)

Lovelady's concerns went way beyond the minuscule capitalization of Liberty National Securities. Falling badly behind schedule in his audit of Franklin American, he felt he had to alert his superiors to his suspicions even before he completed the examination. In February 1999, he wrote to Tennessee's chief examiner:

> *The problem is that Liberty National Securities may be operating outside of its licensed authority and is not of sufficient financial standing that an examiner should place substantial reliance on its confirmation of assets held, especially when solvency of the insurer is dependent upon the validity of the confirmation.*
>
> *There is a possibility that the Company has been looted of its assets. It is possible that Liberty National Securities Inc. may be a front for the interests that created Thunor Trust. If so, this would explain the original backers' agreement to a sole irrevocable trustee. (All funds provided would pass through the Trust, but be returned to their control at the broker level. They would gain control of their original contributions, plus the other reserve assets.)*
>
> *Such an operation could go undeterred for years and could be repeated many times, so long as premiums continued to cover current cash outflows and asset confirmations were accepted from the broker.*
>
> *There are many scenarios that could be played out under these circumstances. If the ultimate recipient of the funds prospers sufficiently, the original funds plus historical earnings on the assets (never truly purchased) could be returned to the Company with no regulatory au-*

thority the wiser. If the situation bombs, the backers abscond with the remaining funds, which in all likelihood, would still exceed the original contributions.

It sounded like the paranoid ramblings of an auditor who'd been cooped up with a bunch of numbers too long.

But it was all true. Lovelady had figured it all out. He only lacked the name of the scamster. Anyone who set his memorandum alongside the report drafted by Mike Henehan unearthing Marty Frankel's identity would have been able to unravel the entire convoluted crime.

There was one problem. Lovelady's memo fell into a deep bureaucratic hole in the insurance department. Although the chief examiner forwarded the memo to several senior officials, including the commissioner himself, they either didn't read it, or they quickly forgot it. Later, the commissioner would say he didn't even recall getting it.

Chapter Fourteen

Escape Plans

Lee Harrell was definitely annoyed. As a special assistant attorney general in Mississippi, assigned to the state's insurance department, he was stuck in an awkward spot. He kept getting reports from insurance examiners that there was something fishy about a brokerage firm called Liberty National Securities, which managed the assets of insurers owned by a trust called Thunor.

But it seemed as if whenever the examiners tried to pin down the insurers' executives in Tennessee, all sorts of powerful people would start pummeling Mississippi's elected insurance commissioner, George Dale, with phone calls. Thurston Little called to argue that if Dale let Liberty National Securities trade the Thunor companies' assets, Thunor would be able to make more on its investments. It would even consider moving its headquarters to Mississippi. That would mean more jobs for Dale's constituents. "George, if you do this, this is going to make you the most popular politician in Mississippi," Little promised.

Little and Larry Martin had another message for the commissioner, too: insurance department personnel—Harrell included—just didn't understand the securities business in general and Liberty National's trading philosophy in particular.

Harrell, then thirty-three, was the first to admit that Little and Martin might have a point. "Some of this stuff is Greek to me," he told the commissioner. But, he insisted, something about the situation "didn't pass the smell test." Harrell and Dale even discussed hiring a securities expert to sort the whole thing out. In March, Harrell met with Dale and pre-

sented a plan for clearing up the misunderstandings. "I will sit down and
I will write all these questions out and we'll send it to them," he said.

There was another reason Harrell was especially anxious to clear
the whole thing up quickly. He'd had a disturbing phone conversation
with Betty Cordial, a freelance insurance-fraud expert who was often
appointed by states to act as receiver when insurers went belly-up.
Harrell had called Cordial and regaled her with his difficulties with the
Tennessee-based empire. Then he mentioned the odd brokerage firm's
role in the problem. Cordial abruptly stopped him.

"Wait a minute," she said. "What's the address?"

Harrell answered that the firm had offices at 82 Wall Street in New
York City.

"Liberty National Securities," Cordial blurted.

Harrell was stunned. He wanted to know how she'd come up with the
name so quickly. Cordial's answer was disheartening. It turned out that
some time before, she'd been called by an insurance regulator in another
state asking her to check out Liberty National Securities' address. She'd
sent someone to the address on Wall Street and found out that Liberty
National's address was nothing but a mail drop. She remembered the incident only because the request had seemed mysterious and the regulator had not told her why he was asking.

Harrell drafted nineteen questions, many of them about Liberty National Securities. They were very much to the point. Where were the
firm's offices? Who were its officers? And who, exactly, was Larry Martin
and what did he have to do with the insurance companies?

For John Hackney and Gary Atnip, the new round of questions from
Mississippi was ample evidence that Larry Martin's strategy had badly
backfired. All his efforts to engage high-flying lawyers and businessmen
like Thurston Little, Brad Dye, and Harlan Mathews had yielded nothing but more questions from regulators with whom Hackney and Atnip
had dealt comfortably for years. On March 11, they called Marty in a
huff about Larry Martin, and they quit.

They had quit at least once before. They had advised Marty to sell the
companies and even told employees in Franklin that their days in the executive suite were numbered. But the two men stayed put, too mired in
lies and quirky corporate crises to walk out the door and slam it behind
them.

Marty, meanwhile, was beside himself as he stayed up nights attempting to answer Harrell's questions. He and Hackney bickered over how to respond. In one draft Hackney faxed to Marty in Greenwich, he answered a question about Larry Martin's role in the insurance empire with a single word: "Nothing." Marty impatiently tossed that aside and drafted a long paragraph that Hackney was sure would arouse even more suspicion. He told Marty the long answer was overkill: "It's like killing a gnat with a shotgun."

With regulators suddenly asking questions about Liberty National Securities, Marty had another little problem, and it was inconveniently located. On the Dun & Bradstreet reports requested by regulators in Mississippi and Tennessee, Liberty National's address was not 82 Wall Street, but 437 Dunham Street, in Dundee, Michigan. That, of course, was the home and office of Bob Guyer.

Guyer had been serving his few local clients and contentedly collecting $2,000 a month from Marty, whom he heard from only irregularly. In 1998 and 1999 the pace of those communications picked up a little bit. First, Sonia told Guyer that Marty was likely to regain his license. Then, in 1999, Marty asked Guyer to obtain a post office box in the name of Liberty National Securities. He also asked him to register the brokerage in several additional states—where he hoped to acquire insurance companies—and sent him $17,000 for filing fees. Guyer didn't have clients in those states, and he had not heard any news about Marty's license, but he followed instructions without asking too many questions.

Though Guyer had usually done his bidding, Marty did not want any mail from state regulators with questions about Liberty National ending up on the front porch where Guyer worked. He didn't feel he could truly trust Guyer with his secrets. At first, Marty had planned to ask a broker who had once worked for Sonia to drive up from the Toledo area to check the mail. But then he decided he couldn't completely trust that man, either. Instead, he sent emissaries from Connecticut, and told Guyer that he was expecting a lot of résumés from job candidates.

Two people shared the task of checking the mail and reporting back to Marty. One was Steve, the real David Rosse's assistant, and the other was Cynthia Allison, who had been banned from the Connecticut mansion after threatening to kill Marty but was still being supported by him. They stayed at a nearby hotel, and Steve, bored to bits, sometimes drove to Ann Arbor for a little entertainment.

One night Cynthia and Steve sat in her hotel room discussing the drill for checking the mail when she started talking about her feelings for Marty. Steve already knew that she had a thing for their boss: he'd stood guard at the trading room door the night Marty threw her out of the mansion. But that evening in Michigan he got an earful as Cynthia, who smelled as though it had been a while since she'd bathed, talked about her feelings. She was in love with Marty, she said, explaining that it wasn't anything sexual. In fact, she said, she didn't even know what it was about him that made her love him so much. She was just in love with him.

Steve wanted out of Dundee, Michigan—and away from Cynthia Allison. He asked her to tell Marty that she could handle the mail on her own, so he could "get the hell out of it."

One Friday in early spring of 1999, Hackney and Atnip called Marty to pass on something one of their lawyers had told them: that if regulators refused to "admit," or recognize, an insurer's assets—a real possibility, because Mississippi and Tennessee had questions about Liberty National—it was an "automatic felony." For the first time, Marty began to realize that he and his empire could be in some serious hot water.

With the situation in Mississippi at a crisis point, Marty took steps to shore up his relationship with the one man he thought might hold sway over Commissioner Dale and other prominent politicians in that state. Through Larry Martin, Marty had sent word that he might be interested in doing some real estate deals with Thurston Little, who had known Commissioner Dale for over thirty-five years. When Little called Marty to find out whether he was serious, Marty summoned him for a meeting in Greenwich, asking him for his date of birth so he could do a little astrological research on his prospective business partner.

It would be hard to imagine two men more different than Marty Frankel and Thurston Little. Called a "redneck" and "good ol' boy" by folks in Mississippi who know what the terms mean, Little was not the type of character who showed up often in Marty's secluded world. He was a large man who knew how to get along in all kinds of business and political circles. Everyone was his pal.

To Marty, Thurston Little was a bit perplexing. "What's an asshole buddy?" he once asked Hackney. "Thurston Little says, 'George Dale is my asshole buddy.'" Although Hackney told Marty that Little was a "blowhard," Marty remained convinced that he was the answer to his problems down South. "He can take care of this so I can trade," he told Hackney.

But Little and Marty had some similarities as well. Like Marty, Little had a knack for saying exactly what people wanted to hear. Even after Marty had received the troubling questions from Lee Harrell, Little was still calling Greenwich to tell Marty that he was in touch with Dale and that things were "under control."

When Little walked through the door of the trading room and they met for the first time, Marty explained that he was interested in investing in real estate, and they discussed the possibility of developing commercial properties in Mississippi and Tennessee. But Little had one small problem that would prevent him from hooking up with Marty. He had some debts to pay off before he could buy more land. That was easily dealt with, Marty told his visitor. He would pay off the debts so that the two could make investments together. Marty explained that he would have to rely on Little to locate potential acquisitions, but that he would put up all the financing.

Little was dumbfounded by the offer. He wasn't about to turn it down.

But Marty was willing to offer even more. He thought that Little should buy himself a new plane so that he could scout out properties. Little said he didn't have the money to buy an airplane and Marty readily agreed to buy one for him. There was just one little thing: Marty didn't want any document acknowledging their understanding.

In the end, Little's lawyers drew up a document describing some of the money, but not all of it, as a loan. Marty signed it. On March 29 he wired $5 million to Thurston Little. Soon afterward, he sent another $1.4 million, which Little spent on a Piper Cheyenne III, a twin-engine turbopropeller plane.

Marty had long tried to avoid thinking about the possibility that he'd be caught. He had no real plan for fleeing his cocoonlike digs in Greenwich. To be sure, the notion had sometimes nagged at him. It was at those times that he came up with childish schemes like escaping on the back of a motorcycle or moving his operation to a yacht anchored safely in international waters. But now he had to come up with an escape plan.

Funds were going to be the big problem if he had to make a speedy exit. In the event of a catastrophe on the insurance front, Marty knew that his accounts at Banque SCS in Switzerland would be frozen. He began to toy with the notion of parking, or investing, money outside the United States in a way that could not easily be traced to him or any of his longtime financial interests. That way, if he did indeed have to vanish, he could tap those investments to live a pretty nice life abroad.

It was possibly with this in mind that he began to seriously court Tom Quinn, who both intrigued and frightened Marty. Over the years Marty had occasionally bandied about some pretty amateurish mob talk. Although he had met Quinn through Larry Martin, he worked at cultivating the Quinn's friendship outside their usual go-between's presence.

One of Marty's many pet projects became getting Quinn's young daughter into Boston College, a Jesuit school in Massachusetts. For this, he prevailed upon Father Jacobs to use his influence. The priest was led to believe that getting the Quinn girl into the school was of critical importance to the man he knew as David Rosse, that he wanted it "terribly." The girl wrote a letter that Father Jacobs found "quite touching," and he did what he could, making the request to a Jesuit acquaintance and turning over the relevant documents. By late March, Marty was feeling hopeful about her college prospects. (Ultimately, she didn't get in.)

The day after Marty met with Thurston Little, he spent a few hours talking with Tom Corbally and Tom Quinn. Several days later, Marty transferred just under $13 million to Quinn. The money was wired to several offshore accounts. Marty told some people in his circle that the money was for an investment, and told at least one other person that Quinn was going to open a London office for him. Quinn was a man who could keep a secret; he didn't talk much, if at all, about his newfound wealth.

But just five days after wiring the money, Marty had second thoughts. He was so afraid of Quinn that he couldn't bring himself to call, so on Tuesday morning, April 6, he phoned Tom Corbally and ordered him to tell Quinn to send the money back. Not surprisingly, Quinn was extremely unhappy at this. He flatly refused and, furious, he called Marty directly.

"I'm going to come in with a baseball bat and bash your fucking head in, you little nerd!" he bellowed at Marty.

Marty got off the phone absolutely terrified. He was sure that Quinn, who was living in a rented house nearby, was going to come over and kill him. In a panic, he once again called Corbally, telling him to call Quinn and say that the real David Rosse was on his way to the mansion to protect Marty. Quinn never showed up.

As his panic eased, Marty began to whine around the house about Quinn having called him a nerd. "Why do people always say that about me?" he complained to one of his women. She thought he was just like a little kid who had given away his baseball cards and then wanted them back.

Apparently $7 million was returned.

At the same time he was feuding with Quinn, Marty received a disturbing letter from James Maloney, Greenwich's zoning enforcement officer. Marty's neighbors had grown impatient with the pending IRS investigation, which so far had resulted in no obvious action. The letter cited "complaints regarding construction at your premises," and used, though it misspelled, Marty's real name. Marty had a lot on his mind, and simply ignored it.

Upsets of the kind he'd had with Quinn were becoming more and more routine at the mansion. His acquisition plan in limbo, the matters in Mississippi and Tennessee also very much up in the air, he began to lash out at everyone around him. He told Corbally that he was going to take back the Park Avenue apartment he was buying for his use. Corbally threatened to "undo the good things," and Marty backed off.

Yet again Marty was feuding with Kaethe, mostly because he refused to invest in a business deal her boyfriend, Alfredo Fausti, was trying to put together in Italy. Alfredo wanted Marty to put money into Sanità Più, an Italian health care company run by Rocco Nuzzaci, a family friend. Marty steadfastly refused and referred Alfredo to a contact at Bear Stearns. Meanwhile he tried to placate Alfredo, who had learned Marty's real name at the New Year's dinner party he'd attended with Kaethe, by promising to pay his tuition if he went to Yale Law School.

That didn't satisfy Alfredo, and now Marty had Kaethe to deal with, which was never easy. In the midst of Marty's battle with Quinn, Kaethe snatched the notebook Marty kept for documenting his many wire transfers from bank to bank, and brokerage firm to brokerage firm.

In a telephone battle at two A.M. on April 7, the day after Marty demanded the money back from Quinn, Kaethe hung up on him. Later that day she told him that Alfredo would kill him if he didn't give her the piano he'd bought for her in the days when they were lovers. The skirmishes went on for days, with Kaethe even calling to bicker from her therapist's office in Manhattan. At one point, Karen Timmins told Kaethe that David Rosse was going to kill her. He didn't.

Marty's relationship with Alfredo and his father was also reaching the crisis point. The Faustis had moved on from their initial assignment helping Marty link up with the Church to more sensitive missions.

In phone conversations with Marty and Corbally, the Faustis had been asked to look at several business opportunities abroad. One assignment was to check into various banking options for the financier, who said he was not happy with Banque SCS and was hoping for more confidentiality than banks in Switzerland could offer. The Faustis spent considerable time hopping from one international banking center to another, racking up huge consulting fees and expenses as Marty changed his mind again and again about what he wanted. Finally they found an option that they considered nearly perfect. They worked out a deal for Marty to purchase between 30 and 40 percent of a bank in Jordan. The Faustis were amazed when Marty changed his mind, and asked them to look into something else.

The Faustis' work had resulted in precious little for Marty. As their bills mounted he became increasingly angry at how little they'd accomplished—although the lack of results was partly his own fault. At least some of the bills went unpaid, and Fausto Fausti fired off a letter to Marty, outlining the work he and his son had done and demanding their money.

In April, as Marty was hunkered over the questions from Mississippi, and fighting with Quinn and Kaethe, the elder Fausti arrived in Greenwich to try to collect. The two fought badly over the course of a week, with Fausti telling Marty that he would no longer work for him. On April 14, Marty threw Fausto and Alfredo out of the mansion. As he left,

Fausto demanded his consulting fees. He wanted $500,000 in three days. "Fausto attempts blackmail," Marty wrote in his astrological calendar. "Wants $500K + gives me 3-days ultimatum or he'll turn me in."

Five days later Marty relented. He wired $542,000 from Banque SCS into one of Fausto's accounts. There were more payments to come.

By then, Marty had spent months ruminating over whether his consultants were ripping him off, often sharing his thoughts with John Hackney over the phone. If anyone tried to steal any money from him, or "mess him over," he'd have them killed, he told Hackney. They would "sleep with the fishes."

"Now you're just talking," said Hackney.

"I'm serious," Marty insisted. "I have people who know how to do that sort of thing."

Hackney said he didn't want to hear any more. As far as he was concerned it was all a bunch of hooey. Though he'd still never laid eyes on his boss, he saw him as fearful and, yes, as a nerd.

As the money fights raged between Marty and his associates, with charges of blackmail and unpaid debts lobbed back and forth, Marty quietly made plans in case the situations in Tennessee and Mississippi grew dire. He started thinking through the logistics of an escape.

Using Mona Kim as a go-between, he bought $16 million worth of Vienna Philharmonic commemorative coins from Monex, a gold dealer based in Newport Beach, California. (He had originally asked the Faustis to look into a gold purchase, but then thought better of involving them.) At the same time he started making arrangements to buy $12 million worth of diamonds through a dealer the real David Rosse knew in California. He said he wanted diamonds because he was worried about Y2K problems. Eventually the dealer agreed to sell him a little more than $10 million worth.

Marty also embarked on a far trickier transaction: passports. After at least one false start, Marty made a contact through Corbally. The contact was referred to only as Mikey by the few in Marty's circle who knew about the plan, and they believed he was from Brooklyn. The actual handing over of the bogus documents, however, was to take place in London, and Tom Corbally orchestrated at least a portion of that transfer. Kaethe and the real David Rosse were dispatched to London. Marty sometimes had Rosse accompany Kaethe on European business matters, in part to keep her from drinking to excess, which Marty feared would lead her to spill his secrets. This time his job was also to keep her from feuding with Corbally.

Kaethe and Rosse met Mikey and Corbally at Claridges. There, Mikey handed the passports to the duo. At least some of the passports were British and were provided through a British ring that over a ten-year period sold about a thousand phony passports, many to criminals. (The passport operation's mastermind, Kenneth Regan, was jailed in London in late 1999.)

The plan was for Kaethe to take the passports to Switzerland and put them in a safe deposit box there. But after she'd done that, Marty changed his mind. Kaethe went back to the safe deposit box, retrieved at least some of the passports, and returned to London. From there they were sent back to Marty by DHL Worldwide Express.

When he opened the envelope in Greenwich, Marty found that the passports were of poor quality, and that the information on them, such as dates of birth, didn't match the phony birth certificates he had bought as well. He had paid over $500,000 for them.

Chapter Fifteen

A Summons to Mississippi

John Woodall, an assistant deputy commissioner of insurance in Spokane, Washington, was sitting in his office one day in April 1999 when he received perhaps the strangest phone call of his twenty-five-plus-year career.

The call came from an investment broker who said he represented the St. Francis of Assisi Foundation. The foundation, the broker explained, wanted to buy Western United, Metropolitan Mortgage's insurance subsidiary. "It's rather an urgent business deal," he explained. "We'd like to have approval by the end of the week."

Woodall was vaguely aware that Metropolitan Mortgage's chief executive, Paul Sandifur, had long been trying to negotiate a sale. But he told the representative from St. Francis that he didn't think his proposed timetable was realistic. "The law requires that you file certain information," he said. "You haven't filed anything yet."

There was a pause on the other end of the line. "Well, would it help if the Pope called you?" the broker asked.

The hair on the back of Woodall's neck stood straight up. "Either there's a scam going on here," he said to himself, "or I'm on *Candid Camera.*"

A call from the Pope, he told the caller, would not help.

It was not the only phone call Woodall received pleading St. Francis's case. He heard from a well-respected lawyer in Seattle and another from Akin, Gump, who made sure to drop Bob Strauss's name. But the reference to the Pope spooked Woodall, and he was not about to grease the regulatory skids so St. Francis could make its deal on an expedited basis. He had heard about the foundation. It had made a pass at another Washington insurer, but had been rebuffed. Woodall put in a phone call to Mississippi, where he'd heard the foundation was also on the prowl.

The subsequent conversation only added to Woodall's alarm. Mississippi, the regulator told him, was concerned about St. Francis. "If I were you I sure wouldn't do anything until I looked very carefully," she said.

Woodall called John Van Engelen, the president of Western United, and ordered him not to sign any contract, transfer any funds, or share any policy lists with St. Francis without permission from the office of the state insurance commissioner. "You better be darned careful," Woodall said.

In mid-April, Lee Harrell finally received the answers to the questions he'd sent Franklin American the month before. He'd granted several requests for extensions and was eager to see how the company had responded after all the confusion of the previous few months. Liberty National Securities was at the top of Harrell's list of worries.

But when he sat down at his desk at the insurance department in Jackson, he didn't make it to the answers about the securities firm. In fact, on the first page of Franklin American's responses he stopped short in amazement. It appeared that the Thunor Trust was now owned by the St. Francis of Assisi Foundation. When an insurance company is sold, it must file a so-called Form A with regulators, explaining the "change of control." Harrell had seen no such filing from any of the insurers in the Thunor family of companies.

Harrell immediately went to see Commissioner George Dale to discuss the startling development. He drafted a letter for the commissioner's signature demanding that Father Peter Jacobs, listed as St. Francis's president, and John Hackney appear at the commissioner's offices to explain the change and who or what St. Francis actually was. It wasn't that Mississippi was satisfied with the answers about Liberty National Securities, Harrell explained to a representative of Marty's team. It was just that the issue of change of control of the companies had to be dealt with immediately.

"CRISIS," Marty wrote in his astrological calendar on Wednesday,

April 21, drawing a circle around the word. "MS threatens to take over co.—wants F.J. [Father Jacobs] there Apr. 29."

The following evening, George Dale was barraged with phone calls at home in Clinton, Mississippi. First Father Jacobs, in Italy, and Tom Bolan, in New York, with Marty on the line, called to ask for an adjournment of the April 29 meeting. Dale, taken aback by the call, responded that a postponement possibly could be arranged and that they should call his office. Then, half an hour later, he received a conference call from Thurston Little and Marty. For thirty minutes Marty tried to convince Dale that Harrell and the other insurance department staffers were overreacting, and that there was nothing to worry about. Dale was polite, but he made no promises.

The next day, it became clear that the direct appeal to Dale had backfired badly. The Thunor folks got a message from Harrell. It was very direct: he forbade any member of Marty's team from contacting the commissioner at the office, at home, or anywhere else. All questions had to go through Harrell.

Meanwhile, Father Jacobs called Harrell to try to postpone the meeting. On April 28, he had plans to attend dinner at the home of Alice Mason, the real estate broker famous for her celebrity-studded dinner parties. Jimmy and Rosalynn Carter were expected to attend.

Over the previous year, since meeting the Carters at another Mason bash he'd attended, Father Jacobs had talked three or four times with the Carter Center's fund-raising office about the possibility that Marty, whom he didn't name, might make a large donation. Now, with the Carters and Father Jacobs all planning to be in New York for the Mason affair, the fund-raisers had set up a breakfast meeting for April 29. The Carter people believed that Father Jacobs would bring along the shy donor—Marty—so that he could meet the Carters and a staffer from the Carter Center's development office. For Marty, who had bragged to Hackney that he could get Carter to join St. Francis's board, meeting the Carters was tempting but anxiety provoking. Once before Father Jacobs had invited him to accompany him to an Alice Mason dinner so he could meet the Carters. Marty had accepted and even arranged for a tuxedo, but had changed his mind at the last minute. (For that reason, Father Jacobs didn't expect him to attend the breakfast.)

But Harrell wouldn't budge from the April 29 date for the meeting, even when Father Jacobs pleaded that he was scheduled to have break-fast with Jimmy Carter that day. The priest called the Carter Center and regretfully told them that the breakfast had to be canceled.

A Southern Baptist from birth, Lee Harrell was no expert on the Catholic Church—in fact, he knew only two Catholics. In preparation for the meeting he started doing some research on the St. Francis of Assisi Foundation and Father Jacobs. He contacted the Reverend Michael Flannery, the vicar general of the local Catholic diocese, who had never heard of the foundation. Flannery had heard of Colagiovanni but doubted that Monitor Ecclesiasticus had millions to invest.

Then he called the Washington, D.C., archdiocese and was told that Father Jacobs had been, as Harrell later put it, "defrocked." (This was not exactly correct. Father Jacobs was still a priest, although he was prohib-ited from performing certain priestly functions.) Though Jacobs was of-ficially attached to Washington, no one at the archdiocese had seen him in years, and the office asked Harrell to have Father Jacobs get in touch if he saw him.

When Harrell called the Vatican office in Washington, D.C., the per-son he spoke to diplomatically declined to answer most of his questions. However, he did say that he was getting many phone calls about Father Jacobs and that the money to buy insurance companies was not coming from the Vatican.

In Greenwich, Connecticut, and Franklin, Tennessee, Marty's troops were also preparing for the summit in Jackson. Harrell had told Thurston Little that he wanted "David Rosse," the mysterious trader who worked for Liberty National Securities, to attend and that Little should make sure he was there as well.

During the week of April 26, Father Jacobs and Monsignor Colagio-vanni flew to the United States. Father Jacobs was already travel weary. He recently had made a grueling fact-finding trip to Kazakhstan at the behest of a Vatican archbishop interested in funneling some of Marty's dollars to poor Franciscans at work in the former Soviet republic. Mean-while there was a flurry of phone calls back and forth among Greenwich, Franklin, and the regulatory lawyers who would represent the group in

Jackson. The plan was for everyone to fly to Jackson a day early for a walk-through by the lawyers.

The other plan was to backpedal furiously and hope that Mississippi would be appeased. Marty's answers had, of course, made it look as though St. Francis had taken control of Thunor and the insurance companies it owned. On April 23, six days before the Jackson meeting, John Hackney sent a letter to Mississippi's chief insurance examiner saying that a "subsequent event has taken place":

"The original grantors [Sonia Schulte, Mark Shuki and Edward Krauss] have decided to remain as grantors of the Thunor Trust. In so doing, the St. Francis Foundation will be an additional grantor to Thunor Trust. All grantors realize that the structure of Thunor Trust shall and will remain in place." The letter was an effort to convince the state of Mississippi that nothing had really changed, that no additional scrutiny was warranted, and that it was not necessary to make the filings required when an insurer changed hands.

Marty's decision to accept Mississippi's invitation to the meeting, of course, necessitated a chartered plane. He was afraid of flying, nervous about leaving Greenwich, and anxious about whether his insurance empire would survive the trip. He ordered that computers and fax machines be loaded on the plane with him. Jackie Ju, an ex-lover who handled minor tasks at the mansion, was assigned to help organize the campaign. There were travel plans to be made, conference rooms to be booked, and hotel rooms to be assigned to lawyers and clergymen and clerical helpers and computer technicians and bodyguards and insurance executives, and most of this was beyond Jackie's capabilities.

Hackney phoned shortly before Marty left Greenwich. "Make sure you dress right," said the insurance executive, who still had never met his boss but knew of his legendary sloppiness. "This is business. Remember to bring a tie."

Marty's contingent met at the airport in Westchester and boarded a large private plane. Monsignor Colagiovanni and Father Jacobs were exhausted because they had flown in from Rome and for them it was the middle of the night. Tom Bolan, a St. Francis trustee, had only reluctantly agreed to attend, and he thought that there wasn't adequate time for the St. Francis contingent to prepare. Marty assured him that only

one simple issue would be on the table in Jackson: whether the foundation was exempt from the exhaustive reporting required when a change
of control occurs. He explained that a Jackson attorney, former Mississippi lieutenant governor Brad Dye, would represent St. Francis.
Nicholas Monaco, a well-known attorney from Jefferson City, Missouri,
who specialized in insurance regulation, would represent the insurance
companies. "Just have bodies there," Marty said Monaco had told him.

On board everyone ate and chatted and Marty calmly assured them
that Monaco would explain everything the next day.

But Marty had not been so calm when he called the real David Rosse
just before the plane took off. "I need you to come to Mississippi," he'd
begged. "Can you be at the airport in twenty minutes?" Rosse was ill. He
had bronchitis and was suffering from terrible back pain that had kept
him away from the mansion much of the time in recent weeks. But
Marty had sounded bad, so he dragged himself out of bed, headed to the
airport in Westchester, and boarded a small jet waiting to whisk him to
an airport outside Jackson. A waiting car took him to a Hilton hotel,
where Marty's entourage had arrived a short time before. There he met
Bob Biddle, a maintenance man from the mansion who had accompanied Marty to Mississippi.

"What the hell is going on?" asked Rosse impatiently. Biddle just kept
shaking his head, which Rosse took to mean that Marty was in a state.
"Where's the boss man?" Rosse asked, and was told that Marty was in
meetings. There was mass confusion as Jackie Ju rushed around trying
to coordinate everything and Bob Biddle chased after her trying to
straighten out her mistakes.

Marty's group had landed at about six P.M. and was met by Brad Dye,
who took them to meet the Most Reverend William R. Houck, bishop of
Jackson's Catholic diocese, at his rectory. Monsignor Colagiovanni and
Father Jacobs made an official presentation of their credentials. The
purpose of the visit was to enable Marty to persuade the bishop to come
to the meeting with Commissioner Dale and formally introduce the St.
Francis contingent, thereby putting a stamp of religious legitimacy on
the group. Though Dye had apparently broached the issue ahead of
time, the bishop said he had to check his schedule and get back to them
the next day. He asked to see an audited report for St. Francis. Marty
spent most of the meeting talking, quoting Don Orione and St. Francis,

and promising to build hospitals in Jackson and elsewhere. Meanwhile, a bodyguard stood by, sipping from a bottle of Coke.

At the Hilton, Father Jacobs and Monsignor Colagiovanni dragged themselves off to bed, and Bolan was introduced to Thurston Little, who with his daughter joined Bolan, Marty, and Brad Dye for a relaxing dinner. To Bolan, none of the guests seemed at all alarmed about what the coming two days would bring. Little, who Bolan thought looked something like Burl Ives, said that Harrell would not be a problem and that Marty shouldn't worry. No more business was discussed.

The next day John Hackney walked into the lobby of the Hilton and was surprised and dismayed to bump into Thurston Little, whom he had once described to Marty as a "blowhard." "We have to fix it so that little smart son of a bitch upstart can trade," Little told Hackney. "He's one of the smartest son of a bitches I ever met in my life."

Hackney went upstairs to a meeting room reserved for the group, which numbered more than a dozen people. On a high floor of the hotel, the room was the size of a large ballroom, and a breakfast spread was available for attendees. Still a little annoyed that Thurston Little was on the scene, Hackney walked over and stood with Gary Atnip. He was looking forward to finally laying eyes on the man he'd been listening to on the phone for nearly ten years.

"That's him," Atnip said, pointing to a skinny six-footer across the room. John Hackney walked over to greet Marty Frankel face-to-face for the first time.

"Good to finally meet you," he said.

Marty immediately recognized Hackney by the sound of his voice. He looked Hackney up and down.

"You're shorter than I thought," he said.

Much of the day was spent reviewing material for the St. Francis representatives, Bolan, Monsignor Colagiovanni, and Father Jacobs, who would be on the spot the next day when Commissioner Dale and Harrell quizzed them on St. Francis's role in the insurance empire. It was a sort of "Insurance 101," as John Hackney later put it, taught by the attorney Nicholas Monaco. Meanwhile, new documents were created to explain the changes in the Thunor Trust companies. A notary public was contacted to stamp an affidavit, signed by Father Jacobs, which stated that in four payments from August 10, 1998, to January 29, 1999, the Monitor

Ecclesiasticus Foundation had contributed a total of $1,259,735,185.28 to the St. Francis of Assisi Foundation. A document prepared by the Franklin-based auditor for the insurers, Leuty and Heath, was discussed with the group. It confirmed the $1.26 billion donation to St. Francis and added, "In April 1999, we have confirmed that a total of $600,000,000 in two transactions were transferred from Saint Francis directly from its Saint Francis Investment Fund account to the separate investment accounts of the Thunor Trust."

That document, Monsignor Colagiovanni's affidavit testifying to the $1 billion donation the Monitor Ecclesiasticus had made to Saint Francis, and the old Thunor Trust document supposedly showing the signatures of Sonia, Ed Krauss, and Mark Shuki, were among the voluminous documents included in several binders of material. The papers were all put together by lawyers and helpers drafting and photocopying and printing in various rooms in the hotel.

From Bolan's point of view, the whole thing was crazy. Marty was lecturing. Monaco was lecturing, and seemed unsure of his strategy. Documents were reworded and retyped. Marty's staff was racing everywhere, trying to deal with new drafts and figure out how to make the argument that there had been no change of control of the insurance companies even though St. Francis was suddenly a big player. Bolan wondered why, if there really hadn't been a change of control, it was necessary to file all those papers.

There were a few odd incidents during the course of the day. Brad Dye, the lawyer representing St. Francis, abruptly announced without explanation that he had a conflict of interest and could no longer represent the foundation. He left. Bolan was deeply disturbed about having to rely on the insurance company's lawyers.

There was also a tense moment when some of the lawyers left the hotel to deliver the binders to the insurance department, only to return in a snit. One of the lawyers called Lee Harrell "a bastard," and told Hackney and a few of the others that Harrell wanted to take over the companies because the department still had questions about Liberty National Securities. This was all the more disturbing to some of the people attending the meetings because they had been told that the only issue to be dealt with the next day was St. Francis's new role with respect to the insurers.

Sometime during the day it was learned that Bishop Houck had declined to perform the introductions the following day. He had become suspicious when, instead of receiving the auditied report he had requested, he received a brochure broadly describing the St. Francis foundation. He also realized that this was the same group that Lee Harrell had contacted Father Flannery about earlier.

The meeting with regulators was scheduled for the afternoon, so on the morning of April 29 the group met once more to discuss strategy. Marty started to argue that Bolan, perhaps the only member of the St. Francis team who would understand the legal arguments that afternoon, should not attend the meeting with the commissioner. Monaco, the lawyer for the Thunor companies, snapped, "I'll make that decision," and decided that Bolan should stay. Bolan was left wondering why Marty suddenly didn't want him there, after persuading him to come to Mississippi in the first place.

They took a break, and Hackney soon bumped into Thurston Little yet again as they ambled around the hotel. "This has nothing to do with you. You're not part of the company," Hackney told him, letting his frustration bubble over. "Well, I understand," was all Little said, and he withdrew to make preparations to depart.

As the time for the meeting grew closer, Marty became more panicked. The idea of going face-to-face with regulators who were so close to figuring out the truth about Liberty National, and so intent on thwarting his efforts to build an insurance empire, completely paralyzed him. He had an uncontrollable desire to flee, even though Harrell had ordered him to be there. And so he decided to leave.

It wasn't until around lunchtime that the other attendees learned that Marty, or "Rosse" as most of them knew him, was heading home. Bolan looked over at Hackney and noticed that he seemed especially upset as they made their final preparations for the meeting that afternoon without their ringleader's presence.

Meanwhile Bob Biddle, Marty's maintenance man, had been standing outside the conference room when he heard his boss referred to as "David Rosse." Not privy to the intricacies and complexities of Marty's business affairs, he had gone in search of the real David Rosse to tell him that Marty was using his name.

Rosse knew that Marty had occasionally used his name for a variety of purposes. But now he was livid. Perhaps he hadn't realized the extent to which Marty was actually impersonating him, or perhaps he finally realized it might get him in a heap of trouble. In any case, the news that Marty was using his name in Mississippi didn't catch Rosse at a good time. He was already angry at having been hauled out of his sickbed just so he could hand around the chaos in Jackson for two days.

As the Greenwich retinue prepared to pull out of Jackson, David Rosse confronted an already anxious Marty. "You're not to use my name," Rosse angrily told him. If he did it again, Rosse said, "I'll hunt you down, you son of a bitch."

Marty looked shocked, almost as if he were choking. "No, God, no," he sputtered. "I wouldn't do that." But of course, both men knew he had, and as Marty and his helpers headed for the airport in three Town Cars and two other rental cars, he began to obsess about Rosse's flash of anger.

After a last-minute fuss at the airport because Thurston Little, who had accompanied the group, didn't like the chartered jet he'd been assigned and wanted another, the exhausted group finally took off for Connecticut. Marty slept much of the way home.

Meanwhile, the phalanx of lawyers and representatives of St. Francis and the insurance companies moved to the offices of the Mississippi Department of Insurance, convening in a conference room high in a building that afforded a view of downtown Jackson. Commissioner Dale, Lee Harrell, and several other officials represented the state.

There were introductions all around, and Father Jacobs chatted amiably with Commissioner Dale. Monsignor Colagiovanni explained to the assembling group that his ring had been given to him by Pope John Paul II. He asked Dale if he'd like to kiss it. At least one member of the Mississippi contingent was appalled by the notion that one man would offer his hand for another to kiss.

After everyone had met, they sat down around a large conference table. One of the Mississippi officials wanted to know why "David Rosse" and Thurston Little weren't there. Someone feebly explained that Marty had to leave because he was going to miss his flight and had to return to New York.

Until that moment, Hackney hadn't even realized that Marty and Little had been *ordered* to attend. He began pulling at his collar and sweating so profusely that it caught the eye of the Mississippi officials. They couldn't help but notice that he looked very, very nervous, even shaken, throughout the meeting.

The discussion began. Bolan told the regulators that he had been advised by legal counsel that since Hackney had remained as Thunor's trustee, there had been no change of control. He pointed out that Thunor had successfully operated the insurance companies for years under Hackney's supervision.

Monaco, the lawyer, also made a pitch to the regulators.

Then Father Jacobs and Monsignor Colagiovanni spoke, arguing that the $600 million that St. Francis had transferred to the insurance companies would go to charitable work and good deeds. They had visited Bosnia with the Pope, they said, and went on at some length about how they had been helping homeless, needy children.

Where had St. Francis gotten all its money? Lee Harrell asked.

Parroting the false affidavit, Monsignor Colagiovanni answered that St. Francis' money came from Monitor Ecclesiasticus. Harrell had trouble understanding him. "I don't understand Northern accents," he said impatiently. "I sure as heck don't understand what you're saying with your accent. You're going to have to slow down."

But even when he did, the Mississippi contingent quite simply didn't get it. Nobody sitting around the table—not Hackney, not Atnip, not Monsignor Colagiovanni, not Father Jacobs or Tom Bolan—could adequately explain St. Francis's role in Thunor, or who from the Catholic Church was overseeing St. Francis's investments. No one could fully explain who Thurston Little represented and who "David Rosse" was. And, for the life of them, the Mississippians couldn't figure out what helping needy children in Bosnia had to do with insurance companies in Mississippi. It was, in the words of one regulator, "a comedy show."

After several hours, Harrell grew tired of it all. He, too, had been nervous about the meeting. There were going to be some powerful people present—representatives from the Vatican and, he thought, Thurston Little, whose tentacles went all over the state. Harrell had even asked another lawyer with the attorney general's office to sit in for a little extra moral support. But after a while he decided that what he was listening to was simply a lot of nonsense.

He suggested a recess and asked to meet privately with the commissioner. Harrell had already drafted orders for the state of Mississippi to take over the two Thunor insurers domiciled in the state. All the commissioner had to do was sign them. As turned out, Commissioner Dale had also heard enough. He was ready to sign.

Lee Harrell asked Monaco and another lawyer to step into the hallway. He told them the news, and Monaco started arguing. Harrell stopped him. "If you like," he said, "you can go to the courthouse."

Hackney was then asked to come to the commissioner's office and was also told the news. He had one question. "If I resign, will that make all the problems go away?"

The answer was no. He was told that the assets belonging to the Mississippi insurers owned by Thunor had to be moved to a financial institution in Mississippi at once.

By the time Hackney got out of the commissioner's office, many of those attending the meeting, including Bolan and the priests, had drifted back to the hotel. They had waited for hours to see whether the meeting would resume.

A very weary Hackney flew back to Tennessee with Gary Atnip. For months they had been telling Marty that ultimately, he was not going to be able to continue trading the assets of the Tennessee and Mississippi companies; now, they knew that as soon as they returned to Franklin they had to call and give him the bad news. They girded themselves for a fit of yelling and screaming, and on the plane made notes of everything they planned to say to their boss. In Tennessee, they went straight to the office and got Marty on the phone.

"Don't yell at us, and don't scream at us, and don't cuss at us," Hackney said, before proceeding to tell Marty that Mississippi had taken over his companies. "This is the truth and reality," Hackney told him solemnly.

"But Father Jacobs and the Monsignor said it went very well," Marty whined.

"Well, they're wrong," Hackney replied firmly. Actually, he was surprised at how calmly Marty seemed to be taking it.

Hackney told Marty that the next day he would start setting up accounts so that Marty could ship the money back to Mississippi. He told him to have the assets transferred by the end of a week, and that he should think seriously about putting the whole insurance empire up for sale.

It was getting late, and as they said their good-byes Marty seemed to be agreeing to Hackney's plan. "He's finally listening to us on this thing," Hackney thought.

Chapter Sixteen

On the Road

Suitcases became a necessity. In the days after Marty returned from Mississippi, he prepared to leave his mansion in Greenwich forever. To some of the women, he said that he was going away for a while and would be back. He then sent them shopping. They returned with more than a dozen pieces of soft-sided luggage. There was a problem. Wrapped in plastic, the suitcases smelled too new. Marty had an extremely sensitive nose and the odor triggered an allergy attack. A smell test was performed, with only the least offensive suitcases making the cut. The rest were stacked to the ceiling of the security office in the garage, still in their plastic wrap.

The real David Rosse had returned to his sickbed, nursing his bad back and fuming over Marty's borrowing of his name. A few days after the chaotic trip, he got a call from Marty, the first since their tense exchange on the way home from Mississippi. "We're leaving. We're out of here. It's over," Marty said. "Are you coming?"

Once, long before, David had asked Marty what he was going to do if he ever got caught. As long as you give the money back it's a slap on the wrist, Marty had answered cavalierly, tossing around Michael Milken's name as an example. So now, Rosse's first question was why Marty didn't just give the money back.

"There is no money to give back," Marty answered.

Rosse was stunned. It finally dawned on him how serious the situation was. He angrily told his boss that he was staying put.

"You're a traitor," Marty said, and slammed down the phone.

220

Marty Frankel had not been indicted. No FBI agents were knocking at his door. But he knew he was in very big trouble. He had returned $57 million to Tennessee after Lovelady had discovered he'd removed it from the Atlanta bank. But there was not enough money to return to Mississippi. Regulators in Missouri, Arkansas, and Oklahoma, where Thunor also owned insurance companies, had not asked for their money back yet, but it was only a matter of time before they caught wind of Mississippi's suspicions.

Quite simply, most of the money was gone, spent on houses and women and bodyguards and surveillance equipment, on Kaethe's wine collection and Tom Corbally, Larry Martin, and Tom Quinn's European travels. And millions more had been spent on consultant fees—or hush money, depending upon one's definition. It was just a matter of time before the law caught up.

Marty sat in his trading room facing his bank of computer screens. But now, instead of studying the market, he did online research into worldwide extradition policies. The safest corners of the world were not particularly appetizing to him. Instead he began to seriously consider Italy, where he hoped that the Faustis, freshly paid over $500,000, would receive him with open arms.

Nervously he transferred money between his many accounts. Typically when he wired money, he had one of his minions fill out and send an Internet wire transfer form by e-mail. Now he frantically handwrote the orders and had them faxed. He sent one fax, and then another rescinding the previous order. Once he called Banque SCS angrily demanding to know why they had failed to execute a transfer. It turned out he had already rescinded it.

Incessantly, he scribbled notes. "Launder money," he wrote on one "to do" list. "Get $ to Israel, get it back in." On a fax transmission form he wrote orders to "buy 15 of each of the Notes and Bonds (U.S. Treasury) listed on the following 2 pages. Then I need to sell 12 of each and then buy 12 back."

He transferred $600,000 to an account at Northern Trust, a Chicago bank. Held in the name of the Chicago lawyer who long ago had handled some of his SEC problems, the money was to pay any legal bills incurred in the future by himself, Karen Timmins, or Sonia. His thoughts and anxieties ricocheted everywhere. For a man who subsisted on veggies and simply prepared fish, the notion of having to dine out in Italy was repugnant. He ordered cases of tuna and bottled water to make the trip with him.

Finally, Marty worked up his astrological charts, asking the stars five pressing questions: "Will I go to prison? Will Tom turn me in? Should I leave? Should I wire money back from overseas? Will I be safe?" The answers, as conveyed to him by the charts, were ominous. He was in danger, danger, danger.

Hackney called. Marty refused to speak to him, and one of the women explained that Marty was busy. David Rosse called and left a message: he wanted a signed statement saying that he had never been part of Marty's schemes.

He called his family back in Toledo. "I'm busy for a few weeks," he told them. "If you don't hear from me, don't worry,"

A worker who took care of Marty's cars arrived at the compound and was told, "Marty's flipping out and he's packing his stuff."

Another low-level employee was astonished by the panic she encountered when she arrived at work that week. Suitcases were everywhere, and she wondered, "How many suitcases does he need for a business trip?" As she wandered around the house she bumped into Karen Timmins, with whom she was friendly. Timmins had a stark message. "Take off and never come back," she told the young woman, suggesting she pass the advice on. Vera, Marty's longtime maid, was ordered to take a vacation.

With David Rosse gone, and Sonia so far away, Marty suddenly started to treat Bob Biddle, the maintenance man, as though he were indispensable. This was partly an act in support of his excuse for leaving. Only a very few in Marty's inner circle knew how devastating the events in Mississippi had been. To some people he simply said he was going on a business trip. But to others, including several of the women and Tom Corbally, he confided that Biddle had uncovered a plot by David Rosse to kill him. "Bob saved my life," he said. He chose Mona Kim and Jackie Ju, the ex-lover who'd made the Mississippi trip, to accompany him into exile.

Marty wanted to get a solid head start on law enforcement. That meant that Bob Guyer was a sticky problem. The moment regulators knocked on his door, they'd figure out that the president of Liberty National Securities knew precious little about what "David Rosse," his trader extraordinaire, was up to. In fact, Guyer called Marty by his real name. Marty suggested that Guyer and his wife needed a little vacation, implying that he would pay for it, and the couple made plans for a road trip. Shortly before they left on their holiday, as they were doing yard work, Cynthia Allison walked up to the house. Recently she'd been keeping an eye on Guyer for Marty, saying that she wanted to watch him in the office because she was planning to become a broker.

"I feel sorry for you people," she said. "I don't think you understand what's going on." This cryptic remark thoroughly confused the Guyers. They soon left on a tour of western Michigan, where they visited churches and did genealogical research.

Marty's last and most significant chore before he took off was to collect the diamonds he'd ordered. He already had received $2 million worth, but it had taken a while for the dealers in California to assemble the other $8 to $9 million worth. Now they were ready to be picked up, and for that Marty turned to Steve, David Rosse's assistant, who had already proved himself trustworthy on two sensitive errands: he had babysat Guyer's mailbox in Dundee, and had recently flown down to Charlotte, North Carolina, with an envelope of papers. Sonia had met Steve at the airport, signed the papers while Steve had a smoke, and handed the envelope back to him. He'd then jumped back on an airplane and returned the envelope to Marty.

Steve's final mission was his most important: collecting the diamonds. Steve flew to San Jose to meet the jeweler Richard Teel, the acquaintance of David Rosse who was supplying the gems. Together they picked up the diamonds, went back to the airport, and prepared to board a private Gulfstream jet for Los Angeles, where they were to pick up another diamond dealer and more diamonds, and then head back to the East Coast just in time for Marty's departure.

Suddenly Marty called the airport used by private planes in San Jose and paged them. Steve answered the page and Marty demanded to be put on with Teel. "I've just come up with some information that causes me to believe that I can't trust this person with the responsibility of this," he told the diamond dealer. "But I trust you." Teel was charged with getting the diamonds to Marty.

Marty asked to speak to Steve again. He ordered him to head for the nearby commercial airport and return to Greenwich immediately. Almost as soon as Steve arrived at the regular airport his cell phone rang. Marty had changed his mind and wanted Steve to head for Dundee. By now, Steve was pretty sure that Marty, or the Rainman, as he called him behind his back, was losing it. He called David Rosse, who ordered him to fly to Los Angeles and try to hitch a ride home on Teel's chartered jet the next day. Steve flew to Los Angeles and checked into the Regal Biltmore Hotel, where he tried unsuccessfully to hook up with Teel. He eventually got home on a commercial flight.

Meanwhile, Marty had arranged for a chartered plane to pick him up at the airport in nearby White Plains and fly him to Rome. As he raced around the compound on the morning of May 4, making final arrangements and issuing orders for the disposal of papers, computers, and cars, Bob Biddle arrived. "Are you still here? You have to go!" Biddle practically screamed, adding to the chaos, Marty, Mona, and Jackie piled into cars, along with more than a dozen suitcases, and the cases of water and tuna were loaded in by helpers. Then they left the compound for the last time.

They got to the airport at 1:30 P.M., just five days after the fateful Mississippi meeting. There Marty sat for five hours, waiting for the diamonds and worrying. Mona and Jackie were scared, too, their fears fanned by Biddle and Marty's panic. Marty drew up a quick astrological chart. The news was not good.

In a new fit of anxiety he decided to take off without the diamonds. He would arrange for their transport later. But, terrified that they would be stolen when the Gulfstream landed in White Plains, he quickly decided that a diversionary tactic was necessary. He had the Gulfstream redirected to Teterboro, New Jersey, where a small airport not far from New York City caters to private planes. He also had someone call Kroll Associates, to arrange for security. The assignment was referred to a Kroll contact in New Jersey, who contracted for several off-duty state troopers to converge on Teterboro shortly before midnight.

At 6:35 P.M., May 4, Marty's plane finally took off.

Back at the mansion, it was total chaos. To the women and support staff remaining it was pretty clear that the boss was not coming back anytime soon. Shortly before he'd left, Marty had ordered that auto titles be distributed to those who drove cars registered to corporate names.

For many of the staff, that was a license to loot. Expensive carpets and stereos were loaded into cars and driven away. So were some of the computers. Marty had left instructions that magazines and video-tapes be boxed up. His minions were supposed to send some items to storage facilities. He had taken a few documents with him, but the re-maining papers were to be fed to the three industrial-strength shredders in the house. Marty's chef calmly cooked for the people swarming around him.

At about seven P.M., David Rosse stormed onto the scene. He'd hoped to get Marty to sign a document absolving him of any wrongdoing in the criminal scheme and was angry to find the boss already gone. He stomped around the house. Everywhere there was disarray, the result of Marty's hurried departure and the frenzied looting afterward. Cameras and the other high-tech security equipment Marty had once obsessed about were shut off. A safe had been emptied and left open. File cabinets were ransacked. There were still a few people running about, but none of them knew where Marty was or how to reach him.

After Rosse left, Marty called home and an employee reported that his chief of security had angrily searched the house looking for him. "7–8 p.m. DAVE TERRORIZES STAFF," Marty wrote in his astrological date-book.

Rosse had just left the compound when his own phone rang. It was Richard Teel, the diamond dealer, who told him he was en route to de-liver the diamonds at Teterboro. Anxious about the delivery, and the bizarre arrangements, Teel beseeched Rosse to come to the airport. With no idea what was going on, Rosse agreed.

Late that night, he arrived at Teterboro to find four men waiting on the tarmac for the Gulfstream carrying Teel and the second dealer, who had been picked up in Los Angeles. Several were jabbering on cell phones, apparently arguing with one another over who should take con-trol of the diamonds. One was Bob Biddle, who was there at Marty's be-hest. Three were the off-duty police officers recruited by the Kroll contact to act as the evening's security detail. And then there was David Rosse, who was fuming—angry about the abrupt departure of his boss, who owed him money and had borrowed his name, and resentful that he'd been left out of this security-sensitive plan.

The Gulfstream landed at about midnight. Rosse boarded the plane and chatted with the diamond merchants. Several bags were unloaded from the plane and left at the bottom of the stairs. Some contained diamonds, which were bagged and marked, and others contained certificates authenticating the gems. When Rosse returned down the steps of the plane, he quickly grabbed two of the bags and put them in his truck. The bags contained several million dollars worth' of diamonds, and some certificates.

The tarmac was not especially well lit and to some on the scene it was not completely clear what Rosse had done. The off-duty troopers raced up and demanded to know what Rosse had taken. One of the jewelers frantically reported that he had taken some diamonds. There was a metal suitcase of stones remaining on the tarmac. The men tussled over the suitcase in the gloom. The hired security men prevailed.

Quickly they put the diamonds into one of their vehicles. "You're coming with us," one of them gruffly told a very frightened Teel. He felt a firm hand on his head as he was shoved into the vehicle, which sped away after Rosse. But the small security force lost sight of the SUV and began debating among themselves what to do next. Finally, one of the officers told Teel that they were going to put him in a motel room and keep him under armed guard for his own protection.

Teel refused the offer and agreed to turn over custody of the diamonds in return for his freedom. They left him on the side of the road, and he was picked up by the other jeweler, who had been following in a taxi. Biddle, swearing into a cell phone in his own vehicle, chased after the diamonds.

What happened next to the stash of diamonds is not completely clear. But later they were were put on a chartered jet bound for Rome by a mysterious older woman with a European accent.

Meanwhile, Marty was somewhere over the Atlantic. On the plane, he told at least one of the women that the $600 million St. Francis had transferred to the insurance companies was completely fictional. "There's really no $600 million, so there's no theft," he explained. "There's no money laundering." The women were not completely sure what he was talking about.

Marty's travel plans were still incomplete: he had yet to tell the Faustis that he was coming to visit. Luckily, they were in when he called from the plane and told them he was on his way to Italy and planned to land at an airport near Rome. He asked them to meet him there. He needed their help, he pleaded, because his chief of security was going to try to assassinate him. He was frightened. They agreed to meet the plane.

The plane landed in Spain to refuel. Marty called back to the United States and learned that David Rosse had stolen some of the diamonds. For Marty, who had decided only a few days before that Rosse was his enemy, it was confirmation of everything he now believed to be true of his longtime protector. The man had threatened to kill him. He'd stolen his diamonds. The situation was dire.

Finally, the next morning, the weary threesome arrived in Rome. They were met at the airport by the Faustis, who were taken aback by the massive amount of luggage that accompanied their guest. They walked Marty and the two women through customs, with Marty wildly tipping everyone he encountered. The Faustis thought that he would want to stay in a luxury hotel, but it turned out that was the last thing he wanted. He emphatically spoke of his fear of Rosse and begged them to help him locate a place to live where he could not easily be tracked down. They quickly found him a temporary apartment. And, since he was a valued—if sometimes difficult—client, they allowed him to use their office and its telephone.

Marty's first priority was to get David Rosse out of his hair. He decided to give Rosse what he wanted, a note absolving him of wrongdoing. He sat down and drafted a one-sentence message. "I, Marty Frankel, used David Rosse's name without his permission or knowledge." The question then was how to get the note to Rosse as quickly as possible without dropping crumbs of information that would lead back to his Italian hideout. The solution was to send it in two steps. First he faxed it to someone in the United States. That person then brought it to a Staples office-supply store and faxed it directly to Rosse. It is not clear who in the United States did the faxing. The message sent, Marty was much relieved. "DAVE RIP," he wrote in his astrological calendar.

Marty also wired about $1.7 million to a trust-type bank account in Germany controlled by Kaethe's brother, a lawyer.

Another priority was to get a substantial amount of cash out of his Swiss account. With the help of the Faustis, Marty retained the services of two trustworthy Italian gentlemen, both veterans of Italian law enforcement agencies. The two were dispatched to Geneva, where they touched base with Marty's banker, Jean-Marie Wery. They were handed a satchel containing $300,000 in currency and returned with this loot to Marty in Rome.

During his first forty-eight hours in Rome, Marty stayed in touch with at least a few of the people busy dismantling the compound. Although much of the house's contents had been either carted off for safe-keeping or looted, two women remained. Their assignment was to shred the mountains of remaining documents, which were a road map to what Marty had been up to for the past ten years. At least one recently re-cruited sexual playmate was still living in the second house, where sec-ond-string paramours and rejected would-be lovers usually boarded.

The two women assigned to the shredding detail, neither of whom was ever in Marty's most intimate circle, had been feeding the shredders for about a day without supervision when they got sick of the boring and mechanical task and started looking for an easy way out. The an-swer, they decided, was the mansion's fireplaces. But the women didn't know what the Greenwich fire inspector George Henehan could have told them about burning file folders: because oxygen can't easily cir-culate between pages, burning them is almost as tedious as feeding a shredder.

When a chair next to one of the fireplaces caught fire, there was little cause for anxiety. The air was smoky, but the flames were contained. What spooked the two women were the alarms and the subsequent call from the alarm company. They fled and contacted someone whom Marty was calling from Europe. "6–7 PM FIRE NY," he wrote in his cal-endar. Worried about the condition of his property and, of course, about what had been found on the premises, he put in a call to the Greenwich Police Department on May 6. Calmly, he asked what had happened at his house and listened as they told him about the fire and the state of the mansion. The police department had already alerted the FBI, although that agency had not yet responded. The officer on the phone told Marty that the police wanted to have a chat with him. He declined to come in for an interview. The officer asked Marty where he was calling from. Marty refused to answer and quickly ended the phone call.

Marty next contacted Mark Durkin, a lawyer in Stamford, Connecti-cut, who had handled some of his local legal needs. Apparently realizing that if the local police were so interested in talking to his client there might be need for criminal expertise, Durkin put a call in to Hugh Keefe. Keefe, a well-known criminal attorney in New Haven, was in the middle of a trial in state court in Hartford when he returned Durkin's call from a pay phone in the courthouse corridor. Durkin explained that he had a client, a gentleman from Greenwich who lived in a big house and was in the securities business. He explained that there had been a fire at his home and that there were some technical, legal questions about what had been going on at the house. If the matter led to anything, asked Durkin, would Keefe be on hand to help with any criminal issues? Keefe said he'd be available and went back to his trial.

For nearly a week, ever since getting back from Jackson, John Hackney had had unwelcome visitors in his conference room. They'd been sent by the state of Mississippi to try to figure out what was going on at the Thunor-owned companies and to wait for the money that Hackney kept telling them was on its way. One of the visitors was Betty Cordial, the insurance-fraud expert whom Special Assistant Attorney General Lee Harrell had brought in to help sort things out. She sat there with her reddish hair, large glasses, and well-manicured nails, shooting questions at Hackney. They were quickly losing patience with each other. She found his answers evasive and often conflicting. He just wanted to get out of there.

Between interrogations, Hackney and Gary Atnip would cross their recently redecorated reception area and enter their private offices, where they were trying to deal with another crisis, one they were trying to keep from Cordial on the other side of the office suite. They were having an unusually difficult time reaching Marty. At one point when they called the Greenwich mansion, one of the women answered and explained that Marty couldn't come to the phone. "You know how he is," the young woman told Hackney. "He'll call you back." But he didn't.

The next day, May 5, nobody answered at the mansion. That had never happened before. Hackney began to panic. In the conference room on the other side of the reception area, Cordial and her assistants plodded on, looking at documents and occasionally pestering Hackney and Atnip with questions. In Hackney's office, the two men were now frantically looking for Marty. They tried to reach Corbally. When that failed, they called Larry Martin, who offered no clues. At his wits' end, Hackney enlisted the woman who was helping Marty with his annuity project to drive over and scope out the Greenwich place. It was a long drive, and every so often her cell phone would ring. It was Hackney checking on her progress and sounding more flustered with every call. He had not fully explained her mission and the woman felt uncomfortable. Finally, she decided she wanted no part of whatever was going on. She made some excuse to Hackney, turned around, and headed home.

Late on Friday afternoon, May 7, Hackney got a phone call from Kay Tatum, the lawyer who represented St. Francis at Akin, Gump. She, too, had been trying to reach Marty. She finally had heard from another Frankel associate, who had driven by the compound. The news was not good. He'd reported that police cars were swarming over the cul-de-sac and driveway of the Greenwich mansion. There had been a fire. And when police and firefighters entered the house it appeared that it had been hurriedly abandoned.

Marty had not returned the assets of the Mississippi insurance companies. Hackney had no idea where to find the assets of some of the other companies, either. He called Franklin American's senior personnel into his office. "I've been trying to find the people at Liberty and I couldn't find them," he told his staff. "And I couldn't find the money that was invested. Nobody's answering the phone. I think he's stolen it."

Hackney called his lawyers. And he also called Ann, who'd been urging him to quit his increasingly stressful job and move on with his life. Now, clearly, it was too late for that. He explained that he wouldn't be home until much, much later. "What's going on?" she asked. He decided not to go into details. "Something really, really bad's happened," he answered.

Then came the hard part. Hackney had to call Lee Harrell and Betty Cordial, who already had left Franklin for the weekend. For several hours he spoke with them by phone, as they grilled him about the money and listened to his befuddled answers. He mentioned some of the names of the people he'd dealt with—Robert Guyer and Eric Stevens. Then he explained that there had been a fire at Liberty National Securities, somewhere in New York.

Late in the evening, Cordial called an FBI buddy in New York, and they started trying to track down this mysterious fire. They got nowhere and finally decided to abandon the search until Monday.

On Tuesday, Cordial was sitting in the offices of Franklin American when the receptionist put a call through to her. The caller was a different FBI agent, and he *was* investigating a suspicious fire—not in New York but in Greenwich, Connecticut. Documents found in the rubble mentioned Franklin American. Suddenly the pieces began to fall into place.

It was only after a few days of questioning by several representatives of Mississippi that Lee Harrell finally heard Hackney utter the true name of his boss. He mentioned it almost in passing, and Lee Harrell stopped him. "John," the lawyer said, "who the hell is Marty Frankel?"

A few days after the fire, John Schulte received a phone call in his spartan office in Oregon, Ohio, from a reporter he'd never met, at a newspaper he'd never read. The reporter asked whether he knew Marty Frankel and Sonia Schulte.

"Yes and unfortunately," Schulte answered. The reporter, Joe Johnson of the *Greenwich Times*, told him that something suspicious was going on in Connecticut. What emerged was sketchy. Apparently a money manager named Marty Frankel had fled without a trace and it looked as if he might have ripped off some insurance companies. Johnson had covered the suicide of Frances Burge and had since tried to keep tabs on the goings-on at the mysterious mansion.

"Wonderful. It's music to my ears," Schulte replied when Johnson explained why he was calling. He told Johnson that he had known Frankel was "bogus from Day One," and that he'd "been waiting for this news for ten years."

Schulte hung up with Johnson feeling that his life had suddenly taken a turn for the better. He hadn't seen his two daughters for years. He'd been litigating with his former wife for more than a decade. He'd attended fathers'-rights rallies and courted press coverage of his plight. "I kiss their pictures every day. I pray they're being looked over by the proper people," he'd told a reporter for the *Plain Dealer* in Cleveland about his missing daughters. Now there was hope. Schulte went into action. He had an intermediary call the cops in Greenwich and learned that his wife had been seen at the Greenwich mansion. Then he alerted his attorney that he was beginning his war anew.

He vowed: "If Sonia gets indicted, I'll file for custody in twenty-four hours."

David Rosse had fled Teterboro Airport with about 330 diamonds and a stack of certificates of authentication stashed in the 1995 Chevrolet Tahoe sport-utility vehicle Marty had bought him. In the following days, no one came knocking at his door in North Salem, New York, looking for the gems. The two diamond dealers thought they'd seen Rosse run off with the bag, but it was not completely clear what had happened and who was who on the tarmac that bizarre and murky night.

And Marty, who had been alerted to the theft, was in no position to go to the police and complain.

It would be an understatement to say that David Rosse was bitter. He knew he was at risk. First of all, there were the myriad tasks he had performed for Marty over the years. He had helped launder insurance company assets as they made their journey from Banque SCS back to the United States in the form of traveler's checks. Then there was Marty's use of his name, which he also felt put him in jeopardy.

Marty also owed Rosse a lot of money—$67,700 in salaries for himself and Steve, his assistant. Marty had promised to provide medical and dental coverage, but the security chief had racked up more than $30,000 in unpaid medical bills, much of it on account of his painful back. Back surgery, he knew, was in his future and Marty clearly wasn't going to be around to foot the bill. Then there were expenses. The boss still owed Ross roughly $100,000 for security cameras, recorders, alarms, lighting and the like for the two-house Greenwich compound.

Increasing Rosse's fury was his constant pain and the fact that he was taking a lot of prescription painkiller medication, maybe too much. Rosse wanted to prepare for the day when someone—he wasn't sure who—came looking for the diamonds. Soon after the Teterboro caper he visited Florida and secreted some of the gems in his uncle's home without his knowledge. He gave other diamonds to several friends for safekeeping. He handed one friend fifteen loose diamonds, two diamond earrings, and a diamond ring.

And some of the diamonds Rosse sprinkled around his home. One three-carat stone, he hid in a bottle of hand cream. Another, he stuck in a package of throat lozenges. Two more, he placed inside a pen. Then he sat in his house mulling over his aching back and contemplating suing Marty Frankel.

Life in Rome was not all bad. The threesome's lives centered around using phone cards to call the United States. When they weren't on the phone, Mona, Jackie, and Marty sat in cafés, basking in the May sun. They went out to eat with the Faustis and planned a sightseeing jaunt to Florence. Marty tried to call Father Jacobs, who spent much of his time in Rome, but didn't reach the priest.

He still had access to his bank accounts in Switzerland and he wired some money to Alfredo, who was helping with the apartment situation. He also checked on his gold in Geneva. Four days after he arrived in Rome, so did the diamonds—except for those taken by David Rosse, that is. Marty still didn't have his hands on them, but they were ready to be picked up. Then he received some good news from the diamond dealers back in California: he was due a sales tax refund of almost $454,000. The money was wired into an account at an Italian bank and put under Mona's name.

Marty had his complaints, of course. He was none too fond of pasta and at one point sent Mona and Jackie out in search of Chinese food. The little household's first dwelling was a tiny, seven-hundred-square-foot apartment. Charm was not among its attributes and it had no television or telephone. Marty called it "a dump."

Marty was no longer hysterical, just somber. His lowest periods came when he worried about where he would go next. He would "never go to Germany," he told Mona. "It's the worst place." He was sure people would "rat" on him there.

In the tiny apartment, Mona, who had never actually been to bed with the boss, sometimes walked around him in her underwear, draping herself over the furniture when she was sure he was looking. He didn't bite. Still, thoughts of romance had not been completely banished from Marty's life. The threesome began talking about finding a mate for Marty—a nice Italian girl. He could settle down, marry, and have children with her. They brainstormed about how they could approach a priest or a local church to help with their quest for the perfect woman. They even drafted a personal advertisement, but that was as far as they got.

By his second week in Rome, Marty was busy making deals. Earlier in the year, the Faustis had helped their friend Rocco Nuzzaci make a deal with a U.S. health care company to buy roughly a half-interest in his Italian firm, Sanità Più, for $20 million. This was the deal that Alfredo had tried desperately to get Marty interested in.

For some reason, Nuzzaci's deal with the U.S. company fell through. Ensconced in Rome, with full access to his remaining $30 million or so at Banque SCS, Marty began talking with Nuzzaci again, using the Faustis as intermediaries. The deal had some advantages. If consummated, it would give Marty a legitimate beachhead from which to conduct business—or make money transfers—in Italy. It was also a convenient, and seemingly legitimate, way to get a large chunk of cash out of his Swiss account, which, he assumed, would eventually be frozen.

On Wednesday, May 12, exactly a week after the fire in Greenwich, Marty signed a contract with Nuzzaci. He paid Nuzzaci $28 million, which was much of the money he had left in Switzerland, in exchange for about 15 percent of Sanità Più. In one sense, it was an odd deal. The U.S. company had been prepared to pay less money for a much higher stake in the company. But the arrangement had some strange advantages as well. There was a provision to cancel the deal. If that happened, Nuzzaci would keep a portion of the purchase price, but most of the money would return to Marty. Presumably, he would be able to put that cash wherever he chose. The deal was consummated as planned, and the money was wired out of Switzerland. The Faustis also did well on the deal. They earned a roughly $2 million commission.

By then, Marty was looking for a way to go into deep hiding if and when the roof fell in and he had to flee again. In Rome, he contacted a man from Libya; the two met on the same day he signed his contract with Nuzzaci. The man offered to get Marty on a flight to Libya, which was not exactly an attractive destination for American Jews, but had the advantage of not having an extradition treaty with the United States. The next day Marty called the owner of Park Avenue Travel, the agency that had made some of his household's travel arrangements in better times. The man counseled him against the trip. "Word is—if I go on plane, I'm toast," Marty wrote in the astrological calendar. He ditched the Libyan plan.

Three days later, on May 16, a federal magistrate in Connecticut issued a warrant for his arrest, which accused him of wire fraud and money laundering. The FBI and federal prosecutors, of course, suspected him of other crimes as well, not the least of which was securities fraud. But they had cobbled together what they could, as quickly as they could, on the basis of the clues left in the Greenwich mansion. Over the coming weeks, agents would fan out across the United States. Sonia had a preliminary meeting with FBI agents in North Carolina. Other agents paid calls on dozens of people in Franklin who knew John Hackney and Gary Atnip. In the next few weeks, all of Marty's insurance companies would be put into receivership as it became clear that most of their assets had simply vanished.

For the FBI agents, the search for Marty was full of frustrations. The rumor mill had him everywhere—in Europe, Brazil, Israel. There was talk that he had ties to the Russian Mob.

Directories of employees had been kept at the house, listing everyone by first name with his or her home number, cell phone number, and pager number, so it was not hard to track down the now dispersed members of the household. The FBI also quickly learned that Marty was calling home. But either because he was using phone cards, or because the women were reluctant to betray him, agents could not figure out where he was.

An added difficulty was that some of the women closest to Marty were nowhere to be found. Kaethe was in Rome, still involved with Alfredo. Karen Timmins had left her small daughter with family members and simply vanished, telling her mother she was going on vacation, but not where.

Marty did not immediately know that a warrant had been issued for his arrest. But within days at least some of his assets in Switzerland had been frozen; by May 26, all of them were. The situation was worsening. He was now a fugitive. Much of his luggage, including his laptop, was in storage. He began hanging out in Rome's cybercafés so he could check on news of the manhunt. The first of what would be thousands of newspaper, magazine, and television accounts began to trickle onto the Internet. On May 21, Joe Johnson of the *Greenwich Time* broke the news on his paper's front page. "Insurance companies in five states may have lost nearly $1 billion from investments the firms made through a securities brokerage possibly linked to a backcountry Greenwich estate," he wrote.

"Where There's Smoke There's Fire? Missing Greenwich Broker Leaves Only Smoldering Clues," read a headline in the *Hartford Courant*. That story was based in part on an affidavit filed in federal court in Connecticut by Special Agent Joseph Dooley of the FBI. Using documents found in the house and information provided by state regulators and others, Dooley had put together many of the disparate pieces of the scam, including the involvement of the St. Francis Foundation. Still, for many of the law enforcement officials and others trying to understand what had happened, there were confusing gaps. Federal agents and state regulators struggled at first to work out how much money Marty had stolen, because he had claimed high investment returns that did not actually exist. Tom Bolan's lawyer announced to reporters that he was seeking up to $1.98 billion belonging to the St. Francis Foundation. That money simply did not exist. Eventually it was determined that about $215 million in insurance assets had been stolen.

Meanwhile, Marty's former associates and bedmates were receiving subpoenas from the U.S. Attorney's Office in Connecticut. The documents asked for information about a long list of "entities," including Liberty National, the insurance companies, and St. Francis, and "individuals," at least six of whom existed only as aliases used by Marty. The subpoenas also sought information about Father Jacobs, Tom Corbally, Thurston Little, and Tom Quinn, and about Marty's women, including Sonia, Miriam, Adriana, Jackie, and Mona.

Marty was not optimistic about his chances of eluding capture. He made an astrological chart to plot how the whole fiasco would end, and he was matter-of-fact about its ominous answer: this matter would end in violence. Previous charts had always shown that he would die of old age.

He began to think about prison life. The prospect of being sentenced to a state prison, as opposed to a federal penitentiary, absolutely terrified him. And the possibility that he would be put in a Mississippi jail was particularly frightening to him; he obsessed about it with his companions. As a liberal Democrat and a Jew, he felt he would be especially unwelcome in Mississippi. Plus, he dreaded that somehow his fellow inmates would learn of his unorthodox sexual tastes.

Marty's days of relative peace were over. His housing situation continued to give him grief. After about three weeks, he, Mona, and the increasingly homesick Jackie moved into a suite in a small hotel in a nice neighborhood in Rome. After they had been there just a short time, someone knocked at the door at about midnight, while Marty slept. The hotel owner wanted to see their passports: the security-conscious Israeli embassy, which was nearby, had raised questions about the little group of tourists. Marty and the women had registered at the hotel using aliases.

Mona woke up Marty, who hurriedly told her not to show the hotel owner their passports. Mona rushed back to the door and explained that the safe in their room was broken, so they had put their passports in a safe deposit box at a bank. An angry Marty then appeared, complaining about the late hour and demanding that the owner return at a reasonable time the next morning. The three left at dawn. With the help of the Faustis they moved to another apartment, in the Trieste section of Rome.

Marty had the cash he'd gotten out of his Swiss account with the help of the Faustis. He had roughly $454,000, from the diamond dealer's tax refund, in a Rome bank under Mona's name. But he knew he would need more. He needed to retrieve the diamonds from wherever they were stored in Rome.

From Marty's notes in his astrological calendar, it appears that the Faustis had control of the gems, and that they wanted money for them. "F. WANTS 30K + etc. FOR STONES," Marty wrote on June 7. The next day he shelled out $43,000 for them, and several days after that he picked them up. He now had them in his possession, but he had not yet figured out how to exchange them for cash, a tricky transaction given that the FBI probably knew about his diamond caper.

But Marty thought he had a financial fallback position. Just in the nick of time, he'd gotten about $30 million out of his Swiss account for the Sanità Più deal. Now that, too, began to come apart. With Marty suddenly in the news, the Faustis and their lawyers realized that there was a strong possibility that dealing with Marty could ensnare them in some sticky legal problems. On the strong advice of their lawyers, the Faustis and Nuzzaci decided to pull out of the deal. Marty had one request. He wanted the money returned to an account in Italy, not to his accounts at Banque SCS, which were frozen.

But that worried the Italian lawyers. Letting Marty keep the money in Italy might look a lot like money laundering, they decided. They advised returning the money to Banque SCS in Switzerland, minus the break-up fee, which Nuzzaci was entitled to keep. (Under the terms of the deal, Nuzzaci was entitled to keep 15 percent of the purchase price. But he agreed to accept only $1.5 million.)

In a late-night phone call on June 24, Alfredo tried to assure Marty that everything would turn out all right. For several days afterward, Marty heard nothing from the Nuzzaci/Fausti camp. Then on Sunday, June 27, he got bad news: Alfredo told him that Nuzzaci was sending the purchase money back to Banque SCS, and that Alfredo was not going to return his own $2 million fee either. He told Marty that Kaethe would pay Marty's bills.

Then came even more devastating news. Fausto Fausti in late June called to say that he wanted nothing more to do with Marty. Fausto told Marty to leave him and his son alone, and not to ask them for any more favors. Marty could not even win over Alfredo, who had always seemed more sympathetic than his father. "ALF ABANDONS ME—TELLS ME TO GO," Marty wrote in his calendar.

The Faustis weren't the only ones anxious to banish Marty Frankel from their lives. Jackie Ju had already left, and shortly afterward, Mona left Italy as well.

Marty had imported a replacement, however. After a flurry of phone calls to the States, Cynthia Allison agreed to fly to Italy to be with the man she loved. By the time she made her decision, Interpol had been alerted and there was a global manhunt on for Marty. Apparently, she didn't care. Cynthia arrived in Italy just a few days before Mona left. They overlapped long enough to change the name on the bank account holding the tax refund from "Mona Kim" to "Cynthia Allison." And then, Marty and Cynthia were left alone.

Mona headed for Paris. With about $20,000 in her pocket, a good-bye gift from Marty, she spent a few days—and a few thousand dollars—shopping, then returned to Westchester. Knowing that she might have legal problems, she almost immediately visited a local criminal lawyer. Then she checked into a mid-priced hotel off a major highway near Stamford, Connecticut. At dawn, the FBI paid her a call there, and she was taken into custody. It turned out that Customs had caught her name when she reentered the country and she'd been followed to the hotel.

Mona was driven to the FBI office in Bridgeport and put in a dingy room with a tuna sandwich and a soda for company. When they let her out some hours later, she was in a hyperactive state, and more than ready to talk. The FBI agents and prosecutors who listened to her tale of hiding with Marty in Italy were in a state akin to euphoria. Each time she dropped an especially helpful hint, agents rushed out of the room to make phone calls. An agent was put on a plane to Italy, although the FBI was already looking for him there. Mona even told the agents about the tax-refund bank account.

The prosecutors were happy enough with Mona's story to allow her to keep the $15,000 or so that remained of her farewell money. Mona apparently made two mistakes. She didn't tell the FBI that she had a car, an SUV, that Marty had supplied her. Some weeks later, when agents fanned out to seize the roughly $1.8 million in cars that Marty had bought his supplicants, Mona's was taken as well. She also apparently neglected to mention that she had helped Marty buy millions of dollars' worth of gold; that omission would come back to haunt her.

After Marty had told Tom Corbally that he was leaving the country because David Rosse was going to kill him, Corbally decided to remove himself from the scene as well. He folded his tent at the Delmonico on Park Avenue and flew to London; there he took a suite at Claridge's, where he kept an extra stash of clothes. But if Corbally thought that Marty's departure would go unnoticed—or that his own name would be left out of the burgeoning scandal—he was badly mistaken.

By June, Marty Frankel's story was all over the national press in the United States and was spreading abroad as well. Very much to his dismay, Corbally's name and that of Kroll Associates were beginning to make it into press accounts. The FBI had requested an interview. A reporter for ABC News had checked in to Claridge's and was camped out in its lobby.

For several weeks Corbally lay low. But finally he decided to emerge from seclusion. He called the Kroll offices in New York and in his signature gravelly voice asked for his messages. The receptionist refused to relay them. He asked to speak to Jules Kroll, his friend and ally for thirty years. The receptionist refused to transfer him.

Instead, she transferred him to Michael Cherkasky, Kroll's president. A steely former prosecutor, Cherkasky had little patience for Corbally's cloak-and-dagger style. His top priority was to protect the firm's image, a matter all the more important because Kroll had recently gone public. Unbeknownst to Corbally, he had already called New York prosecutors and invited them to examine the contents of Corbally's office if they wished. (Sitting on Corbally's desk were frantic messages from Lee Iacocca, who had started trying to reach Corbally when the Frankel scandal erupted in the press.)

By the time Corbally heard Cherkasky's voice on the other end of the line, he was enormously upset. Frantically, he proclaimed his innocence. Apologizing for bringing the firm's name into the brewing scandal, he insisted he had done nothing wrong. "If anyone is innocent, it's me," he told Cherkasky. "My name is being dragged through the mud." In short, he argued, he was a "victim."

Cherkasky said very little until Corbally was done. "Tom," he finally said, "your stuff is packed up."

Corbally got off the phone. There was only one thing to do. He had to find Frankel—and even capture him—before the FBI got to him. He had to turn himself into a hero. It was the only way to save his reputation. Corbally had the kind of contacts who could do something like that. It would be the most important maneuver of his career.

Just as things were getting uncomfortably hot in Rome, Marty heard from Tom Corbally, who had long been friendly with the Fausti family and had a much easier time than the FBI in making contact with the fugitive. Marty was anxious to take off. There was, after all, no reason to stay. And there was the distinct possibility that either the Faustis or

Mona would reveal his whereabouts to the international teams of police who were out to get him.

Corbally offered to help. Marty said he wanted to flee to a country that had no extradition treaty with the United States. He was terrified because he didn't trust the quality of the passports he was traveling with, and he wanted fresh fake documents. For all this, he said, he would pay roughly $500,000. Corbally said he had contacts who could arrange those things, and put him in touch with a fixer in London.

Anxious to depart, Marty hired a Mercedes and driver, and he and Cynthia hit the road on June 29, heading toward Germany. Marty kept in touch with Corbally's contact by phone as he and Cynthia traveled. The plan, as Marty understood it, was to fly him in a private jet to northern Cyprus, from which the United States could not extradite him. He was supposed to meet up with the mysterious Corbally contacts in Munich.

But unbeknownst to Marty, some of the people making the arrangements for him were reporters from the *Express,* a London tabloid. Corbally had set Marty up. He had told the *Express* that he didn't want any money for himself; he only wanted Marty captured. So while Marty talked to his contact in his frenzied, erratic, and sometimes paranoid way, an *Express* reporter was listening in, taking notes. Marty told the contact that he was driving north from Sicily, and that he would never turn himself in. "No way. I'm not doing any deal," he said. Finally, he called from the road to say that he would meet his contact at a Munich hotel.

The reporters and editors of the *Express* hoped to get an interview, take a few pictures, and then turn their information over to the police and assist with the capture, generating worldwide headlines in the process. Though their escape plan for Marty was a hoax, they had a plane on standby: they were impressed enough by Marty's smarts to think that they might actually have to have a plane idling on the tarmac in order to entice him into their web.

On Tuesday evening, June 29, Marty and Cynthia arrived in Munich, checking into a small hotel. Marty called Hugh Keefe, the New Haven criminal lawyer who was now advising him. Keefe had had some preliminary discussions with the U.S. Attorney's Office in Connecticut. He told Marty that the feds had informed him that two groups were trying to find and kill him, and that the FBI had learned about these threats from European intelligence sources. If the FBI had given Keefe this tidbit simply to spook his client, it worked. Convinced that Tom Quinn had Mob connections, and worried that his efforts to have the Pope visit Russia had made him dangerous enemies there, Marty thought the threats were all too real.

He quickly switched hotels, and early in the morning of Thursday, July 1, he called his contact in the U.K. He said that he had checked his astrological chart and that the time was not ripe for the Munich meeting. "It's a bad day for me. It has to be tomorrow," he explained. He was on his way to Paris, he said, and would phone again to arrange the meeting. He never called again.

In his astrological calendar, Marty noted, "I CANCELLED COR[BALLY] MAN APT." He had narrowly escaped the plot. It turned out that he had also left Rome in the nick of time. With fresh information, the FBI had stepped up their efforts in Italy, asking Italian investigators to interview Fausto Fausti. The Italian system moved slowly, and it wasn't until the beginning of July that the Faustis were placed under police surveillance. By then, Marty and Cynthia were gone, heading not toward Paris, as he had told the *Express*, but toward Hamburg.

Chapter Seventeen

Betrayal

***

Patched together from three nineteenth-century villas, the Hotel Prem is a comfortable, but hardly luxurious, hotel on the shores of Lake Alster. To the south are Hamburg's wealthy suburbs; to the north, the city itself. Hamburg lacks the Old World charm of many European cities and it is not on most tourists' itineraries. For the most part it is modern, rebuilt after being decimated in 1943 by Allied bombers, whose handiwork is still evidenced by the sooty remains of the St. Nikolai church. Once the church was the third tallest building in Germany. Now it is a grim public shrine to the 55,000 citizens of Hamburg who died during the onslaught.

Even in the summer, Hamburg can be a little grim, especially when a stiff wind blows off the huge lake into the trees and shrubbery that line the water in front of the Prem. It was midafternoon on July 7 when Marty Frankel pulled up to the hotel in a taxi. He had left Munich at dawn, the day after canceling his appointment with the London scamsters, and had arrived in Hamburg early the same morning. After six days at another hotel, Marty chose the slightly out-of-the-way Prem as his new home.

His face pasty white, his mouth clamped shut, he checked in to the hotel, paying cash for several weeks in advance on a suite. The name he used was Roger Ellis, and he had a phony British passport to prove it. But nobody asked.

Marty and Cynthia squeezed into the Prem's minuscule elevator and were escorted to Room 5. Marty carried his black suitcase himself. It was a circuitous journey up and down stairwells and through quirky passages created when the villas had been joined together some eighty years before. At last they came to a short corridor with oriental-style runners on a highly polished wood floor.

They had a suite, but it was nothing like the spacious surroundings Marty had once enjoyed at his stone mansion back in Greenwich, Connecticut. The living room was tiny, and so narrow that there was only enough room for an upholstered loveseat. The bedroom was large enough for two beds, as long as they were pushed nearly together. The beds faced a television set. The furnishings were sparse and the wall-to-wall carpet was pink. A narrow balcony spanning both rooms overlooked a well-kept garden in the back. A room facing the lake, and the road that ran around it, would have been too noisy.

Marty had never been so alone. To be sure, he had Cynthia at his side, but the somewhat overweight redhead had never been a favorite of his, even before he had banished her from the mansion for threatening to kill him. Her conversation was as erratic as she was, and at times was even hard to follow. In Rome, Marty had spent his days making phone calls and wangling deals. In Hamburg, he knew nobody. He was sure that somewhere out there, the two groups the FBI had informed his lawyer about were looking for the right moment to kill him.

Marty slept a lot. He worked on his astrological charts, and for fun read the British tabloids. Occasionally he and Cynthia ventured downstairs to La Mer, the Prem's acclaimed seafood restaurant. They even sometimes walked several blocks to the elegant restaurant at the Hotel Atlantique. More often, they ordered room service. Several times they toured Hamburg's notorious Reeperbahn, the sex district, where the neon signs were easily translated into English: "Club d'Amour," "Das Jungle Internet Café," and "Cats," the musical.

Every day Marty and Cynthia carefully monitored press reports of the unfurling scandal back home. Although one U.S. newspaper called him a "primo doofus," others were almost admiringly chronicling his flight, as bumbling federal investigators scrambled to track him to Italy and then appeared to lose his scent. The press described him as a "fugitive financier," an "on-the-lam scammer," a "high-flying" broker with no fewer than "six identities," a "cache of diamonds," and a "sexy German girlfriend."

The truth was a lot less glamorous. Marty was no longer flying so high. He had only about $250,000 left in his valise. The $8 million worth of diamonds would be very difficult to turn into cash with the world's police forces on the lookout. The tax refund account now in Cindy's name was inconveniently located in a bank in Italy, as was much of his luggage. And the "sexy German girlfriend" was now romantically entwined with Alfredo, who had betrayed him.

Marty's only contact with the outside world was his lawyer in New Haven, whom he had never actually met. Their talks were long and rambling and the news was not so good. Hugh Keefe, known to some of his competitors as Huge Keefe for his own estimation of his legal prowess, had continued to chat with the two young federal prosecutors handling Marty's case in Connecticut. On July 13, Keefe told Marty over the phone that the government was talking about a twenty- to thirty-year sentence. But two days later, after speaking with prosecutors again, Keefe revised that figure. Now the government was talking about three twenty-year sentences, or forty to sixty years.

Marty was beside himself. He was forty-four; the prospect of thirty years behind bars was unfathomable. The possibility that some of those years might be spent in Mississippi continued to haunt him. He saw himself as puny and defenseless. He continued to worry that his sexual tastes, if they somehow became public, would make him a target in the rough-and-tumble prison population of the South.

Already feeling low, he sank into an even deeper depression as he obsessed. For a ten-year sentence he would consider turning himself in, he told Cynthia. But he couldn't see spending the rest of his life in jail. Continually he berated himself. The man who had once looked up to the fugitive financier Robert Vesco as his hero had not had the forethought to plan his own escape. Here he was, running through his money, in a country that would extradite him the moment he got caught. He wanted to kill himself, he told Cynthia. It was a threat he repeated again and again.

For Cynthia, life on the lam with the man she loved was not turning out to be a honeymoon. Her daily routine revolved around errands to pick up fruit, yogurt, and newspapers, and monitoring her companion's sagging spirits.

In her bag, she had the phone number of a lawyer back in the States.

After several weeks in Hamburg, she bought a phone card, walked to a nearby outdoor public phone, and called him. She was upset. Her account of life in Germany was disjointed, but she talked until the phone card ran out. Over two or three weeks she had five or six conversations with the lawyer.

Her conversation was a little hard to follow, but it was clear that she was sick of life in Hamburg and worried about what would happen if she got caught. She had another concern as well, and it was almost as pressing as her own well-being and safety. Marty, she confided, was going crazy, and she feared he would take his own life. More than almost anything, she wanted to protect him.

Sometimes Cynthia would run out of time on her phone card, and she'd have to buy another. She began to run through various scenarios with the lawyer, discussing the inevitable capture and reviewing her legal options. Soon, she was sprinkling her conversation with details. She was in Germany. She was in Hamburg. With each conversation she was more worried about herself and Marty, whose mood was spiraling ever downward and who was doing nothing to save himself.

During her last conversation with the lawyer, she made up her mind to take action. She told him that she was at the Hotel Prem, in Room 5. And she gave him permission to pass on the information to the federal authorities who were so desperately looking for Marty Frankel.

On the morning of September 4, the Landeskriminalamt Hamburg, the local police, were asked to arrest Martin Frankel. The order came from the Bundeskriminalamt, or federal police, who in turn had received a request from the FBI in Washington, D.C. A copy of a May 16 arrest warrant issued in Connecticut and an Interpol arrest warrant issued on May 31 were transmitted from Washington. In the afternoon, the Hamburg police received another fax from the U.S. embassy in Berlin. It contained personal information about Martin Frankel and Cynthia Allison, including their exact address in Hamburg—right down to the suite number at the Hotel Prem. Frankel, the fax noted, was unarmed. A photo followed.

The Hamburg police were curious. How had American officials fig-

ured out where he was, let alone learned his suite number at the Hotel
Prem?

That night Marty and Cynthia were sitting on their beds watching
Patch Adams, a movie about a sympathetic doctor they had watched
many times before. They had just finished a halibut dinner. Suddenly
there was a noise at the door. Marty asked Cynthia if she thought it was
the authorities, and almost immediately two German police officers entered, using a key. They pointed their guns at Marty and Cynthia.

Marty dug the British passport in the name of Roger Ellis out of his
black valise and attempted to fake an accent. But when the policemen
confronted him, insisting that the passport was a fake—and noting that
there were a handful of other British and Greek passports in his bag—he
gave up. "You got me," he finally said.

The policemen handcuffed Marty and then he and Cynthia were escorted to the old police headquarters in Hamburg's St. George district, a
forbidding slab-concrete tower. The two were separated and questioned.
Cynthia told her captors that she wanted to consult with a lawyer in the
United States, but declined to name one. She was kept for several hours.
It turned out that the FBI had not sent along a warrant for her arrest. Although she had checked into the Prem using the name Susan Kelly, she
was carrying a U.S. passport in her own name. She had not violated German law and there was no reason to keep her. She was released and returned to the hotel.

Marty was led into a duty room, containing tables, desks, and computers, and was questioned by two lieutenant inspectors. He was afraid
for his life, he told them. There were groups trying to kill him. If he was
imprisoned in an American jail, he insisted, he would not survive. He
began to ramble. He hinted that he had important information about
the Italian government, and the Mafia, as well. He mentioned the names
of the Italian prime minister, Massimo D'Alema; the Russian president,
Boris Yeltsin; and Vernon Jordan, a friend of President Clinton and former law partner of Bob Strauss.

To the police officers, Marty's tale seemed confusing and wild. Perhaps, they thought, he was offering to trade information. They listened
awhile and then consulted a list of volunteer crisis counselors and called
a lawyer for him. Marty didn't stop talking until the lawyer, Thomas
Piplak, arrived and convinced him to shut up for his own good.

But it didn't matter, anyway. For the German police, the matter was a simple case of traveling with a false passport. The rest was for American officials to deal with. And as for the complicated tale this strange, scrawny man kept telling and retelling, and the fancy names he was throwing about—they simply didn't believe any of it.

Epilogue: The Homecoming

On a gray day in early March 2001, Marty Frankel came home. Disheveled, manacled in plastic handcuffs, he was accompanied by federal marshals on a commercial Lufthansa flight from Germany. The trip had been delayed by bad weather, and when Marty finally landed he was met by dozens of police officers and a helicopter hovering overhead. It was as though he were a dangerous criminal capable of escape.

In fact, U.S. officials were worried that Marty would make a sudden break for freedom. Press reports from Germany said that he had made a pathetic attempt to saw through the bars of his prison cell—directly in view of a video camera. German officials had informed their American counterparts that Marty at times had been extraordinarily depressed while incarcerated in Germany. They worried, as had Cynthia Allison, that he would attempt suicide.

Marty steadfastly denied that he'd tried to escape or that he was a suicide risk. But still, home was the last place on earth he wanted to be.

Almost as soon as he'd entered his Hamburg jail cell, Marty had begun to whine. He couldn't eat the food, he complained. He demanded kosher meals, something he'd never asked his personal chefs to prepare back in the old days in Greenwich. The jail, which mostly housed street criminals, was not set up to cater to the complex needs of a neurotic white-collar criminal of international renown. Marty's various demands typically went unmet.

Although he was usually isolated and spoke no German, Marty soon became a celebrity of sorts among his fellow inmates. He doled out ad-

249

vice on everything from their criminal cases to their personal finances. Some inmates called him Herr Wirtschaft, Mr. Economy, because of his stock market advice. He took a little advice too, switching German lawyers on the basis of what he heard behind bars.

Marty had serious German legal problems of his own. He had traveled on a false passport and had failed to pay customs taxes on the roughly $8 million in diamonds he had imported into Germany to fuel his flight. The charges carried a prison term, but nothing like what he faced from the courts back home.

After doing a little research, he came up with his own legal and public-relations strategy. He realized that in Germany people convicted of white-collar crimes of the kind he was accused of received much lighter sentences than they would under U.S. law. Plus there was no capital punishment.

In the United States he was eligible to receive a lengthy sentence that might stretch until the end of his life. A life sentence, he felt, was essentially capital punishment. That, he began to argue to anyone who would listen, would fly in the face of human rights and German law.

Marty's lawyer in the United States had been approached by Barbara Walters and other television journalists but had refused requests for interviews. With his new strategy in place, Marty reversed course and granted an audience to Brian Ross, an investigative reporter at ABC News. In an interview broadcast on *20/20*, he spent roughly half an hour making the case that he should be allowed to remain in Germany. He refused to talk about the charges against him, or what exactly had been going on inside his Greenwich mansion.

He repeated the performance in a Hamburg courtroom. First he tried to delay his trial by unexpectedly requesting that foreign witnesses, including Mona Kim and Alfredo Fausti, be called to testify. Then a few days later he pleaded guilty. He used his court appearances, which were heavily covered by U.S. and European reporters, to plead his case against extradition to the United States.

"The law says everybody should be treated with human dignity," he lectured, his beard scruffy and his fingernails dirty and long. "That's been interpreted by the German courts to mean you cannot execute anybody, you cannot kill them. Also human dignity means they have to have a chance to get out of prison some day."

On the day he pleaded guilty, he read a statement to the judge explaining that "my parents always taught me to help people, help society. Although it may be hard for people to believe, that's all I ever tried to do my whole life." In handcuffs, he was returned to his prison cell. He was sentenced to three years in jail.

Back home, Marty's former associates had cause for concern. FBI agents paid visits to everyone from Marty's women to John Schulte. Lawyers for Tom Corbally and Larry Martin, among others, declined invitations for their clients to meet with federal officials. Kaethe thought it best not to return to the United States, and flew to Bermuda where she met with a lawyer. She charged some of her expenses to the Greenwich household's American Express account, which had not immediately been canceled.

A few of Marty's associates decided to confront their fate. In December 1999, just a few months after Marty was nabbed in Hamburg, David Rosse made a deal with two young federal prosecutors, Mark Califano and Kari Pedersen Dooley. (Dooley was the prosecutor Michael Henehan, the private investigator, had spoken with about a year earlier.) Rosse pleaded guilty to one racketeering conspiracy charge related to money laundering. He remained free, pending sentencing. At first he denied having stolen any diamonds, but then confessed and turned the stones over to the feds. The law-enforcement officials compared the gems to records meticulously kept by the diamond salesmen and realized that some were missing. They confronted Rosse again, and he turned over more diamonds. Still, more were missing. Agents finally searched his home and found several diamonds scattered about, including one under a sink. Rosse was jailed and about 60 of the diamonds remained unaccounted for.

Soon after Rosse's plea, Karen Timmins, who had returned from her "vacation," pleaded guilty to helping conceal money-laundering activities. Federal authorities learned about Marty's plans for her baby and questioned witnesses about the child, now a toddler. Although they were worried, the little girl remained in the care of Karen and her family.

One by one, Marty's compatriots fell. Bob Guyer made a deal with Califano and Dooley, and so did John Hackney, who convinced prosecutors that although he had broken the law, he hadn't actually known that

Marty was stealing the insurers' assets. He pleaded guilty to federal conspiracy and money-laundering charges and to state charges in Tennessee
and Mississippi as well.

Sentencing for all those who pleaded guilty was put off, and some of
the new felons were led to believe that they might not be sentenced until
after Marty's trial—whenever that might be. Some hoped that if they
cooperated they would get lighter sentences. One federal official told
Hackney that they would rather have him arrive in a courtroom to testify against Marty in business attire than in a prison jumpsuit.

Hackney was consumed with thoughts of prison and being away
from his family. He spent hours telling federal officials all he knew about
Marty's empire—hoping to keep his prison time to a minimum. The
Hackney household had been turned upside down. The feds seized their
beautiful house in Franklin and sold it at auction in early 2001 for
$670,000. Feeling like pariahs in Franklin, the family retreated down to
their country house in Guntersville, Alabama. Then that was seized and
they moved to another Guntersville house. Finding a job while awaiting
sentencing was not easy for John Hackney. He sold used cars and water-
proofing for house foundations. He spent many days covered with muck
digging out the basements of construction sites.

One evening FBI agents stopped Sonia Howe Schulte Radencovici as
she returned to her house in Charlotte, North Carolina, having made
sure that her children were not home. They arrested and handcuffed
Sonia and began to lead her away. She and Stefan Radencovici had a hurried conversation about transferring money between accounts, but
when she tried to give him a code for an account, the agents stopped her.

Prosecutors worried that Sonia might flee and she was held without
bail. One federal official called her the number-two person in Marty's
scheme. After several weeks her family finally arranged bail, and she was
released to her parents, pending trial.

Sonia safely under federal control, a judge unsealed a superseding indictment charging Marty, Sonia, Mona Kim, Gary Atnip, and John Jordan, the lawyer who had helped set up the Thunor Trust, with a slew of
federal charges ranging from securities fraud to racketeering conspiracy.
Jordan soon after pleaded guilty to conspiracy and money laundering.
Mona decided to take her chances. She turned down a deal that might

have gotten her thirty-eight months in jail. If ultimately she was found guilty for her role in buying Marty's gold, she risked a substantially higher sentence.

Marty, Sonia, and Gary Atnip all said they could not afford lawyers and were appointed counsel. Meanwhile prosecutors tried to have Kaethe arrested in Germany and extradited. When their efforts were unsuccessful, they unsealed a remaining portion of the indictment. Kaethe, too, had been charged.

By mid-2001, seven of Marty's associates had pleaded guilty to federal charges. Four others awaited trial. The rest of Marty's associates waited in fear that they, too, would be indicted. Many were sued by state insurance commissioners trying to recoup insurance-company losses. They watched as Marty's fleet of twenty-one cars and David Rosse's motorcycle were auctioned off. The U.S. Treasury Department took in more than $750,000. The highest price for a car, $88,000 was paid for a black 1999 Mercedes-Benz S-600.

They tried to put their lives back together. Greg and Oksana ran a small Internet company, and lived together as husband and wife. They used a mail drop as their company's address. Tom Corbally continued to lunch at Cipriani's, although, at eighty, walking the few blocks to get there from his Park Avenue hotel was increasingly difficult.

For a while in 2001, Marty's old crowd relaxed. It seemed that for the moment prosecutors Califano and Dooley were easing off the case. But that changed suddenly in late August. Monsignor Colagiovanni, then eighty-one, was visiting an elderly sister in a Cleveland suburb. He was about to say a mass for another sister, who had recently passed away, when he was suddenly arrested. After being flown to Connecticut, he was jailed overnight and then released on bail. It was a sign to the others that the case was far from dormant.

For Marty, his new life back in Connecticut was definitely an adjustment. He was miserable. At first he was kept under strict surveillance. Lights were kept on in his cell twenty-four hours a day and he wasn't allowed to have his glasses. His court-appointed lawyer, Jeremiah Donovan, told a judge that his client was "agitated," "sleep deprived," and felt like Hannibal Lechter in the movie *The Silence of the Lambs.* Marty complained that he didn't have enough to read. Many of the books on the prison bookshelf were Christian texts and Marty, his days of religious fervor apparently behind him, just wasn't interested. He even lost interest in the stock market.

Eventually Marty was moved into the regular population of the Suffield, Connecticut, prison where he was awaiting trial. He was depressed. He was scared. He felt abandoned by all but a few family members and friends from Toledo. He begged them for money and books. He explained that he feared for his life, that he'd witnessed guards beating up inmates. His tooth hurt.

Still there were bright spots. "The people in prison are the nicest people you'd like to meet," he told a Toledo friend. He vowed to "fight for the rest of my life for prisoners' rights." He played chess with his new friends and decided that he wanted to restudy the works of William Shakespeare. After cutting through a lot of prison red tape he ordered an annotated collection of Shakespeare's works from a Toledo bookstore.

But always, he came back to his own plight. He hinted that he could pull powerful people into his case, and groused about Jeremiah Donovan.

"This is just a white-collar crime. Why are they making such a big thing about it?" he said to a Toledo phone pal. "People stole millions from me. You'll never believe how many millions people stole from me."

Notes

This book is based primarily on about four hundred interviews I conducted between 1999 and 2001. I spoke with people who worked with Frankel and a number of his girlfriends. I also interviewed many lawyers and government officials involved in the Frankel case. In the best of all possible worlds, all sources would talk on the record. But this was a complicated situation. When I started working on this book, it still was very unclear who would be indicted by the federal government and who would be sued by states trying to recoup losses suffered by insurance companies. Many of my sources had a lot to worry about. While some people were willing to speak on the record, many spoke on a "not for attribution" basis.

I also relied on court and other documents, and published articles, many of which are mentioned below.

The dialogue in this book is as close to verbatim as possible. Most was reported by people who participated in or witnessed the conversations. A few quotations come from third-hand sources who heard about the conversations directly from participants.

I met Marty Frankel once, in a German courtroom. I gave him my card and asked him to write to me from his German prison cell. "Send me money," he said, as he was led away by guards.

I sent him stamps. But he never wrote, and he subsequently declined to be interviewed.

CHAPTER ONE

Frankel described hanging around at brokerage firms and opening various accounts in Toledo in a deposition he gave to the Securities and Exchange Commission in 1988. His quote about predicting stock prices comes from that deposition.

For devotees of astrology, and the author confesses to being a hopeless skeptic, Frankel and Bill Gates are both Scorpios. Frankel was born on November 21, 1954, at 8:46 P.M., EST, and Bill Gates on October 28, 1955, at 10:00 P.M. PST. Both birth times come from Lois Rodden's Astrodata bank. See www.astrodatabank.com. Scorpios are "intense, secretive, and mainly concerned with handling other people's resources and talents," according to a description that can be found at www.zodiachouse.com.

CHAPTER TWO

This chapter is based largely on interviews and litigation documents stemming from the demise of the Frankel Fund. Complaints were filed by Herlihy and Bitter and by the SEC.

Much of the dialogue in this chapter between Frankel and Maxwell was reported by Frankel in his 1988 SEC deposition. Some of Frankel's comments were reported by Elizabeth Maxwell in a deposition. Douglas Maxwell was not deposed, and he declined to be interviewed for this book.

A letter Frankel wrote to Queen Anne, as well as a receipt for $50,000, was collected by lawyers involved in the litigation stemming from the collapse of the Frankel Fund. Surviving also are copies of checks Frankel wrote for his expenses, statements sent to clients, and many other records. Some information in this chapter comes from the complaint filed against Frankel by the SEC.

A lawyer for Queen Anne says she remembers few details of her involvement with Frankel and that she does not recall seeing the letter he wrote her. The lawyer describes Queen Anne as a "victim."

CHAPTER THREE

Years after the Schulte divorce, Frankel told one of the women who worked for him that he had taught Sonia Schulte how to make such a mark on her neck. The description of the tussle between John and Sonia Schulte comes in part from a police report.

CHAPTER SIX

The vast majority of the information in this chapter came from interviews with people who worked at Frankel's mansion, as well as with lawyers and law enforcement officials.

David Rosse's motorcycle was sold for $10,500 at an IRS auction in April 2001.

Robert Guyer pleaded guilty to charges stemming from the Frankel case.

Jeff Moreau has exhibited his work at the White Street Studio, 50 White Street, New York, NY. The studio's web address is www.whitestreetstudio.com.

Moreau, who says he met Frankel once, insists that he lived with Kaethe Schuchter in the East Village until her abrupt departure for Europe in 1999. However several people who were close to Schuchter—and some who were not—say she lived on West Fifty-seventh Street before she went to Europe. In 2001 Moreau said that he had not heard from his wife since she'd left and that he wanted a divorce.

The description of Frances Burge's suicide and the events leading up to it comes in part from police reports and police interviews. In some cases, recollections of the members of Frankel's household involved in the incident varied somewhat. That Burge received packages of money for Frankel comes from a July 2, 1999, Associated Press story by Brigitte Greenberg, "Fugitive Financier Not Blamed for Woman's Death."

The Eulenspiegel Society's website includes the group's history and a description: www.tes.org.

Phil Miller pleaded guilty to federal charges related to the Frankel case.

Greg's Lexus was sold at the IRS auction of Frankel's cars in April 2001.

CHAPTER SEVEN

For more on Frankel's trading problems, see "Frankel, Choked with Anxiety, Traded Few Securities," *The Wall Street Journal,* September 2, 1999.

Details of the Frankel household's spending come from American Express statements. Kaethe Schuchter's wine is described in a document filed by the federal government when it seized the wine.

Ari Kiev declined to confirm his treatment of Frankel, citing patient confidentiality. It is not clear whether Frankel used his real name when he consulted the psychiatrist.

For more on Dewi Sukarno, Kaethe Schuchter, and Marty Frankel see Mike MacIntire, "High Society Gets Low: Wealthy Widow's Wrath Could Undo Fugitive Financier Martin Frankel," *The Hartford Courant,* August 15, 1999.

CHAPTER EIGHT

This chapter is based primarily on interviews conducted with people who were privy to Frankel's relationship with Corbally, and with people who have socialized and worked with Corbally over the decades both in New York and Europe.

Corbally's involvement in the Profumo affair is described in declassified FBI files available on the Internet. See www.foia.fbi.gov. The FBI code name for the Profumo case is "Bowtie." For Corbally's account of Ambassador Bruce's request that he look into the Profumo matter, see *An Affair of State: The Profumo Case and the Framing of Stephen Ward,* by Phillip Knightley and Caroline Kennedy (New York: Atheneum, 1987).

For more on Tom Quinn and some of his associates see two articles by Gary Weiss, entitled "The Mob on Wall Street" in *Business Week,* December 16, 1996, and March 24, 1997.

A biographical sketch of Robert S. Strauss can be found on Akin, Gump's website, www.akingump.com.

Kay Tatum has since left Akin, Gump and joined Wiley, Rein & Fielding, also in Washington.

Frankel's planned purchase of the apartment at 515 Park Avenue for Corbally's use is detailed in a forfeiture complaint filed in U.S. District Court in Connecticut in October 2000 demanding payments of $596,013 and $855,000 held in escrow for the purchase. "Records reviewed to date and information provided by a cooperating witness reveal that this apartment was being purchased for the use and benefit of Thomas Corbally under the name of Endurance Investments Limited," the document states.

For more on 515 Park Avenue, see "An Aerie for the Super-Rich with Room for the Servants," by Robert D. McFadden with Rachelle Garbarine, *The New York Times,* April 25, 1998.

The apartment Frankel planned to buy for Corbally's use is described in the "Manhattan Transfers" column of the *New York Observer,* April 25, 2001. The apartment was resold in 2001 for $7.1 million.

CHAPTER NINE

This chapter is based primarily on interviews with clergy and lay people in the United States and Rome, as well as documents drafted by Frankel.

Three articles about the Catholic Church's involvement with Frankel informed some of the reporting for this chapter: "Washing Money in the Holy See," by Richard Behar, *Fortune,* August 16, 1999; "How 2 Priests Got Mixed Up In a Huge Insurance Scandal," by Alessandra Stanley, *The New York Times,* June 26, 1999; "Foundation Funds and Claims Appear to Be Shaky," by Mitchell Pacelle and Deborah Lohse, *The Wall Street Journal,* June 22, 1999.

A Vatican spokesman and the Vatican's representative to the United States did not respond to my letters in 2001. In an official statement issued in June 1999, a Vatican spokesman, Joaquin Navarro-Valls, said that the Vatican did not have a relationship with Father Peter Jacobs and didn't give or get money from St. Francis or Monitor Ecclesiasticus. The spokesman also said that St. Francis had no legal standing with the Vatican. The comments were reported by the Associated Press on July 1, 1999.

Roy Cohn's home at Saxe, Bacon & Bolan and his tax problems are described in several articles in *The New York Times,* including "Roy Cohn Finds Politics Brings New Prominence," by Paul L. Montgomery, February 19, 1981, and "U.S. Sues Cohn for $7 Million in Taxes and Fees," by Arnold H. Lubasch, April 4, 1986. Mr. Bolan's remark about Mr. Cohn's affinity for people and dogs comes from "Legal Tiger, Social Lion: His Life & Trying Times," by Margot Hornblower, *The Washington Post,* December 22, 1985. Cohn was disbarred in 1986, just months before his death.

For more on Kaethe Schuchter's visit with Michele Spike, see "The Bikinied Emissary and the Monks: Fugitive Martin Frankel Apparently Sought to Launder Money via a Monastery in Italy," by Mike McIntire, *The Hartford Courant,* July 16, 1999.

Bolan says that he never saw the Federal Express package that Schuchter showed Spike, or the documents it contained. Nor does he recall receiving a phone call from Florence that afternoon.

Some of Father Jacobs's nicknames, as well as his pet Dalmatians and his restaurant, were mentioned in "Priest in an Unholy Mess," by Dennis Duggan, *Newsday,* June 29, 1999.

Father Jacob's relationship with Cardinal Spellman, and Pope Paul VI's visit to Rice High School, were reported by Sidney Zion in his column " 'Jewish Priest' in Ponzi Scam Is Not a Sinner," *Daily News,* July 1, 1999. However, Joseph Zwilling, director of communications for the Archdiocese of New York, doubts whether Zion's account is correct. Mr. Zwilling says that a contemporaneous account of the Pope's visit, published in book form in the 1960s, mentions the Pope's unscheduled stop at Rice, and an invitation by the school's students, but makes no mention of Father Jacobs. Mr. Zwilling, who was six years old at the time, has no firsthand knowledge of the trip.

Cardinal Laghi's letter to Father Jacobs was included in an "information package" about the St. Francis Foundation put together by Frankel. In 1999 Thomas Bolan commissioned Decision Strategies Fairfax International (DSFX) to do an investigation of Father Jacobs. A DSFX investigator interviewed Father Jacobs and a senior Vatican official in Rome. The DSFX report stated that Cardinal Laghi had intervened on "Rosse" 's behalf at the Vatican. The report also stated that "Rosse" had sent Jacobs $3,300 a month between November and March.

Father Jacobs said in an interview that money he received from "Rosse" was to compensate him for expenses or to make donations to various charities. He confirmed the gift of the Volkswagen.

A lawyer for Father Jacobs says his client was "a babe in the woods dragged ino Frankel's web."

Father Jacob's motorbike was described in the *New York Times* article by Alessandra Stanley mentioned above.

Bolan's explanations about not having seen the August 22 letter were made through his lawyer, Maurice Nessen.

Zbigniew Brzezinski was not contacted by Frankel or any of Frankel's representatives.

On Frankel's apparently false claim that Iacocca and Cronkite had agreed to be on St. Francis's advisory board, see "Foundation Funds and Claims Appear to Be Shaky," in *The Wall Street Journal,* June 22, 1999.

In response to a letter asking questions about Martin Frankel or "David Rosse," a spokeswoman for Mr. Iacocca's office said that she could not comment because he "does not remember Mr. Frankel or anybody by that name, nor does he remember the information that you were asking about, something about the private jet." There was no specific reply to my question about whether Mr. Iacocca had agreed to sit on an advisory board.

CHAPTER TEN

A Decision Strategies spokesman says that the company official who called Frankel's neighbor said only that the firm had checked out the mansion's security and said nothing about having checked out Frankel.

CHAPTER ELEVEN

Frankel quoted Archimides incorrectly. The quote should read, "Give me somewhere to stand, and I will move the earth."

As he withdrew from the Capitol Life deal, Alexander was told to refile the Form A, which he did.

The circumstances surrounding Colagiovanni's signing of the second affidavit remain murky. According to notes Frankel made in his "Daily Planetary Guide, 1999," Colagiovanni and Bolan were with him in Greenwich on Saturday, February 13, 1999, the day Colagiovanni signed the affidavit. "11AM–3:30 PM—COLA + BOLAN HERE—COLA SIGNS AFFIDAVIT," Frankel wrote on February 13.

Bolan says he was not present when Colagiovanni signed the affidavit.

Colagiovanni has given several accounts of the signing of the affidavit. One of his versions of the events makes it appear that he and Frankel were not together when he signed it. He told federal agents that "Rosse" had faxed an affidavit to him for his signature, and that he faxed it back to him on February 13.

"He identified his signature on a copy of the affidavit and admitted that it was false," according to a statement sworn to on August 29, 2001, by Charles Cooney, an agent of the IRS's Criminal Investigation Division.

At other times, Colagiovanni said that the affidavit wasn't valid because it hadn't been witnessed by a notary public. See "Frankel Link Poses Problems for Vatican," by Steve Stecklow, *The Wall Street Journal,* July 6, 1999. Colagiovanni told Stecklow that he signed the affidavit while he was meeting with Frankel in Connecticut.

Finally, Monsignor Colagiovanni told me that someone else had signed his name to the February 13, 1999, affidavit.

In a letter to Bolan, dated January 16, 1999, Colagiovanni says that he made "declarations," including the first affidavit, "having been assured that right after these declarations, the promised account would be trasnferred [sic] through the I.O.R. [Vatican Bank] to the M.E. [Monitor Ecclesiasticus] Nothing happened."

Frankel's explanation to Colagiovanni about why he needed him to sign the affidavit was reported in the story by Steve Stecklow in *The Wall Street Journal* mentioned above.

Colagiovanni's request for Bolan's help came in the January 16 letter mentioned above.

The Vatican's one-sentence note to Sandifur was quoted in "Washing Money in the Holy See," by Richard Behar, *Fortune,* August 16, 1999. It is also quoted in the Cooney affidavit.

Archbishops Giovanni Battista Re and Agostino Cacciavillan were named cardinals in 2001.

CHAPTER THIRTEEN

This chapter is based on interviews with lawyers, insurance executives, and associates of Frankel in New York, Tennessee, Mississippi, and Italy. Frankel made notes in his "Daily Planetary Guide, 1999" about many of the events of that year. Some of the descriptions in this chapter are based on his diary entries. Some details about his and his associates' efforts to straighten out their problems in Tennessee are based on a Special Report issued by the state's Department of Commerce and Insurance after a review of what the report called "inaction on the part of [state] employees" in the Franklin American situation. The report was issued in July 2000.

Frankel described his New Year's weekend in the diary.

General D'Avossa told Bolan of his communications with Jean-Marie Wery and Cardinal Angelo Sodano during a lunch meeting in Rome.

On February 3, Frankel wrote, "LARRY THREATENS TO HAVE DALE RIP

UP LETTER UNLESS I GIVE HIM 850K" (George Dale was Mississippi's insurance commissioner).

"LARRY MARTIN PROMISES 100M IN 10 DAYS," Frankel wrote in his diary on Tuesday, January 19, 1999. Frankel's final arguments with Martin over the $850,000 and Thurston Little's report that Tom Quinn wanted him to hold back the letter from the Tennessee department are detailed by Frankel in his diary.

That the insurance commissioner, Douglas Sizemore, had a favorable attitude toward Harlan Mathews and his clients is shown in an interview with him by the auditors who prepared the Special Report mentioned above.

Larry Martin's suggestion to Frankel that he would talk to Tennessee's governor is mentioned by Frankel in his diary.

Lovelady's February memo stating that Franklin American might have been "looted of its assets" is reproduced in the Special Report. The failure of insurance department officials to take note of the memo is also detailed in the report.

CHAPTER FOURTEEN

The March 11, 1999, phone call between Frankel, Hackney, and Atnip is mentioned in Frankel's diary.

Hackney and Atnip's call to Frankel about the "automatic felony" is mentioned in the diary, as was Little's report to Frankel that things were "under control."

Details of payments made to Guyer and his plans to register Liberty National in several states come from the SEC's complaint against Robert Guyer, filed September 18, 2000, in Connecticut.

Frankel's payments to Little are noted in the diary. That the plane was a Piper Cheyenne III was reported in "Frankel 'Gift' of Plane Is Denied," by J. A. Johnson, Jr., in *Greenwich Time*.

The term "asshole buddy" has several meanings. It was first used, apparently, in some gay communities. *Wizard's Gay Slang Dictionary*, compiled by Robert Owen Scott Jr., provides three definitions, including, "two who are not lovers but come together for sexual gratification."

"Asshole buddy" is also used in heterosexual settings and usually refers to particularly close guys. For example, Jack Nicholson was referred to as Warren Beatty's asshole buddy in Frank DiGiacomo's "The Transom" column in *The New York Observer*, on October 18, 1999. I believe this was Thurston Little's meaning in his conversation with Martin Frankel. *Wizard's Gay Slang Dictionary* can be found at http://hurricane.net/~wizard/19.html.

On Sunday, March 21, Frankel wrote in his diary: "11AM—F. Jac. Says Tom Q Daughter in BC."

Frankel's conversation with Corbally and Quinn and his wiring of money to Quinn are mentioned in the diary. On April 2, he wired $12.9 million to Quinn, in increments of $2.5 million, $4.8 million, $2.9 million, and $2.7 million.

On April 6, Frankel wrote in his diary, "I tell Tom C to tell Tom Q to wire $ back." Two days later he wrote, "Corbally tells Tom Q Dave is coming over— Tom Q gets crazy and threatens to kill me." The diary makes it look as though $7.5 million was returned to Marty, although it is not absolutely clear that the money came from Quinn. It is also not clear what Quinn did with the money he apparently kept. Quinn could not be reached for an interview. A lawyer who once represented him said Quinn did not want to be interviewed for this book.

Frankel recorded his bickering with Corbally and Schuchter in the diary.

Paul Goldberger, a lawyer for Alfredo and Fausto Fausti, says Alfredo knew nothing about a piano and made no murderous threats. Goldberger also says that Fausto did not attempt to blackmail Frankel.

Mona Kim's gold purchase is detailed in a superseding indictment of Frankel and four alleged conspirators, including Kim, in January 2001.

Two articles in U.K. tabloids linked Frankel's passports to Kenneth Regan. See "Huge Fake Passport Racket Smashed," *The Express*, December 7, 2000, and "Fake ID Crooks Sell New Lives for £1000; Fugitives and Immigrants Snap Up Papers," by Charles Beaton, *The Scottish Daily Record*, January 23, 2001.

CHAPTER SIXTEEN

The details of David Rosse's handling of the diamonds—and how he hid them—come from documents filed by prosecutors in federal court in New Haven, Connecticut. Rosse turned over some of the diamonds to the government. Although he was awaiting sentencing on charges related to money-laundering, to which he pleaded guilty, Rosse was jailed because of the diamond caper and his subsequent efforts to keep prosecutors in the dark about them. His lawyer at the time, Thomas Williams, told a judge during a hearing that Rosse was having trouble with prescription pain medication.

The details of the money Frankel owed Rosse come from a lawsuit Rosse filed against him after Frankel left the country.

Some of the details of Frankel's life in Rome come from interviews. Others are from his diary.

Frankel wrote about his deal with Nuzzaci in the diary. Other details come from a source familiar with the transaction.

Frankel's entries in his diary make it appear that the Faustis were involved in at least some elements of the transport of the diamonds. However the Faustis' New York lawyer, Paul Goldberger, says that his clients were in no way involved with the transport of the diamonds and that they received no money in connection with the diamonds' delivery.

The diary makes clear that Kaethe Schuchter was in Rome. From interviews, it seems that Marty never saw her there.

Most Franklin American's assets were still in a bank, where Marty had put the money after Lovelady discovered he'd removed it. Tennessee recovered about $57 million of the money the insurer had "invested" at Liberty National. After a settlement between the various states where Thunor ran insurers, Tennessee paid out $17.5 million to the other states. The state comptroller's July 2000 report states "the net recovery, to this point, is approximately $40 million of the company's funds, out of the approximately $69 million in alleged total assets" of Franklin American.

I learned of Mona Kim's problems with a suspicious hotel owner from interviews, as well as from "On the Run: A Special Report, A Fugitive, Hiding in Plain Sight, Eludes a Target," by Katherine E. Finkelstein, Joseph Kahn, and John Tagliabue, *The New York Times*, August 16, 1999. Frankel's preference for Chinese over Italian food also comes from that article.

Mona Kim's detention is mentioned in "Life on the Run: Frankel's Spirits and Funds Dwindle," by Ellen Joan Pollock and Mitchell Pacelle, *The Wall Street Journal*, August 26, 1999.

On June 27, Frankel wrote in his diary: "ALF—PM—TELLS ME ALL $ STOLEN—HE WON'T GIVE BACK 2M + ROCCO SENT 30M BACK TO SCS—BUT K WILL PAY MY BILLS!"

K apparently refers to Kaethe Schuchter. But Alfredo Fausti's attorney, Paul Goldberger, says that his client never said that Kaethe would pay Frankel's bills.

My efforts to reach Nuzzaci were unsuccessful.

Details of Frankel's negotiations with *The Express* come from interviews with sources in New York and London, Frankel's diary, and articles in *The Express*. Frankel's refusal, "No way. I'm not doing any deal," comes from *The Express*, as does the remark "It's a bad day for me. It has to be tomorrow."

Chapter Seventeen

Frankel's diary describes some of the details of his flight from Italy to Germany.

Cynthia Allison described her life in Hamburg to reporters of the *Toledo Blade* and *Time*. See "On the Lam with Marty, Cindy Allison, One of Embezzler Martin Frankel's Gal Pals, Tells of His Not-So-Secret Life in Europe," by Karl Taro Greenfeld, *Time*, November 8, 1999, and "Frankel Associate Recalls Life on the Lam," by Michael D. Sallah, *The Toledo Blade*, December 19, 1999. Allison and Frankel's life in Hamburg is also described in "Life on the Run: Frankel's Spirits and Funds Dwindle," *The Wall Street Journal*, by Ellen Joan Pollock and Mitchell Pacelle, August 26, 1999.

The description of Frankel's capture is based partly on interviews with officials in Germany. Also see "Frankel's Life on the Lam Ends in Arrest—German

Detectives Capture Financier at Hamburg Hotel," *The Wall Street Journal,* by Ellen Joan Pollock, Mitchell Pacelle, and Christopher Rhoads, September 7, 1999.

Allison "denied rumors that she called the police" when she was in Hamburg with Frankel, according to the December 19, 1999, article by Michael D. Sallah mentioned above. "Absolutely not true," she told Sallah. "I don't know how they found us."

Epilogue

That Frankel was called "Herr Wirtschaft," or Mr. Economy, comes from "Frankel Lands in U.S. Jail," in the *New York Post,* by Alan Hall, Maria Alvarez, Dan Mangan, and Dan Kadison, March 3, 2001.

Acknowledgments

I owe a tremendous debt of gratitude to the reporters at *The Wall Street Journal* with whom I reported the Marty Frankel story in 1999. Mitch Pacelle and Deborah Lohse were the best of colleagues as we tried to unravel Frankel's scheme. For this book I also relied on the reporting of Mike Allen, Steve Stecklow, Aaron Lucchetti, Christopher Rhoads, Greg Zuckerman, and other *Journal* reporters. All of them were unbelievably supportive as I worked on this book. I can't thank them enough.

Journal editors Larry Ingrassia, Mike Siconolfi, Leslie Scism, John Brecher, Dan Kelly, and Jeff Sutherland were all, quite simply, fantastic.

The idea for this book came from Dan Hertzberg, a *Journal* deputy managing editor. Steve Adler, who oversees book projects at the paper, made it happen. He was a wonderful sounding board throughout. This book also could not have been written without Paul Steiger, the *Journal*'s managing editor, who has supported me through twelve years of sometimes controversial stories. There is no one like him. Carol Hymowitz, my long-time editor at the paper, was at my side throughout this project. She's the best. As always, I went to Barney Calame with my toughest questions.

At Simon & Schuster, Fred Hills's enthusiasm and encouragement constantly bolstered me during the complicated reporting and writing of this book. Many thanks to Jolanta Benal for her thoughtful copyediting, and to Frances Tsay.

Two lawyers reviewed this book, and both went well beyond their role as lawyers. Stuart Karle, at *The Wall Street Journal,* was a source of support and ideas from the very beginning of the project. This book was in its final stages when New York was attacked on September 11, 2001, and Elisa Rivlin, a lawyer at Simon & Schuster, was a voice of comfort and stability in the several days after my family had to leave our home in lower Manhattan.

Many of the photographs for this book were collected by Allison Nowlin of *The Wall Street Journal,* who was fabulously tenacious. I thank her and Greg Leeds, also of the *Journal* graphics department. Leah Bourne helped me fact check the book. She was meticulous, enthusiastic, and great to work with. Almut Schoenfeld, of *The Wall Street Journal Europe,* helped arrange the logistics of my trip to Hamburg. The *Journal's* Roe D'Angelo acted as liaison between the paper and Simon & Schuster.

Several journalistic competitors generously helped me with this book. They are Brian Ross, Jill Rackmill, and David Rummel of ABC News, and Joe Johnson of the *Greenwich Time.*

My colleagues at *The Wall Street Journal* put up with a lot from me over the eighteen months I spent working on the book. They witnessed bizarre conversations with sources and, quite frankly, some peculiar behavior on my part. (For awhile, I vowed to wear a baseball cap until I finished writing, and I won't go into the details of my chocolate fetish here.) Ann Podd, Wade Lambert, Dorothy Gaiter, Erin Friar, Eileen Daspin, Edward Felsenthal, Michael Moss, Jonathan Kaufman, Charlie Gasparino, and Steve Barnes are just a few who deserve praise for putting up with me during those months. Mark Robichaux was my constant weekend pal in the office.

Likewise I relied on some long-time friends for support. I spoke often about the book with Denise Martin. More significantly, she gave my family a temporary home on September 11. This is the second book I've written with the Abramson-Griggs clan at my side. Jill Abramson encouraged me to write this book and helped keep me going throughout. Henry Griggs's hospitality defies description. He and Elizabeth Griggs provided a sanctuary for my family in the days before we returned to our home in the wake of September 11. Many, many, many thanks to Kathy and Bob Burke, Amy Singer, Richard Einhorn, Fran Black, and Leah Rozen. And many apologies to those I'm inadvertently leaving out.

The members of my book group were my unofficial cheerleading

squad. Jerry Patterson, Bill Borders, Walter Mead, Meg Cox, Becky Sale-
tan, Bob Seidman, and Geri Thoma—who imparted some professional
advice at the onset of this project—helped keep me excited about the
project.

Also, many thanks to my new friends in Tribeca—especially the
mommies and daddies of Sylvia, Ian, Felix, Grace, Margaret, Truman,
Simon, and the other three year olds who play in Washington Market
Park, and to the remarkable Judy Stevens.

I would still be writing this book had not my mother, Iris Pollock,
spent many a Sunday entertaining my daughter so that I could plow
ahead in my office. My sister Rachel Pollock and her family, John, Alex,
and Jason Aerni, were beyond patient, as were my in-laws, Steve Meier
and Iris Osman, and Gerta Meier.

My little daughter Lily was a never-ending source of delight.

My greatest debt of gratitude goes to my husband, Barry Meier. At a
crucial point in the reporting of this book Barry, whose skills as an investigative reporter far exceed mine, dug in and helped unearth an important puzzle piece, without which writing this book would have been
more difficult. Barry also carefully read the manuscript. His journalistic
contributions were only outstripped by those on the home front, where
he is the perfect daddy and a constant source of comfort and strength to
his wife.

Index

269

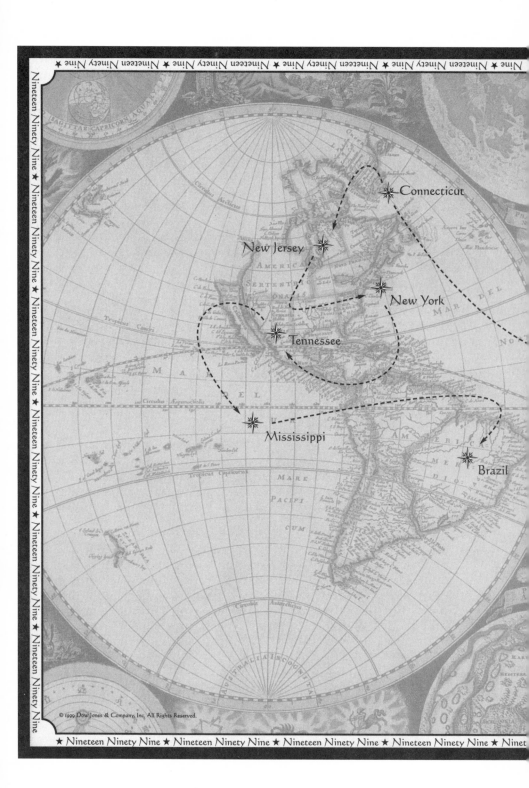